STATE OF LOUISIANA

MINERAL CODE
AND FORMS

2023

This is a reprint with addenda made available from the Louisiana Legislature website as a public service by the Louisiana Legislature and Secretary of State Kyle Ardoin

R.S. Title 31, Chapter 1 through 13, enacted by Act 50 of 1974 including laws through the 2023 Regular Sessions of the Legislature

Baton Rouge
CLAITOR'S PUBLISHING DIVISION

Published and for sale by
CLAITOR'S PUBLISHING DIVISION
3165 S. Acadian at I-10, P.O. Box 261333
Baton Rouge, LA 70826-1333
Tel: 800-274-1403 (In LA 225-344-0476)
Fax: 225-344-0480
Internet address:
e mail: claitors@claitors.com

World Wide Web: http://www.claitors.com

Mineral Code Preface 2023

Drilling for oil took place in Louisiana as early as 1866. It was not until September 1901 when oil was discovered at Jennings, Louisiana, that the state's oil and gas industry began its modern development. The Civil Code of Louisiana had not been drafted with any thought to minerals, so the courts were left with the responsibility for fashioning a body of law governing the rights for development of petroleum. Colonel John H. Tucker spoke of the mineral law of Louisiana as being explicable by the aphorism "au-dela du code civil mais par le code civil" — beyond the civil code but through the civil code.

The earliest book on Louisiana mineral law was published in 1922. Its author, George G. Dimick of the Shreveport bar, made the following observation:

> The discovery of oil in Louisiana found the State with no mining laws, as that industry was unknown in this section. The few antiquated sections of the Codes and statutes which might apply were evidently casual and accidental expressions and illustrations enacted without the remotest idea that they would ever apply to the production of oil and gas. ---George G. Dimick, *Louisiana Law of Oil and Gas* 3 (1922).

Harriet S. Daggett, an LSU law professor, dedicated her treatise on Louisiana oil and gas law to the Louisiana judiciary during the years 1900-1939 for their role in shaping Louisiana mineral law. She observed:

> The law of oil and gas is new and without precedent.... [T]he courts of Louisiana were without aid from the legislature. They could receive little from counsel, though the members of the Louisiana Bar who are concerned in these issues have not

been unmindful of the complexity of the problems. The decisions of other states were of small value because Louisiana is a civil-law state with an old civil code. The French, Spanish, and Roman sources furnished no precedents because the problem was unknown to those forefathers. The judiciary has ever been a determining factor in defining frontier interpretation of new social and economic policies. The history of legal thought cannot neglect the role of judge-made law. Louisiana jurisprudence on oil and gas is a continuing tribute to the patience, research, wisdom, and fairness of the members of the bench of the state. Harriet S. Daggett, *Mineral Rights in Louisiana* xxxiv-xxxv (1939).

A hazard of this method of legal development was a degree of doctrinal inconsistency and unpredictability that appeared in some cases, and occasional application of principles ill-suited to the industry. It is not surprising that comprehensive legislation was seen as desirable.

A proposed Mineral Code appeared as early as 1938 after Mr. Sidney Herold was appointed by the governor to head a Commission to propose such a code. The Commission of seven was appointed pursuant to Act 170 of 1936. They were charged by the statute to prepare a draft to be known as A Code of the Oil, Gas and Mineral Laws of the State of Louisiana. The act was a joint resolution submitted to the people at the general election of 1936 and was adopted as a constitutional amendment.

The Louisiana Law Institute, with the concurrence of the Mineral Law Section of the Louisiana Bar Association, undertook a project for adoption of a Mineral Code under the direction of Professor Eugene Nabors of the Tulane Law School. That work was continued by Professor George W. Hardy of the LSU Law School after he was appointed Reporter in July, 1963. In 1971 an *Exposé des Motifs* was published setting forth the statements of general principles that the Reporter and Advisory Committee were submitting to the Law Institute as a basis for legislation. Professor Hardy in his "Reporter's Foreword" described the concerns with the state of Louisiana mineral law that the proposed Mineral Code would address upon its completion:

> The bending and warping of Civil Code concepts, the application of articles from varying parts of the Code in sometimes awkward circumstances, and the flimsiness of some of the analogies which have been made inhibit, if not prohibit, intelligent, organized consideration of Louisiana mineral law in the conceptualism of the Civil Code.

Most of the Recommendations in the 1971 *Exposé* were incorporated by the Louisiana Legislature when it enacted the Mineral Code in 1974, effective January 1, 1975. 1974 La. Acts No. 50; La. R.S. 31:1 et seq. The Mineral Code has removed from question some areas of existing judicial decisions that may have been of doubtful authority. Because the Code is now statute rather than a body of judicial decisions, the principles embodied in the articles will not be capable of being changed by judicial decision even when the courts are no longer persuaded of the wisdom of the judicial decisions which were codified.

The Mineral Code is a specialized extension of the Civil Code. La. Civ. Code art. 561, comment (a). As provided in Article 2 of the Mineral Code, the Civil Code or other laws are applicable in instances in which the Mineral Code "does not expressly or impliedly provide for a particular situation." The courts do have occasion to go to the Civil Code for matters not expressly resolved by the Mineral Code. Nevertheless, Louisiana citizens and courts have had since the Mineral Code's adoption a comprehensive body of legal provisions and principles to govern the creation and operation of mineral interests and the resolution of disputes among landowners and owners of mineral rights. There have been very few amendments to the Mineral Code since its initial adoption, reflecting both the care and comprehensiveness with which the Mineral Code was crafted and a legislative reluctance to interfere with a body of law that is still in development. In 2005 Professor Thomas A. Harrell, Director of the Louisiana Mineral Law Institute, surveyed three decades of operation of the Mineral Code and concluded: "The Mineral Code has worked extremely well."[*]

Patrick H. Martin, Campanile Professor of Mineral Law, LSU Paul M. Hebert Law Center

1/7/09

---

[*] Thomas A Harrell, "The Mineral Code After Thirty Years," 52 *Ann. Inst. on Min. Law 251* (Claitor's and LSU Paul M. Hebert Law Center, 2005, 2008). The LSU Law Center has held an annual Mineral Law Institute since 1953. Most of the papers from these programs have been published or are presently being published and are available from Claitor's Law Books. They are an indispensable source for scholarly commentary on the Louisiana Mineral Code and on other aspects of Louisiana mineral law as it has developed over the past century.

PREFACE 1974

(Contained herein at the request of the
Louisiana State Law Institute)

The Louisiana Mineral Code, adopted as Act 50 of 1974, is the result of a study begun by the Louisiana State Law Institute with the concurrence of the Mineral Law Section of the Louisiana State Bar Association under the, direction of Professor Eugene Nabors, deceased, of Tulane, and completed in 1974 by George W. Hardy III, formerly Professor of Mineral Law at the Louisiana State University Law School and presently Dean of the University of Kentucky Law School. Dean Hardy accepted appointment as reporter for the project in 1963. He was assisted by an advisory committee composed of sixteen members of the Louisiana Bar possessing considerable experience in the mineral law area both from the standpoint of the landowner and the mineral operator. The resulting product, a proposed Mineral Code, was considered in detail over several years, and approved by the Council of the Louisiana State Law Institute, first in the form of "Suggested Principles of Louisiana Law - A Basis for Reform," and again in the form of the Code itself.

The Mineral Code is designed in: large measure to supplant by way of codification the extensive jurisprudence that developed in this area of the law. Louisiana's existing mineral law was a product of jurisprudential development principally by way of analogy to the provisions of the Louisiana Civil Code relating to servitudes but including particularly also the general rules of conventional obligations and leases. In other words, before the adoption of the Mineral Code, the mineral law reposed in decisions of the courts, principally the Louisiana Supreme Court, rather than in a codification. The basic result of the judicial determination that sales and reservations of minerals do not constitute a dismemberment of ownership in perpetuity but merely give rise to servitudes is that under the provisions of the Civil Code the servitudes so established expire for nonuse in ten years and the land is no longer burdened by them. There has been general agreement with the wisdom that characterized the adoption of these basic principles by the courts; nevertheless, the extensive volume of jurisprudence that had been developed was lacking, as must necessarily be the case, in the coherence that is characteristic of a code.

The Mineral Code contains comments explanatory of the articles contained therein. In brief, it can be said that no basic change has been made in the prior law. The jurisprudential rules covering the nature of mineral servitudes, how they may be created and how extinguished, have been retained. Some modifications have been made, however, mostly by way of clarification.

Section 2 of Act 50 of 1974 provides for the continuous revision of the Code under the direction of the Law Institute. This will include the integration of new statutes with the Code, necessary renumbering, and possible reconciliation of overlapping legislation affecting the same articles.

Section 6 of Act 50 of 1974 delays the effective date of this Code until January 1, 1975. This will give the judiciary, the members of the bar and the industry generally a reasonable time to become familiar with its provisions and will provide time needed for its official printing and distribution.

The legislative charter of the Institute recognizes its general purpose to be to promote and encourage the clarification and simplification of the law of Louisiana and its better adaption to present social needs. The Mineral Code was recommended for adoption in response to this purpose.

In keeping with established practice, great care was exercised in the preparation of the Code by the reporter and his advisors and in its detailed consideration by the Institute Council and general membership. It is hoped that It will facilitate the administration of the mineral law of this state and will better serve the needs of the oil and gas industry, and the public generally.

MINERAL CODE

TABLE OF CONTENTS

CHAPTER 1. PRELIMINARY PROVISIONS

Art. 1. Title and form of citation

This Chapter shall be known as the Louisiana Mineral Code. The provisions hereunder may be referred to or cited either as Articles of the Mineral Code or as Sections of the Revised Statutes. Thus Article 30 of the Louisiana Mineral Code may also be referred to or cited as R.S. 31:30.

Whenever reference is made herein to an Article of the Mineral Code, the same shall also relate to the corresponding Section of the Revised Statutes.

Acts 1974, No. 50, §1, eff. Jan. 1, 1975.

Comment

Although the authorized forms of citation include reference to provisions of this code by using the traditional form for citation of the Revised Statutes, it is hoped that because of the relationship of this code to the Civil Code and the attempt to structure it more in the style of a code than a statute, the preferred practice will grow to be that of citing particular provisions as Articles of the Mineral Code.

Art. 2. Relation to Civil Code

The provisions of this Code are supplementary to those of the Louisiana Civil Code and are applicable specifically to the subject matter of mineral law. In the event of conflict between the provisions of this Code and those of the Civil Code or other laws the provisions of this Code shall prevail. If this Code does not expressly or impliedly provide for a particular situation, the Civil Code or other laws are applicable.

Acts 1974, No. 50, §1, eff. Jan. 1, 1975.

1

Comment

The mineral law of Louisiana sprang from the Civil Code. Transactions involving mineral rights have involved use of forms and application of principles of the Civil Code. Disputes concerning mineral rights have been resolved in terms of the principles of the Civil Code, directly or by analogy. The Mineral Code is a specialized extension of the Civil Code, and in instances where the Mineral Code does not make express or implied provision for a particular situation, it is intended that the principles of the Civil Code will continue to be applicable, either directly or by appropriate analogy. However, the provisions of the Mineral Code will govern in the absence of a hiatus as to its coverage, and it is of particular importance that the Mineral Code prevail in any instance in which there is conflict with the Civil Code. An additional purpose of Article 2 is that of preventing the inappropriate transfer of the principles of the Mineral Code and interpretive jurisprudence to resolve questions that are properly governed by the general principles of the Civil Code. There has been concern among some for a number of years that principles evolved in mineral law decisions, specially tailored to meet the special needs of Louisiana's mineral industries, would, by inverse analogy, be doubled back into other types of controversies that should properly be resolved under the Civil Code without the necessary liberties sometimes taken in the decision of mineral cases. It is the intent of Article 2 that this undesirable process be avoided.

Art. 3. Freedom of contract and limitations thereon

Unless expressly or impliedly prohibited from doing so, individuals may renounce or modify what is established in their favor by the provisions of this Code if the renunciation or modification does not affect the rights of others and is not contrary to the public good.

Acts 1974, No. 50, §1, eff. Jan. 1, 1975.

Comment

Comment
Article 3 is, in principle, intent, and wording, much like Article 11 of the Civil Code. It is to be noted that Article 3 does not contain the first sentence of Article 11 of the Civil Code: "Individuals can not by their conventions, derogate from the force of laws made for the preservation of public order or good morals." That general principle is one of those in the Civil Code that is intended to remain applicable to all mineral transactions. The purpose of Article 3 is somewhat more limited. In many instances in the process of drafting the Mineral Code, individuals working on the project desired to make it plain that parties could contract in a manner contrary to the provisions of the code. This resulted, in early drafting stages, in the presence of a multitude of references of this kind to the role of freedom of contract as to particular provisions of the code. After completion of an initial draft, it was decided that it would be preferable technique to utilize one general article such as Article 3 and eliminate thereby the multiple references to the right of parties to alter code rules by contract. Accomplishment of this purpose did not require repetition of the first sentence of Article 11 of the Civil Code, and it is intended that in accordance with Article 2 of the Mineral Code, parties will continue to be governed by the prohibition against contracting contrary to laws for the preservation of public order or good morals.

The role of freedom of contract, however, is not unlimited under the Mineral Code. There are certain principles in the Louisiana mineral property system that are based on public policy. As an example, special attention should be paid to the provisions of Article 73 through 75, applicable to mineral servitudes. These articles respectively prohibit the creation of one servitude on two or more noncontiguous tracts of land, contracting for a prescriptive period greater than ten years, or making the rules of use of mineral servitudes less burdensome than those provided by the Mineral Code. Under Article 103, these same limitations are imposed on contractual freedom in the creation of mineral royalties. Similarly, the requirements of Article 1901 [changed to Art. 1983 by Acts 1984, No. 331] of the Civil Code, repeated as to parties to mineral leases in Article 119 and 122 of the Mineral Code, that all agreements legally entered into be performed in good faith would seem to be one that cannot be contracted away on grounds of public policy. These are specific examples of limitation of the power of parties to contract freely, and others, based on the combined principles of Article 11 of the Civil Code and Article 3 of the Mineral Code, might be found by a court in the presence of particular circumstances.

CHAPTER 2. THE LANDOWNER'S RIGHTS IN MINERALS

PART 1. OWNERSHIP AS INCLUDING MINERALS OR RIGHTS THERETO

Art. 4. Substances to which Code applicable

The provisions of this Code are applicable to all forms of minerals, including oil and gas. They are also applicable to rights to explore for or mine or remove from land the soil itself, gravel, shells, subterranean water, or other substances occurring naturally in or as a part of the soil or geological formations on or underlying the land.

Acts 1974, No. 50, §1, eff. Jan. 1, 1975.

Comment

Article 4 determines the application of the provisions of the Mineral Code. It does not attempt a firm definition of the term "minerals." The purpose of including oil and gas within the meaning of the term minerals is solely to indicate the applicability of the code to those substances and has no relationship whatsoever to the problem of construing particular conveyances to determine whether specific substances are included or excluded from the terms of an instrument. Insofar as construction of instruments for this purpose is concerned, the Supreme Court has stated in Holloway Gravel Co. v. McKowen, 200 La. 917, 925, 9 So.2d 228, 231 (1942), that the "term 'mineral' is not a definite one....but is susceptible of limitation according to the intention of the parties using it and in determining its meaning, regard must be had not only to the language of the deed in which it occurs, but also to the relative positions of the parties interested and to the substance of the transaction which the deed embodies." In Huie Hodge Lumber Co. v. Railroad Lands Co., 151 La. 197, 91 So. 676 (1922), the court was required to determine whether an instrument reserving rights to "iron, coal, and other minerals" included oil and gas. The *ejusdem generis* doctrine was applied and oil and gas were held not to have been included. This article of the Mineral Code is not intended to alter the jurisprudence in this regard.

Making the code applicable to rights to remove other substances is a furtherance of what is felt to be the policy of the civil law system of land tenures. That is, that it is undesirable for land to be burdened by ancient claims or use rights. The free and continuing utilization of land to the highest economic advantage should not be inhibited. Thus, it is undesirable that a right to remove gravel, shells, sand, or clay remain outstanding against the land except under the terms of the code. A lease to remove any such substances is governed by the principle of Article 115 that it may not permit maintenance of the lessee's rights without development for a period greater than ten years. If the instrument cannot be classified as a lease, a right to remove such substances is a mineral servitude subject to the prescription of nonuse.

Art. 5. Ownership of solid minerals

Ownership of land includes all minerals occurring naturally in a solid state. Solid minerals are insusceptible of ownership apart from the land until reduced to possession.

Acts 1974, No. 50, §1, eff. Jan. 1, 1975.

Comment

Article 5 acknowledges ownership of solid minerals but imposes limitations on the landowner's right to alienate them. The jurisprudence is inconclusive concerning this theoretical problem though the servitude analogy is clearly applicable to conveyances of solid minerals. Two early cases of approximately the same vintage as Frost-Johnson Lumber Co. v. Salling's Heirs, 150 La. 756, 91 So. 207 (1922), expressly avoid the question of ownership versus nonownership of solid minerals by construing particular conveyances as having been intended by the parties to create no more than a servitude in the first instance. Huie Hodge Lumber Co. v. Railroad Lands Co., 151 La. 197, 91 So. 676 (1922); Wetherbee

v. Railroad Lands Co., 152 La. 1059, 97 So. 40 (1923). In Lee v. Giauque, 154 La. 491, 97 So. 669 (1923) and Wemple v. Nabors Oil & Gas Co., 154 La. 483, 97 So. 666 (1923), both decided in the same year as the *Wetherbee* case, the Louisiana Supreme Court considered conveyances susceptible to construction as grants of solid minerals in place in addition to oil and gas. In the *Wemple* decision the court went to some length in citing authorities regarding Louisiana's simple system of land tenures, asserting that the recognition of ownership and servitude as the only permissible estates or interests in land is a doctrine clearly traceable through the lineage of civil law. On this basis it was held, without qualification, that there could be no "mineral estate" distinct from and independent of the surface estate, the so-called "mineral estate," by whatever term described or however acquired or reserved, being a mere servitude upon the land in which the minerals lie and giving only the right to extract such minerals and appropriate them. Justice Overton dissented from both of these opinions insofar as they applied to solid minerals. A conveyance purporting to divide the subsurface by horizontal planes and to sell certain portions of the subsurface by description according to such planes was considered in Iberville Land Co. v. Texas Co., 14 La. App. 221,128 So. 304 (1st Cir. 1930). In reliance on Wemple v. Nabors Oil Co., *supra*, the Court of Appeal rejected the contention that the deed created ownership of the specified planes separate from ownership of the surface.

The foregoing jurisprudence makes it clear that the servitude theory is applicable to solid minerals. However, it does not specifically deal with the question whether the landowner, in view of Article 505 of the Louisiana Civil Code [changed to Art. 490 by Acts 1979, No. 180], is considered the owner of solid minerals. Though there may be some basis for criticism, it seems that there is a distinction drawn between solid minerals on one hand and liquid and gaseous minerals on the other in this regard. The rationale of the servitude theory as applied to liquid and gaseous minerals is based on their fugacious character, which has been said to make them insusceptible of ownership in place. On the other hand, it seems that one cannot deny the principle stated in Article 505 of the Civil Code regarding ownership of the soil and all that lies beneath it. Further, it does not seem that the jurisprudence in fact denies the validity of this principle. However, the judicially evolved theory does seem to contemplate that though the

7

landowner may own the subsoil and its components, his capacity to alienate them is limited by what the court has regarded as an established policy of prohibiting horizontal fractionation of ownership. Thus, the servitude theory is applicable to solid minerals, not because such minerals are not owned in place, but because public policy prohibits their alienation separately from the surface.

In the light of the jurisprudence and the conclusions drawn from it, Article 5 specifies previously established law. Subsequent to the *Frost-Johnson* case, the court was importuned to consider the factual error regarding the migratory character of oil and gas. The issue was directly raised in Wetherbee v. Railroad Lands Co., *supra*. The court, however, sustained a ruling denying admission of evidence to show the relatively static location of oil and gas within defined reservoirs, noting that the evidence in question could succeed in modifying the basis for the nonownership theory only in degree. Further it was stated that even assuming the correctness of the contention concerning the static character of oil and gas, no change would be wrought in the principle upon which Frost-Johnson Lumber Co. v. Salling's Heirs, *supra*, had been based. This remark, coupled with the later decisions in the Wemple and Lee cases, might furnish a premise for arguing that the theoretical base of Louisiana's mineral law was changed subsequent to *Frost-Johnson* from a strict nonownership theory to one recognizing ownership but, for policy reasons, prohibiting alienation apart from title to the surface. It must be admitted that in the abstract such a theory has advantages in terms of conceptual symmetry. Nevertheless, the better interpretation of the jurisprudence is that the servitude theory is still applied to liquid and gaseous minerals on the assumption, however mistaken, that they are insusceptible of ownership in place and to solid minerals for reasons of policy without regard to their susceptibility to ownership because of their physical nature. This article contemplates continuance of the idea reflected in *Frost-Johnson* and subsequent cases that a conveyance purporting to sell minerals in place is not invalid but merely creates a right in the nature of a servitude. The Louisiana mineral conveyancing system has a strong flavor of those in ownership jurisdictions. Little change has been noted in standard conveyances since *Frost-Johnson*, and no change is required or intended by this article.

Art. 6.   Right to search for fugitive minerals; elements of ownership of land

Ownership of land does not include ownership of oil, gas, and other minerals occurring naturally in liquid or gaseous form, or of any elements or compounds in solution, emulsion, or association with such minerals.   The landowner has the exclusive right to explore and develop his property for the production of such minerals and to reduce them to possession and ownership.

Acts 1974, No. 50, §1, eff. Jan. 1, 1975.

Comment

Article 6 is a retention of the theory articulated in Frost-Johnson Lumber Co. v. Salling's Heirs, 150 La. 756, 91 So. 207 (1922).

PART 2. REDUCTION OF MINERALS TO POSSESSION

Art. 7. When minerals reduced to possession

Minerals are reduced to possession when they are under physical control that permits delivery to another.

Acts 1974, No. 50, §1, eff. Jan. 1, 1975.

Comment

In view of changing technology and the wide variety of possible mining methods for different substances, Article 7 does not attempt to determine the point in time or space at which minerals are reduced to possession. It provides only that possession is had when delivery to another becomes possible. Insofar as oil and gas are concerned, the jurisprudence construing the severance tax laws indicates a generally accepted view that severance occurs at the wellhead. See La.R.S. 41:634(3) (1950). Sartor v. United Carbon

Co., 183 La. 287,163 So. 103 (1936); United Gas Public Service Co., 186 La. 555, 173 So. 103 (1937); Texas Co. v. Fontenot, 200 La. 753, 8 So.2d 689 (1942); Wall v. United Gas Public Service Co., 178 La. 908, 152 So. 561 (1934); State ex reI. Boykin v. Hope Producing Co., 167 So. 506 (La.App. 2d Cir. 1936). A few other cases contain vague language of some relevance. Dixon v. American Liberty Oil Co., 226 La. 911, 77 So.2d 533 (1955); Federal Land Bank of New Orleans v. Mulhern, 180 La. 627,157 So. 370 (1934); Liles v. Texas Co., 166 La. 293,117 So. 229 (1928); Breaux v. Pan American Petroleum Corp., 163 So.2d 406 (La. App. 3d Cir. 1964), writs refused, 246 La. 581, 165 So.2d 481. The severance tax cases, technically construed, deal with the question of who is the "owner" within the meaning of the severance tax laws at the time of severance. Although none of the decisions denies the possibility that possession might be had at another point in the extractive process for property law purposes, all of them are based on the common understanding that in the case of ordinary oil and gas operations severance occurs, possession is taken, and ownership vests at the wellhead as to liquid and gaseous substances such as oil and gas. There is no reason why this common understanding should not be accepted, for, within the meaning of Article 7, this would ordinarily be the point at which possession is sufficient to deliver the substances to another.

Article 7 eschews further definition or another approach, such as defining possession as having occurred at the surface of the land or water where extraction takes place because new technology holds out the possibility of sufficient control being had at some point below ground or, for example, on the seabed. Thus, the court will be required to determine, considering the kind and character of mining operations in question and viewing the customs of particular industries, the point at which one extracting minerals has possession.

The vesting of possession is of great importance for legal purposes. For a landowner extracting fugitive minerals, it will mark both the vesting of title and mobilization of the substance in question. In the case of solid minerals, the landowner is regarded by Article 5 as the owner of such substances, but vesting of possession will still determine when minerals extracted become subject to the law of movables. As to others than the landowner, vesting of possession will have the dual effect of marking the vesting of title and mobilization. Despite the fact that Article 5 recognizes that the owner of land also owns solid minerals, such minerals are insusceptible of ownership apart from the land, and the landowner may therefore only convey or lease the right to explore for them and reduce them to possession and simultaneously to ownership. Accordingly, the nature of the substance involved has no impact on the significance of reduction to possession and consequent vesting of title.

PART 3. RIGHTS OF LANDOWNERS TO EXPLORE FOR ANDPRODUCE MINERALS AND LIMITATIONS THEREON

Art.8. Landowner's right of enjoyment for mineral extraction

A landowner may use and enjoy his property in the most unlimited manner for the purpose of discovering and producing minerals, provided it is not prohibited by law. He may reduce to possession and ownership all of the minerals occurring naturally in a liquid or gaseous state that can be obtained by operations on or beneath his land even though his operations may cause their migration from beneath the land of another.

Acts 1974, No. 50, §1, eff. Jan. 1, 1975.

Comment

Article 8 preserves established law governing the landowner's right to operate and his liability for damages. There is no attempt to change or to define the specific limitations upon the landowner's right to operate. Definition of the landowner's rights has been achieved by use of various legal institutions. The *sic utere* doctrine set forth in Article 667 of the Civil Code has been utilized in some instances. *E.g.*, Higgins Oil & Fuel Co. v. Guaranty Oil Co., 145 La. 233, 82 So. 206 (1919) (landowner leaving a well uncapped to decrease pumping efficiency of neighbor's well); Adams v. Grigsby, 152 So.2d 615· (La. App. 2d Cir. 1963) (right to full and free use of subterranean water for secondary recovery operations sustained).

Several other cases, though not directly in point as they involve leases, are nevertheless appropriate to this area. In Fontenot v. Magnolia Petroleum Co., 227 La. 866, 80 So. 2d 845 (1955) the court, citing Article 667 of the Civil Code, imposed what amounts to a strict liability for damage to neighboring property resulting from geophysical operations which included blasting. Whether the earlier decisions rendered in McIlhenny v. Roxanna Petroleum Corp., 122 So. 165 (La.App.1st Cir. 1929), Le Bleu v. Shell Petroleum Corp., 161 So. 214 (La. App.1st Cir. 1935), and Watkins v. Gulf Refining Corp., 206 La. 942, 20 So.2d 273 (1944), all of which disposed of similar cases under the law of negligence, were overruled by the *Fontenot* case is not clear.

Regardless of the theory utilized to dispose of cases involving liability for conduct of oil and gas operations, two conclusions emerge. One is that the jurisprudence indicates a strong tendency to impose liability on the operator for damage to persons or to adjacent or neighboring property resulting from the conduct of otherwise lawful operations when they are inherently dangerous. The second is that the conceptual articulation of this result has not been of great importance. The *Fontenot* decision utilizes the language of Article 667 to impose strict liability for operations entailing blasting. The Watkins case utilizes negligence concepts to impose liability for damage resulting from a blowout and holds that the facts of the case required application of the doctrine of *res ipsa loquitur*. Because the conceptual approaches of these cases vary while the results are the same, it can be further concluded that the courts are giving great weight, in keeping with the national trend, to the hazardous aspects of oil and gas operations, with .the result that a high degree of responsibility is placed upon such enterprises when they involve inherent risks of damage through escape of oil or gas or the use of explosives. In essence, this is simply a tendency to examine the nature of the enterprise involved rather than property relationships, which is the substance of the principle specified in Article 667 of the Civil Code.

As noted, Article 8 does not attempt, and it is felt that as a rule legislation should not attempt, a full definition of the rules governing the landowner's freedom to operate and his liability for abuse of his property rights. Thus, the general law should be allowed to control such questions. The unsatisfactory condition of present law is more than offset by the extreme dangers involved in attempting to define rules which would be applicable not only to the petroleum industry but to all other mining industries which might be affected. Additionally, it appears unwise in terms of basic policy to remove mining activities from the ambit of the general law except when necessary to accommodate peculiarities warranting a distinction.

Art. 9.   Correlative rights of owners of common reservoir or deposit

Landowners and others with rights in a common reservoir or deposit of minerals have correlative rights and duties with respect to one another in the development and production of the common source of minerals.

Acts 1974, No. 50, §1, eff. Jan. 1, 1975.

Comment

Functionally speaking, the doctrine of correlative rights is based on the notion that those whose property and mineral interest overlie a common source of supply of oil or gas have certain rights in the common reservoir even though their surface property lines encompass only a small portion of the area underlain by it. Analytically, these shared rights fall into two basic categories: (1) rights concerning the opportunity to produce a fair share of the common reservoir, and (2) rights to utilize the natural reservoir energy. See La. R.S. 30:11(B) and La.R.S. 30:9(0) (1950). The cited portions of the Conservation Act assure to those with interests in a common source of supply the rights stated when the Commissioner of Conservation exercises his powers. Thus, the act is based on the assumption that these rights pre-exist in the property law.

The following passage from an article by Professor Eugene Kuntz of the University of Oklahoma presents a good functional analysis of the basis for the doctrine of correlative rights:

13

"Because of the reciprocal effect which the conduct of the parties who own interests in a common source of supply of oil or gas will have on one another may be described as operating in a special community, and the conduct which will or will not be tolerated in connection with such operations will be determined by the social acceptability of such conduct within such special community. In determining whether a form of conduct is or is not socially acceptable, we may not look to generally accepted standards, but we must look to the utility of such conduct in the light of the special consequences which may be expected to follow for the other parties in the same special community. The term 'correlative rights' is simply a term to describe such reciprocal rights and duties of the owners in a common source of supply." Kuntz, "Correlative Rights of Parties Owning Interest in a Common Source of Supply of Oil or Gas," 17th Inst. on Oil and Gas Law and Taxation, 217, 224-225 (1966).

For further discussion, see Article 10 and the comment thereon.

Art. 10. Liability to others with interests in common reservoir or deposit

A person with rights in a common reservoir or deposit of minerals may not make works, operate, or otherwise use his rights so as to deprive another intentionally or negligently of the liberty of enjoying his rights, or that may intentionally or negligently cause damage to him. This Article and Article 9 shall not affect the right of a landowner to extract liquid or gaseous minerals in accordance with the principle of Article 8.

Acts 1974, No. 50, §1, eff. Jan. 1, 1975.

Comment

Article 10 is a limited restatement of the obligation of good neighborhood contained in Article 667 of the Louisiana Civil Code. It views the relationship between those with rights in a common source of supply as one of neighborhood. It is to be noted that the phrasing of Article l0 is both broader and more limited than that of Article 667 of the Civil Code, which merely states that a proprietor may not "make any work....which may deprive his neighbor of the liberty of enjoying his own, or which may be the cause of damage to him." Article 10, however, provides that one owning rights in a common source supply of minerals may not "make works, operate, or otherwise use his rights so as to deprive another of the liberty of enjoying his rights or that may cause damage to him." The intent is to assure that the article will not be limited in its application to making works as such but will govern the entire range of exploratory and extractive activities in a common source of supply of minerals.,

The applicability of the principle of Article 667 of the Civil Code to mineral matters in Louisiana is sustained in the case of Higgins Oil & Fuel Co. v. Guaranty Oil Co., 145 La. 233, 82 So. 206 (1919), in which a landowner left a well uncapped to decrease the pumping efficiency of his neighbor's well. An injunction was granted against such conduct. See also Adams v. Grigsby, 152 So.2d 619 (La.App.2d Cir. 1963).

In Anglo-American jurisdictions oil and gas decisions have granted relief for waste of the common resource resulting from various causes. See Kuntz, "Correlative Rights of Parties Owning Interest in a Common Source of Supply of Oil and Gas," 17th Inst. on Oil and Gas Law and Taxation, 229 et seq. (1966). Relief has also been granted where an attempt was made to disguise waste beneath the cover of a sham, low magnitude economic utilization ofresources. Louisville Gas Co. v. Kentucky Heating Co., 117 Ky. 71, 77 S.W. 368(1903). Similarly, an owner of rights in a common source of supply has been protected against negligent waste of the common resource, as for example by a blowout which due care could prevent. Eliff v. Texon Drilling Co., 146 Tex. 575, 210 S. W. 2d 558 (1948). There does not, however, seem to be any instance to date in which courts have been willing to impose liability for waste of the common source of supply without either intent or negligence. This reflects a determination that the public interest in utilization of the resources is such that the ordinary risks of waste occasioned by occurrences which are not the result of intent or negligence should not be shifted from one party engaged in extraction to other engaged in the same utilitarian endeavor. It is in this sense, in view of the general jurisprudence, that Article 10 of the Mineral Code is more limited than Article 667 of the Civil Code. Under Article 10, the obligations of those having correlative rights in a common source of minerals result in liability only if damage is intentionally or negligently caused. The fact that ordinary risks have not been shifted among those engaged in extraction does not, however, mean that relief cannot be granted if, once an event has taken place, an operator .does not take reasonable steps to remedy a situation resulting in waste. If, for example, a producing formation is menaced by a blowout resulting from an unavoidable accident causing waste of the common resource, the operator suffering the accident cannot fail to take all necessary and reasonable measures to minimize the damage to other interests in the common source of supply. Larkins-Warr Trust Co. v. Watchorn Petroleum Co., 198 Okla. 12, 174 Pac. 2d 589 (1946).

Other cases in Anglo-American jurisdictions have dealt with spoilage of the common reservoir. For example, excessive rates of withdrawal causing intrusion of water in the producing formation, Manufacturers Gas and Oil Co. v. Indiana Natural Gas & Oil Co., 155 Ind. 461, 57 N.E. 912 (1900); failure to plug an abandoned well, permitting intrusion of water, Atkinson v. Virginia Oil & Gas Co., 72 W.Va. 707, 79 S.E. 647 (1913); and negligence is "shooting" a well, Commanche Duke Oil Co. v. Texas & Pacific Coal Co., 298 S.W. 554 (Tex. Comm. 1927), have all been situations warranting relief. These types of conduct can cause damage either to production or energy rights or both.

Modern techniques of pressure maintenance and secondary recovery are beginning to cause problems in other jurisdictions. In one instance, water flood operations deprived an owner of his right to primary production, and relief was granted. Tidewater Oil Co. v. Jackson, 329 F.2d 157 (10th Cir. 1963).

This brief review of cases involving correlative rights in other jurisdictions is not intended to suggest that the Louisiana Supreme Court must necessarily adopt the holding of any or all of those cases as a result of the enactment of Article 10. The review is given merely to point out the general nature of the doctrine of correlative rights and the types of interests which have been protected in other states. It is believed that this article furnishes the necessary flexibility to Louisiana courts to deal with problems of correlative rights in a common source of supply of oil, gas, or other minerals in Louisiana, and it is thus intended that this device be used to make it clear that correlative rights of those with interests in a common source are protected.

It should be noted that if by exercise of the policy power the correlative rights of the parties are regulated or fixed by an administrative agency, the rule of private property in Article 10 limiting liability to intentionally or negligently caused damage would not excuse the party for violation of the regulatory order.

The reference to Article 8 is intended to assure that although the obligation of neighborhood exists, the so-called "rule of capture" as stated in Article 8 will not be infringed by application of Articles 6 and 7. Thus, a landowner conducting lawful operations on his own property is not in violation of his obligation of good neighborhood simply because some of the fugitive minerals that he recovers may have been drawn from beneath land belonging to another. It should. be noted, however, that the Louisiana Supreme Court has held that although the rule of capture protects a landowner or one procuring rights from him in reducing minerals to possession even though migration from the land of another may result, if intentional or negligent conduct damages the property values of another as a result of waste of the common source of supply, the party damaged has a cause of action for such diminution of his property value. McCoy v. Arkansas Natural Gas Co., 175 La. 487, 143 So. 383 (1932). The rule of capture is not applicable to solid minerals. Article 13 provides that a landowner may recover for unauthorized withdrawal of such minerals "by any means." Therefore, the limiting words of Article 10 referring to Article 8 are applicable only to the fugitive minerals.

Art. 11. Reasonable regard for concurrent uses of the land burdened by mineral rights

A. The owner of land burdened by a mineral right or rights and the owner of a mineral right must exercise their respective rights with reasonable regard for those of the other. Similarly the owners of separate mineral rights in the same land must exercise their respective rights with reasonable regard for the rights of other owners.

B.(1) A reservation of mineral rights in an instrument transferring ownership of land must include mention of surface rights in the exercise of the mineral rights reserved, if not otherwise expressly provided by the parties.

(2) In the absence of particular provisions in the instrument regulating the extent, location and nature of the rights of the mineral owner to conduct operations on the property, the requirements of this Subsection are satisfied by inclusion of the following language in the reservation of mineral rights: "The transferor (Seller) shall exercise the mineral rights herein reserved with reasonable regard to the rights of the landowner, and shall use only so much of the land, including the surface, as is reasonably necessary to conduct his operations. Such exercise of mineral rights shall be subject to the provisions of Articles 11 and 22 of the Louisiana Mineral Code. The transferee (Buyer) recognizes that by virtue of the mineral reservation herein made, the mineral owner shall have the right to use so much of the land, including the surface, as is reasonably necessary to explore for, mine and produce the minerals."

Acts 1974, No. 50, §1, eff. Jan. 1, 1975. Amended by Acts 1982, No. 780, §1; Acts 2006, No. 446, §1; Acts 2023, No. 88, §1.

Comment

Article 11 is intended to provide a flexible formula governing the relationship between the mineral servitude owner and the owner of the servient estate. There are several articles in the Civil Code which could conceivably be applied to this relationship. Article 777 of the Civil Code [changed to Art. 748 by Acts 1077, No. 514] provides that the owner of the servient estate can do nothing tending to diminish the use of the servitude or make it more inconvenient. He cannot change the condition of the premises or transfer the exercise of the servitude to a different place from that on which it was assigned in the first instance. It is felt that application of this article to the relationship between landowner and mineral servitude owner might be unsatisfactory. To make a flat proscription that a landowner could not change the economic utilization of the surface of his property because of the existence of the mineral servitude would be unwise.

Article 778 of the Civil Code [changed by Acts 1977, No. 514] provides that the owner of predial servitude can use it only according to his title, without being at liberty to make either in the estate which owes the servitude, or in that to which the servitude is due, any alteration by which the condition of the first may be made worse. It is felt that application of this article to the relationship between the landowner and mineral servitude owner would also be difficult.

Article 779 of the Civil Code [changed to Art. 750 by Acts 1977, No. 514] provides that if the manner in which the servitude is to be used is uncertain, as if the place necessary for the exercise of a right of passage is not designated in the title, the owner of the estate which owes the servitude is bound to fix the place where he wishes it to be exercised. This article is clearly inappropriate to mineral servitudes.

As a substitute for these articles of the Civil Code it is intended that the general specification of Article 11 be adopted and that the relationship be one in which the parties each must exercise their rights to use the land with reasonable regard for those of the other. This standard does not present the difficulties noted in the articles applicable to predial servitudes. It should permit concurrent uses of land by the owner of mineral rights and the owner of the land and those deriving use rights from him. Further, the standard does not attempt to suggest that rights and liabilities must always be based on negligence. Uses by one party which may be considered ultra-hazardous as to the other's right to concurrent use of the land may in proper circumstances result in the imposition of liability without regard to the manner of performance of the activity in question.

Comment -1982
The second sentence of this article has been added to provide an express statement that the rights and duties pertaining to a mineral right extend directly to other owners of mineral rights.

PART 4. PROTECTION OF THE LANDOWNER'S RIGHTS IN MINERALS

Art. 12. Protection of landowner's interest in minerals

Except as provided in Article 14, the owner of land may protect his rights in minerals against trespass, damage, and other wrongful acts of interference by all means available for the protection of ownership.

Acts 1974, No. 50, §1, eff. Jan. 1, 1975.

Comment

Article 12 is a statement of established law. The landowner can protect himself in numerous ways, including assertion of the real actions, La. Code of Civil Procedure arts. 3651-3671 (1960), *e.g.*, Dixon v. American Liberty Oil Co., 226 La. 911, 77 So. 2d 533 (1954), Wetherbee v. Railroad Lands Co., 153 La. 1059, 97 So. 40(1923); actions in trespass, e.g., Layne Louisiana Co. v. Superior Oil Co., 209 La. 1014, 26 So. 2d 20 (1946), State v. Jefferson Island Salt Mining Co., 183 La. 304, 163 So. 145 (1935); actions in quasi contract against one who has produced minerals without authorization, *e.g.*, Lilesv. Producers Oil Co., 155 La. 385, 99 So. 339 (1924), Liles v. Barnhart, 152 La. 419, 93 So. 490(1922), Martin v. Texas Co., 150 La. 556, 90 So. 922 (1921); actions for. an accounting from owners of other fractional interests, *e.g.*, Huckabay v. Texas Co., 277 La. 191, 78 So. 2d 829 (1955), Wetherbee v. Railroad Lands Co., *supra*, and other means available for the protection of interests embodied in title to land or severed minerals. The right to recover damages for removal of minerals from beneath the land is treated expressly in Articles 13 and 14.

20

Art. 13. Damages for removal of solid minerals

A landowner may recover damages for the unauthorized removal from his land by any means of minerals occurring naturally in a solid state.

Acts 1974, No. 50, §1, eff. Jan. 1, 1975.

Comment

In the case of both solid and fugitive minerals the landowner is protected against unauthorized removal resulting from operations involving surface trespass on his property. However, it seems necessary to protect the landowner against removal of solid minerals as a result of operations conducted from locations on other property. It is conceivable that in some industries, such as the sulphur industry, which involve mining by processes of liquification below ground, there would be difficulty in proving the volume of minerals removed so as to substantiate a claim for damages. Such problems were at least partial motivation for the nonownership theory regarding liquid and gaseous minerals and are also among the reasons why Louisiana courts have been strict in their attitude toward claims by landowners for damages resulting from drainage of fugitive minerals from beneath their premises. However, problems of proof in the case of solid minerals should relate only to the manner in which courts administer the landowners exercise of his right to recover damages and not deny existence of the right. If there are problems created by the nature of the mining process, the courts might simply take a rather strict view in administering the rules regarding burden of proof. This is not to indicate support of any such attitude but merely to demonstrate that the problems of proof are more properly considered in the judicial administration of the landowners rights than in defining those rights in terms of basic property law.

The essence of Article 13 is supported by the decision rendered in State v. Jefferson Island Salt Mining Co., 183 La. 304, 163 So. 145 (1935).

Art. 14.   Drainage of fugitive minerals; exclusion of liability; exceptions

A landowner has no right against another who causes drainage of liquid or gaseous minerals from beneath his property if the drainage results from drilling or mining operations on other lands. This does not affect his right to relief for negligent or intentional waste under Articles 9 and 10, or against another who may be contractually obligated to protect his property from drainage.

Acts 1974, No. 50, §1, eff. Jan. 1, 1975.

Comment

Article 14 sustains established law. Louisiana Gas & Fuel Co. v. White Bros., 157 La. 728, 103 So. 23 (1925); Adams v. Grigsby, 152 So.2d 619 (La. App. 2d Cir. 1963); Frost-Johnson Lumber Co. v. Salling's Heirs, 150 La. 756, 91 So. 207 (1922) (by implication); McCoy v. Arkansas Natural Gas Co., 184 La. 101, 165 So. 632 (1936) (dictum); Higgins Oil & Fuel Co. v. Guaranty Oil Co., 145 La. 233, 82 So. 206 (1919) (dictum). Although the landowner cannot recover for removal of liquid or gaseous minerals so long as the operations take place on the neighboring premises, he is protected against both surface and subsurface invasions that result in unauthorized removal of minerals. *E.g.*, Gliptis v. Fifteen Oil Co., 204 La. 896, 16 So.2d 471 (1944) (subsurface invasion); Liles v. Texas Co., 166 La. 293, 117 So. 229 (1928); Liles v. Producers Oil Co., 155 La. 385, 99 So. 339 (1924); Liles v. Barnhart, 152 La. 419, 93 So. 490 (1922); Martin v. Texas Oil Co., 150 La. 556, 90 So. 922 (1921).

Articles 12 and 13, *supra*, and Article 14 do not deal with the possibility that the landowner may have property values which can be protected against damage as a result of operations on neighboring lands or that he may have certain correlative rights in a common reservoir overlying his property as well as that of others. These matters are treated in Articles 9 and 10.

The reference to "others who may be contractually obligated to protect his property from drainage" is intended principally to leave undisturbed the obligation of a mineral lessee to protect his lessor's premises from drainage. Williams v. Humble Oil & Refining Co., 290 F.Supp. 408 (E.D. La. 1968), affirmed, 432 F.2d 165 (5th Cir. 1970); Swope v. Holmes, 169 La. 17, 124 So. 131 (1929); Breaux v. Pan American Petroleum Corp., 163 So. 2d 406 (La. App. 3d Cir. 1964), cert. denied, 246 La. 581, 165 So. 2d 481 (1964). The fact that landowner A might not be able to recover from landowner B for drainage of oil or gas from beneath A's land would not prohibit A from obtaining appropriate relief against X, the lessee of both properties, whose operations caused the drainage, because X is contractually obligated to A to protect his property from drainage.

PART 5. CREATION OF MINERAL RIGHTS BY THE LANDOWNER

Art. 15. Right of landowner to convey, reserve, or lease right to explore and develop

A landowner may convey, reserve, or lease his right to explore and develop his land for production of minerals and to reduce them to possession.

Acts 1974, No. 50, §1, eff. Jan. 1, 1975.

Comment

Article 15 is a retention of the theory articulated in Frost-Johnson Lumber Co. v. Salling's Heirs, 150 La. 756, 91 So. 207 (1922).

Art. 16. Basic mineral rights; status as real rights

The basic mineral rights that may be created by a landowner are the mineral servitude, the mineral royalty, and the mineral lease. This enumeration does not exclude the creation of other mineral rights by a landowner. Mineral rights are real rights and are subject either to the prescription of nonuse for ten years or to special rules of law governing the term of their existence.

Acts 1974, No. 50, §1, eff. Jan. 1, 1975.

Comment

Use of the generic term "mineral rights" to describe the three basic interests may give rise to questions in the minds of some. First, the phrase "mineral rights" is sometimes used in reference to "mineral servitudes." This is loose usage, and it should not prevent utilization of the term to describe all types of interests arising from the landowner's conveyance, reservation, or lease of his own "mineral rights."

There are many types of transactions which may create interests which should be regarded as mineral rights and, therefore, real rights. For example, a production payment (limited royalty) carved from the landowner's interest in minerals should be characterized as a real right under present law: By analogy to Hodges v. Norton, 200 La. 614, 8 So. 2d 618 (1942), the production payment is a fixed-term interest subject to prescription, the only salient difference being that the term of existence for the production payment is usually fixed by money or amounts of production rather than an agreed number of years. On the other hand, many contracts are merely personal in nature (e.g., drilling contracts) though they may be closely related to the development or exploitation of property for mineral production. It would be impossible to attempt by limited definitions to compete with the creativity of the business community and legal profession in framing mineral transactions. Further, it would be improper to inhibit this creativity and to bind the courts to a specified list of real rights relating to minerals.

The characterization of all "mineral rights" as real rights in land reflects present law insofar as mineral servitudes, mineral royalties, and similar interests are concerned. However, the characterization is at least a superficial change fron the judicial attitude toward the mineral lease. *E.g.*, Harwood Oil and Mining Co. v. Black, 240 La. 641, 124 So. 2d 764 (1960); Reagan v. Murphy, 235 La. 529, 105 So. 2d 210 (1958); Arnoldv. Sun Oil Co., 218 La. 50, 48 So. 2d 369 (1950); Gulf Refining Co. v. Glassell, 185 La. 143, 168 So.

755 (1936). It is intended that this article make it clear that the mineral lease is a species of mineral rights and, as a result of that classification, is a real right. However, this does not· mean that the mineral lease is necessarily subject to rules of liberative prescription governing such rights as mineral servitudes. The functional distinctions between the mineral lease and the mineral servitude are fully accommodated in the articles regarding the lease. See Articles 114-148. It is desirable to recognize that the combined substance of the patchwork of existing jurisprudence and statutes together with the functional realities of the mineral leasing transaction make it clear that though the mineral lease is a hybrid institution, it is a real right and should be recognized as such. By way of functional comparison, the lease, like the mineral servitude, conveys rights to explore and develop, to produce minerals, to reduce them to possession, and to assert title to a specified portion of the production. The mineral lease has long been subject to the registry laws, La. R.S. 9:2721-24 (1950). See Article 18 of the Mineral Code. It has been subject to assertion and defense as real right by use of the real actions, La.R.S. 9:1105 (1950) [changed to Articles 31:18 and 31:114.et seq. by Acts 1974, No. 50); La. Code of Civil Procedure Art. 3664 (1960). It has been subject to mortgage as a corporeal immovable, La. R.S. 9:5101 (1950), now Articles 203 and 204 of the Mineral Code. And it has been given protection in the event of a partition by licitation, La. Civil Code Art. 741 (1870, as amended), now Articles 178-187 of the Mineral Code. All things considered, the lease has the major characteristics of a real right: the mineral lessee may follow the land, regardless of transfers of ownership; the mineral lessee may assert his rights against the world just as the proprietor of any other real right; he may enjoy directly and draw from the land a part of its economic advantages by appropriating a wasting asset; he has certain rights of preference; and he holds a right that is in reality susceptible of a type of possession through exercise. Regarding these as salient characteristics of real rights, see generally, 1 Yiannopoulos, Civil Law of Property Ch. 6 (1966). It is true that there are certain distinctions from the normal real right which give the mineral lease markings of kinship to personal rights. Not all obligations created by the lease are binding on a subsequent owner of the land. However, these distinguishing marks are susceptible of recognition and are dealt with appropriately in the articles of this code governing mineral leases. The basic purpose of this article is to recognize that insofar as the mineral lease transfers both operating

rights and rights to production it is a real right and not a mere personal contract.

The reservation stating that all mineral rights are either subject to prescription or specified rules of statutory law is intended to allow the establishment of desired principles necessary to accommodate peculiar features of the mineral lease. Principal among these is the limitation that a mineral lease must have a term and may not be continued for more than ten years without drilling or mining operations or production. Article 115. The reservation also makes allowances for the so called "imprescriptible" mineral rights that arise from conveyance to the United States, or any of its agencies or subdivisions, or to the State of Louisiana or any of its subdivisions. See Articles 149 through 152, formerly La. R.S. 9:5806 (1950, as amended).

Art. 17. Rescission for lesion beyond moiety unavailable

A sale of a mineral right is not subject to rescission for lesion beyond moiety.

Acts 1974, No. 50, §1, eff. Jan. 1, 1975.

Comment

The right to rescission for lesion beyond moiety is granted in La. Civil Code Arts. 1861-62 [changed to C.C. Arts. 1965, 2593 by Acts 1984, No. 331]. Article 17 represents existing law as to mineral transactions on undeveloped property. Haas v. Cerami, 201 La. 612, 10 So. 2d 61 (1942); Wilkins v. Nelson, 155 La. 807, 99 So. 607 (1924). This is appropriate to the speculative character of such transactions. A case could be made for application of the principle of lesion when the rights sold are in a fully developed property, thus permitting rather accurate determination of reserves and computations of values. However, considering the nature of transactions in developed properties and the facts that parties to them are usually experienced and lending institutions involved are highly conservative, the opportunities for the kind of overreaching which the concept of lesion was designed to prohibit are small indeed. Thus it is reasonable to make the doctrine of lesion beyond moiety inapplicable to all mineral transactions.

CHAPTER 3. THE NATURE OF MINERAL RIGHTS AND THE CAPACITY, AUTHORITY, AND FORMALITIES NECESSARY TO THEIR CREATION

Art. 18. Nature of mineral rights

A mineral right is an incorporeal immovable. It is alienable and heritable. The situs of a mineral right is the parish or parishes in which the land burdened is located. All sales, contracts, and judgments affecting mineral rights are subject to the laws of registry.

Acts 1974, No. 50, §1, eff. Jan. 1, 1975.

Comment

The term "mineral rights" as defined by Article 16 includes the mineral servitude, the mineral royalty, and the mineral lease. Characterization of the mineral servitude as an incorporeal immovable is consistent with the jurisprudence and with the provisions of Articles 460 and 471 of the Civil Code. Though the heritability of the mineral servitude was not determined in Frost-Johnson Lumber Co. v. Salling's Heirs, 150 La. 756, 91 So. 207 (1922), this question was definitely answered and the mineral servitude was declared to be a heritable right in Ford v. Williams, 189 La. 229, 179 So. 298 (1938). See also Munn v. Wadley, 192 La. 874, 189 So. 561 (1939) (mineral rights characterized as "realty", transfer of which is controlled by Louisiana law). The statement that the situs of a mineral servitude is the parish or parishes in which the land burdened by it is located is also a concept embodied in present law. La. Code of Civil Procedure Art. 80 (1960); Payne v. Walmsey, 185 So. 88 (La.App.2d Cir. 1938). All "mineral rights," which includes mineral leases, are subject to the laws of registry. Article 18; La. Civil Code art. 2662 (1870); La.R.S. 9:2721-24 (1950).

Though the jurisprudence has sometimes spoken of the mineral royalty as a "real obligation," there is no doubt that it meets the definition of a real right and that, as such, it has the characteristics included in this article. For language regarding the real obligation concept, see e.g., Vincent v. Bullock, 192 La. I, 187 So. 35 (1939). The royalty is, however, also referred to as a real right. See. e.g., Continental Oil Co. v. Landry, 215 La.. 518,41 So.2d 73 (1949). Professor Yiannopoulos suggests that the Civil Code articles on real obligations are superfluous. 1 Yiannopoulos, Civil Law of Property, § 115 (1966). Insofar as heritability and situs are concerned, there is no reason for distinction between a mineral royalty and a mineral servitude.

Although there has been considerable confusion over whether the interest of the lessee under a mineral lease is a real right or merely a personal contract, there is no doubt that the lease creates an incorporeal immovable. Incorporeal things are categorized as movable or immovable "according to the object to which they apply." La. Civil Code art. 470 (1870). Doubts which have been raised by the jurisprudence were fully dispelled by the combination of the statutory law and judicial decisions. See La. R.S. 9: 1105 (1950) [now R.S. 31:16, 31:18, 31:141 et seq.]; La.R.S. 9:2721-24 (1950); La. Code of Civil Procedure art. 3664 (1960); Succession of Simms, 250 La. 177, 195 So.2d 114 (1966); St. Charles Land Trust v. St. Amant, 253 La. 243, 217 So.2d 385 (1969).

Art. 19.   Capacity to create mineral rights

Capacity to create a mineral right is established by the laws governing capacity to alienate immovables.

Acts 1974, No. 50, §1, eff. Jan. 1, 1975.

Comment

Article 19 makes no changes in the law and merely expresses the idea that questions of capacity are to be controlled by appropriate provisions of the general law.

THE NATURE OF MINERAL RIGHTS

Art. 20. Authority to create mineral rights

The authority of a tutor, curator, succession representative, or trustee to create a mineral right on property subject to his administration is governed by the laws applicable to each.

Acts 1974, No. 50, §1, eff. Jan. 1, 1975.

Comment

Regulation of authority to act for persons under disability or for successions is now adequately governed by provisions of general law. See La. R.S. 9:711-13 (1950) [repealed; now C.C.P. arts. 4268, 4271]; La. Code of Civil Procedure art. 4271 (1960) (authorization of tutor); La. Code of Civil Procedure art. 4554 (1960) (interdicts); La. Code of Civil Procedure arts. 3224-25 (1960) (continuation of business by succession representative); La. Code of Civil Procedure arts. 3261-82 (1960) (sale of property by succession representative); La. Code of Civil Procedure art. 3227 (1960) (performance of executory contracts by succession representative).

Under Louisiana law a trustee is allowed to alienate immovable property unless prohibited by the trust agreement and even then any such prohibition is limited to a period of fifteen years from the settlor's death. La.R.S. 9:2119 (1950, as revised, 1964). The power to alienate immovables would certainly include power to create mineral rights. No changes are intended in any laws regarding authorization to create mineral rights.

CHAPTER 4. THE MINERAL SERVITUDE

PART 1. THE NATURE OF THE MINERAL SERVITUDE

Art. 21. Nature of mineral servitude

A mineral servitude is the right of enjoyment of land belonging to another for the purpose of exploring for and producing minerals and reducing them to possession and ownership.

Acts 1974, No. 50, §1, eff. Jan. 1, 1975.

Comment

Article 21 is amply supported in the jurisprudence. *E.g.*, Frost Johnson Lumber Co. v. Salling's Heirs, 150 La. 756, 91 So. 207 (1922); Wemple v. Nabors Oil and Gas Co., 154 La. 483, 97 So. 666 (1923); Union Sulphur Co. v. Andrau, 217 La. 662, 47 So.2d 38 (1950) (dictum); Horn v. Skelly Oil Co., 224 La. 709, 70 So.2d 657 (1954); Scott v. Hunt Oil Co., 160 So.2d 433 (La.App.2d Cir. 1964), writs denied, 245 La. 950, 162 So.2d 8.

Art. 22. Certain rights and obligations of mineral servitude owner

The owner of a mineral servitude is under no obligation to exercise it. If he does, he is entitled to use only so much of the land as is reasonably necessary to conduct his operations. He is obligated, insofar as practicable, to restore the surface to its original condition at the earliest reasonable time.

Acts 1974, No. 50, §1, eff. Jan. 1, 1975.

Comment

Article 22 is supported in the jurisprudence cited in the comment following Article 21.

Art. 23. Right of servitude owner to operate; protection thereof

The owner of a mineral servitude may conduct his operations with the freedom and subject to the restrictions that apply to a landowner. He may protect his right against interference or damage by all of the means available to a landowner.

Acts 1974, No. 50, §1, eff. Jan. 1, 1975.

Comment

For discussion of the landowner's right to explore for and produce minerals and the means of protecting his interest, see the comments following Articles 8 through 14.

PART 2. WHO MAY CREATE MINERAL SERVITUDES

Art. 24. Right of landowner to create mineral servitude

Except as provided in Article 25, a mineral servitude may be created only by a landowner who owns the right to explore for and produce minerals when the servitude is created.

Acts 1974, No. 50, §1, eff. Jan. 1, 1975.

Comment

This article reflects firmly established jurisprudence. See e.g., Hodges v. Long-Bell Petroleum Co., 204 La. 198, 121 So.2d 831 (1960); Bourg v. Herbert, 224 La. 535,70 So.2d 116 (1954); Long-Bell Petroleum Co. v. Granger, 222 La. 670, 63 So.2d 420 (1953); McMurrey v. Gray, 216 La. 904, 45 So. 2d 73 (1950); Long-Bell Petroleum Co. v. Tritico, 216 La. 426, 43 So. 2d 783 (1950); Gulf Refining v. Orr, 207 La. 915, 22 So.2d 269 (1945); Superior Oil Producing Co. v. Leckett, 189 La. 972, 181 So. 462 (1938).

Art. 25.   Right of conditional landowner to create mineral servitude

A mineral servitude may be created by a landowner whose title terminates at a particular time or upon the occurrence of a certain condition but it is extinguished at the specified time or on occurrence of the condition divesting the title.

Acts 1974, No. 50, §1, eff. Jan. 1, 1975.

Comment

This Article gives those with conditional titles the same rights to create mineral servitudes as they have to create other servitudes. La. Civil Code art. 736 (1870) [now C.C. art. 712]; *cf.,* La. Civil Code art. 735 (1870) [now C.C. art. 713] (allowing the purchaser with a reservation of redemption to impose servitudes on property acquired by him, subject to extinction if the right of redemption is exercised).

Art. 26. Usufructuary may not create mineral servitude

A usufructuary cannot establish a mineral servitude on the estate of which he has the usufruct even for the period of his usufruct.

Acts 1974, No. 50, §1, eff. Jan. 1, 1975.

Comment

The rule against usufructuaries creating mineral servitudes is consistent with the general prohibition. La. Civil Code art. 737 (1870) [now C.C. art. 711]. For full explanation of the rights of usufructuaries regarding minerals, see Articles 188 through 196 and the comments thereon.

PART 3. MODES OF EXTINCTION OF MINERAL SERVITUDES

Art. 27. Extinction of mineral servitudes

A mineral servitude is extinguished by:

(1) prescription resulting from nonuse for ten years;

(2) confusion;

(3) renunciation of the servitude on the part of him to whom it is due, or the express remission of his right;

(4) expiration of the time for which the servitude was granted, or the happening of the dissolving condition attached to the servitude; or

(5) extinction of the right of him who established the servitude.

Acts 1974, No. 50, §1, eff. Jan. 1, 1975.

Comment

Article 27 is a partial restatement of Civil Code Article 783 [now c.c. arts. 751, 753,765,770,771,773, and 774] stating the modes of extinction of predial servitudes. See also Article 2130 of the Civil Code [now c.c. art. 1854] regarding extinction of obligations.

The first ground stated for extinction of mineral servitudes is prescription resulting from nonuse for ten years. The evolution of a system of terminable mineral intersts was one of the principal purposes of the original servitude analogy. Article 27 perpetuates the principle of prescriptibility. La. Civil Code art. 789 (1870); Wise v. Watkins, 222 La. 493, 62 So.2d 653 (1953); Haynes .v. King, 219 La. 162, 52 So.2d 531 (1951); Standard Oil Co. v. Futral, 204 La. 215, 15 So.2d 65 (1943); Hightower v. Maritzky, 193 La. 998, 195 So. 518 (1940); Lynn v. Harrington, 193 La. 877,

34

192 So. 577 (1939); Coyle v. North Central Texas Oil Co., 187 La. 238, 174 So. 274 (1937); Palmer Corp. of Louisiana v. Moore, 171 La. 774,132 So. 229 (931); Frost-Johnson Lumber Co. v. Salling's Heirs, 150 La. 756, 91 So. 207 (1922). Regarding the matter of date of creation of mineral servitudes, see Article 28 and the comment thereon.

Excluded as causes of extinction are the destruction of the servient estate and abandonment of "that part of the estate which owes the servitude." Both are deemed inappropriate to the law applicable to mineral servitudes. It is difficult to envision "destruction" of an estate owing a mineral servitude considering the level of technological advancement in drilling and production techniques. As to abandonment of the part of the servient estate owing the servitude this mode of extinction is reasonable in the case of predial servitudes, such as servitudes of passage, but it is inappropriate to the law of mineral servitudes. First, identification of "the part...which owes" a mineral servitude is usually impossible before it is used and difficult even in the development stage. Second, it is unlikely that a landowner would "abandon" his surface ownership to the mineral servitude owner. In such an unlikely event, means are available for conveyance to the servitude owner.

It should be noted that the provisions of paragraph 5 that mineral servitudes are extinguished by the extinction of the right of him who established the servitude is subject to one important qualification deriving from the public records doctrine. In Jefferson v. Childers, 189 La. 46,179 So. 30 (1938), plaintiff executed a deed of sale of certain land. The court found that the purchase price had never been paid and thus annulled the deed. Prior to the court's action, a mineral lease had been taken from plaintiff's vendee. The court held that the mineral lease, having acquired on the faith of the public records, could not be prejudiced by the setting aside of the deed of sale. Thus, the rule stated in paragraph 5 must be taken as subject to this limitation where a party in good faith has acquired a mineral servitude in reliance on the public records. The court emphasized the fact that the mineral lessee in that case not only relied on the public records but was in good faith in doing so.

PART 4. COMMENCEMENT OF PRESCRIPTION
SUBPART A. GENERAL PRINCIPLES

Art. 28. Commencement of prescription of nonuse

Prescription of nonuse of a mineral servitude commences from the date on which it is created.

Acts 1974, No. 50, §1, eff. Jan. 1, 1975.

Comment

Article 28 is a statement of established law. See La.R.S. 30: 112 (1950); Ober v. Williams, 213 La. 568, 35 So. 2d 219 (1948); Chicago Mill & Lumber Co. v. Ayer Timber Co., 131 So. 2d 635 (La. App. 2d Cir. 1961). However, it must be noted that the Article does not afford great relief to those concerned over pinpointing the date of creation of a mineral servitude and the possibility of some degree of manipulation which may permit a landowner to control mineral rights for a period in excess of ten years. In Ober v. Williams, *supra*, the landowner executed a contract to sell land on a specified future date subject to a reservation of minerals in the sale. The sale was on the condition that the buyer would complete certain improvements on the property and was later executed. Ultimately, the date from which liberative prescription commenced to run became an issue of significance to the parties. It was determined that no servitude existed until the sale itself was executed. Noting the possibility that the holding presented opportunities for evasion of the public policy underlying the servitude theory, the supreme court stated that when faced with a scheme to avoid the public policy, it could adequately deal with such a situation. By itself, this decision suggests that personal contracts regarding future conveyances resulting in creation of mineral servitudes are innocuous as long as they are executed by the parties in good faith, in the normal course of commerce, and without intent to defraud the public policy.

Some doubt has been cast on the meaning of Ober v. Williams, *supra*, by the decision of the Second Circuit Court of Appeal in

Chicago Mill & Lumber Co. v. Ayer Timber Co., *supra*, which was disposed of on an exception of no cause of action. In that case, the landowner had granted a predial lease with an option to the lessee to purchase the property at the end of the five-year term of the lease, subject to the reservation of minerals at the time of sale. In the original lease-option contract the landowner specifically reserved from the predial lease all rights to explore and drill for oil and gas. The lessee exercised the option. Production occurred within ten years from exercise of the option but more than ten years from the date of the original lease-option contract. Plaintiff expressly alleged that the lease-option contract was entered into with the intent of circumventing the public policy embodied in the rules of liberative prescription applicable to mineral servitudes. On original hearing, the exception of no cause of action was denied. On rehearing, however, the exception was sustained on the ground that the parties have a right to make contracts for the future sale of immovables. As no servitude came into being until execution of the sale, prescription could not begin to run until that time, and the principle of Ober v. Williams, *supra*, was deemed applicable. The court, in disregarding the allegation of intent to circumvent the public policy, stated that "there can be no attempt to evade, prolong or extend the ten year prescription of nonuse until the mineral servitude is created." The public policy,it was stated, "is directed against attempts to renounce prescription in advance, or to suspend or interrupt prescription by means other than usual or by other means expressly recognized by the law, such as acknowledgments made specifically for the purpose and with the intention of interrupting the running of prescription. What the courts have considered as contrary to public policy are agreements which seek to cause the lands to be burdened with mineral servitudes for more than ten years without use."

The Louisiana Supreme Court denied writs in the Chicago Mill case. This decision and the denial of writs might be taken as some indication that the courts may be moving in the direction of exercising somewhat less control over the incidents of entry into otherwise legal contracts concerning future dealings with mineral rights than one might have expected.

By comparison with the Chicago Mill case, the decision of the Second Circuit Court of Appeal in Ober v. McGinty, 66 So.2d 385 (La.App.2d Cir. 1953) should be considered. In that case a vendor of land reserved both minerals and a right to extend the servitude for an additional ten years by payment of consideration after the first ten years expired. This was found to be an attempt to evade the law of prescription and enforcement of the contract was refused. This decision provides insight into the remarks of the second circuit in the Chicago Mill case regarding its interpretation of the public policy embodied in the rules of prescription. In this instance, the servitude was created, and there was an accompanying attempt to guarantee to the purchaser a right of renewal for a trifling amount of consideration, which was viewed as an illegal attempt to waive prescription in advance of its accrual. As framed, the McGinty transaction contemplated extension of the servitude created in the original deed. Thus, it was properly viewed as an attempt to waive prescription in advance. If upheld, the contract would have burdened the land and bound future purchasers.

A variant of the problem is found in the recent decision of LeBleu v. LeBleu, 206 So.2d 551 (La.App.3d Cir. 1968), in which the servitude owner executed instruments with the landowner by which the servitude owner: (1) appointed the landowner as agent, granting full executive rights over the outstanding mineral servitude; (2) conveyed or released a portion of the outstanding mineral servitude rights to the landowner; and (3) received from the landowner a promise that if the outstanding servitude interest expired by the accrual of prescription, the landowner would convey to the servitude owner a one-fourth mineral interest, a larger mineral interest than was held by the servitude owner. The third circuit denied the servitude owner's demand for specific performance of the agreement to convey the new interest upon expiration of the old one, relying on Ober v. McGinty, *supra*, and other authorities, and on the principle of the Civil Code that one cannot renounce the benefit of prescription not yet accrued. Chicago Mill & Lumber Co. v. Ayer Timber Co., *supra*, was considered distinguishable.

It is arguable that the court need not have struck down the LeBleu contract. In return for a present benefit—a larger share of the mineral rights and executive rights over the servitude owner's interest—the landowner made a promise to convey a different, larger mineral servitude to the plaintiff if a certain condition occurred, that is, if the then outstanding interest expired for nonuse. It might have been concluded as in Chicago Mill, that no real right was created by the contract. The life of the existing mineral servitude was not in any way affected, and the accrual of prescription against it continued in the manner contemplated by law. It might have been held that this contract is like any other based on the occurrence of a future condition. The problem in this instance may have been that the consideration given by the plaintiff and the promise given by the defendant landowner centered on a condition involving the life of an existing mineral servitude.

Despite the confusion presented by this group of decisions, it was deemed impractical to attempt to foresee all available contractual approaches which parties might make toward the creation of mineral servitudes. Some can be sustained and other cannot. The problem of definition is best left to the courts.

SUBPART B. INTERRUPTION OF THE PRESCRIPTION OF NONUSE

Art. 29. How prescription of nonuse is interrupted

The prescription of nonuse running against a mineral servitude is interrupted by good faith operations for the discovery and production of minerals. By good faith is meant that the operations must be

(1) commenced with reasonable expectation of discovering and producing minerals in paying quantities at a particular point or depth,

(2) continued at the site chosen to that point or depth, and

(3) conducted in such a manner that they constitute a single operation although actual drilling or mining is not conducted at all times.

Acts 1974, No. 50, §29, eff. Jan. 1, 1975.

Comment

Article 29 is a broad restatement of the rule evolved for oil and gas. It is intended to be sufficiently general in structure so that it can be adapted and applied to fit any mining industry. In speaking of "operations for the discovery and production of minerals" it is intended that the rule of Goldsmith v. McCoy, 190 La. 320, 182 So. 519 (1938) be incorporated. That case held that mere exploration or prospecting by geophysical methods is not sufficient to constitute a use of a mineral servitude. It is contemplated that the operations must involve use of equipment of the type necessary to produce minerals if they should be located.

Insofar as the petroleum industry is concerned, Article 29 perpetuates the rule that dry hole drilling operations satisfying the stated criteria will interrupt prescription. See Taylor v. Dunn, 233 La. 617, 97 So. 2d 415 (1957); White v. Frank B. Treat & Son, Inc., 230 La. 1017, 89 So. 2d 883 (1956); McMurrey v. Gray, 216 La. 904, 45 So. 2d 73 (1947); International Paper Co. v. Louisiana Central Lumber Co., 202 La. 621,12 So. 2d 659 (1943); Hunter Co. v. Ulrich, 200 La. 5368 So. 2d 531 (1942); Ohio Oil Co. v. Cox; 196 La. 193, 198 So. 902 (1940); Lynn v. Harrington, 193 La. 877, 192 So. 577 (1939); Louisiana Petroleum Co. v. Broussard, 172 La. 613, 135 So. 1 (1931); Keebler v. Seubert, 167 La. 901, 120 So. 591 (1929); Kellogg Bros. Inc. v. Singer Mfg. Co., 131 So.2d 578 (La.App.2d Cir. 1961). What will constitute drilling to a point at which there is reasonable expectation of commercial production varies from case to case depending on the circumstances. Reasonableness of expectation in a wildcate area may not be similar in any respect to reasonableness in a known productive area. The courts have reflected a commendably sound attitude in these situations, applying an objective standard to determine the reasonableness of the expectation.

Some comment is appropriate on the rather curious mixture of subjective and objective standards in Article 26. Operations must be in "good faith," but "good faith" is proven only if the operations meet evidentiary standards requiring that there be a "reasonable" expectation of production, an objective standard. This is, however, the test evolved by the courts and it has proven workable. Short of the standards stated in Article 26, then, no amount of subjective good faith or effort will sustain a contention that a use has occurred. See Louisiana Petroleum Co. v. Broussard, *supra*. The standard which has developed is a statement of a basic requirement--*i.e.* good faith operations for the discovery and production of minerals--accompanied by the statement of an evidentiary standard--*i.e.* drilling to a depth at which there is a reasonable expectation of commercial production. The evidentiary requirement is a well-conceived judicial device for assuring a reasonably certain and administrable standard of proof that "good faith operations" have been conducted and a use has resulted. Any lesser standard would inject the court into an impenetrable forest of cases involving the good faith of operators who have fallen short of the evidentiary standard now applied and would introduce an undesirable degree of subjectivity and, thus, uncertainty into the law of use. What the courts have done, then, is to shape a subjective standard --"good faith"-- into an objective one by addition of the requirement of reasonableness of the expectation of production.

Article 29(3) takes cognizance of the fact that actual drilling operations may be suspended without destroying the continuity of a single operation ultimately constituting a use. It is necessarily stated in a loose fashion as no workable definition can be conceived of what will constitute a "single operation." The circumstances of McMurrey v. Gray, 216 La. 904, 45 So. 2d 73 (1947), support the statement of this Article.

Art. 30. Date on which prescription interrupted and commenced anew

An interruption takes place on the date actual drilling or mining operations are commenced on the land burdened by the servitude or, as provided in Article 33, on a conventional or compulsory unit including all or a portion thereof. Preparations for the commencement of actual drilling or mining operations, such as geological or geophysical exploration, surveying, clearing of a site, and the hauling and erection of materials and structures necessary to conduct operations do not interrupt prescription. Prescription commences anew from the last day on which actual drilling or mining operations are conducted.

Acts 1974, No. 50, §30, eff. Jan. 1, 1975.

Comment

>Article 30 is in substantia! accord with the present law. See generally the authorities cited in the comment on Article 29, *supra*. Although it is not entirely clear, the statement that prescription is interrupted only on the date "actual drilling or mining operations" are begun may constitute a change in the present law. It might have been inferred from La. R.S. 30: 112 (1950) (repealed) that an interruption by drilling or mining operations would commence only from the date of actual drilling or mining operations. However, the jurisprudence is apparently contrary to any such inference. See Keebler v. Seubert, 167 La. 901, 120 So. 591 (1929). See also the opinions in Mire v. Hawkins, 177 So. 2d 795 (La. App. 3d Cir. 1965); writs granted 178 So. 2d 657; 249 La. 278, 186 So. 2d 591 (1966). The district court apparently sustained commencement of preparatory operations as marking the date of interruption. However, this holding was not appealed and the question, though assumed as a basis for decision, was not at issue before the court of appeal or the supreme court. Article 30 excludes preparatory operations principally because doing so provides a more definite, ascertainable date for the interruption of prescription than the less definite time of when "operations for drilling" were begun. Determinations of when prescription is interrupted as to a mineral servitude are most often made after the passage of substantial time periods after the operative facts occurred. This being the case, it seems that customary business records will more reliably reveal the date a well is "spudded in" than when preparatory operations began.

Art. 31.   Operations beyond prescriptive date; effect as interruption

Actual drilling or mining operations commenced within the prescriptive period interrupt prescription although the operations are not completed until after the date on which prescription would have accrued.

Acts 1974, No. 50, §31, eff. Jan. 1, 1975.

Comment

Article 31 does not alter the law, though there is no clear holding to this effect. The decision in McMurrey v. Gray, 216 La. 904, 45 So.2d 73 (1949), is necessarily based on the assumption that the principle stated is valid. In that case the landowner was enjoined from preventing prosecution of operations begun prior to the prescriptive date which the servitude owner's lessee was attempting to resume after the prescriptive date. The right to resume operations was upheld by the grant of the injunction, though at that point it was held that no use had occurred because drilling had not proceeded to a depth at which there was reasonable expectation of production in paying quantities.

Art. 32. Interruption by additional operations

When prescription has commenced anew following the cessation of drilling or mining operations, it may later be interrupted by a good faith attempt to complete the well or mine or place it in production conducted in accordance with the general principles stated in Articles 29 through 31.

Acts 1974, No. 50, §32, eff. Jan. 1, 1975.

Comment

Article 32 contemplates a situation which has not been dealt with in the jurisprudence. It is one which apparently has not arisen because the occasions on which it might be of importance are rare. However, it is nevertheless a situation that might arise and become crucial to the life of a servitude. The article intends that if operations sufficient to interrupt prescription have terminated, prescription may be interrupted again by operations in the same hole or in the same mine so long as such operatons are conducted in accordance with the general principles stated in Articles 29 through 31. Concerning the types of operations contemplated by this article, it is intended to include such operations as testing by actual surface production, plugging back, side-tracking, and similar operations conducted by use of equipment in the well bore. The mere gathering of geological or geophysical data should not be deemed sufficient to constitute an interruption, but the gathering of such data might, under proper circumstances, be viewed as a legitimate part of operations for completion of a well or placing it in production.

Art. 33. Unit operations; effect as interruption of prescription

Operations conducted on land other than that burdened by a mineral servitude and constituting part of a conventional or compulsory unit that includes only a part of the land burdened by the servitude will, if otherwise sufficient to interrupt prescription according to Articles 29 through 32, interrupt prescription only as to that portion of the tract burdened by the servitude included in the unit provided such operations are for the discovery and production of minerals from the unitized sand or sands.

Acts 1974, No. 50, §33, eff. Jan. 1, 1975.

Comment

Article 33 is consonant with Trunkline Gas Co. v. Steen, 249 La. 520, 187 So.2d 720 (1966) insofar as it applies to operations on the servitude premises. It is also harmonious with Mire v. Hawkins, 249 La. 278, 186 So.2d 591 (1966) in applying the "dry hole" rule to unit operations. Further, it is consonant with the prior decisions on the effect of compulsory unit production. Jumonville Pipe & Machinery Co. v. Federal Land Bank, 230 La. 41, 87 So.2d 721 (1956); Childs v. Washington, 229 La. 869, 87 So. 2d 111 (1956); Frey v. Miller, 165 So. 2d 43 (La. App.3d Cir. 1964) writs denied, 167 So.2d 669. The principle articulated in Article 33 is also made applicable by Article 34 to the situation in which a servitude tract is unitized with a well that is or becomes shut in and to unit production by Article 37.

Article 33 also preserves the rule of Matlock Oil Co. v. Gerard, 263 So.2d 413 (La.App.2d Cir. 1972), writs denied, 265 So.2d 241 (1972), that the operations off the servitude tract though conducted within the unitized area and even through the hole designated as the unit well, must be directed toward discovery and production from the unitized sands. For further discussion of the effects of unit operations, see the comments following Articles 34 and 37.

Art. 34. Shut-in well; testing as interruption of prescription

When there exists on a tract of land burdened by a mineral servitude, or on a conventional or compulsory unit that includes all or part thereof, a shut-in well proved through testing by surface production to be capable of producing minerals in paying quantities, prescription is interrupted on the date production is obtained by such testing. If only a part of the tract burdened by the servitude is included in such a unit and the unit well is on land other than that burdened by the servitude, the interruption of prescription extends only to that portion of the tract burdened by the servitude included in the unit. Prescription commences anew from the date on which the well is shut in after testing.

Acts 1974, No. 50, §34, eff. Jan. 1, 1975.

Comment

The jurisprudence has recognized that the presence of a shutin well capable of producing in commercial quantities has an effect on the running of prescription. Delatte v. Woods, 232 La. 341, 94 So. 2d 281 (1957); LeBlanc v. Haynesville Mercantile Co., 230 La. 299, 88 So.2d 377 (1956); Union Oil Co. of California v. Touchet, 229 La. 316, 86 So. 2d 50 (1956); Sohio Petroleum Co. v. V.S. & P.R.R., 222 La. 383, 62 So. 2d 615 (1952); Lee v. Goodwin, 174 So. 2d 651 (La. App. 2d Cir. 1965). writs denied 248 La. 149, 177 So. 2d 118. But see Pan American Petroleum Corp. v. O'Bier, 201 So. 2d 280 (La. App. 2d Cir. 1967), the special facts of which provide a sound limitation on the prior jurisprudence. Most of these cases deal with prescription accruing against a royalty interest. However, there is little doubt that the same principles apply to mineral servitudes. .

It is required that the commercial capability of the well be proven by surface production tests. However, in requiring that the well be capable of producing in "paying quantities" it is not intended that the well be proven to be one which will return investment costs. The concept of "production in paying quantities" is defined in Article 124 for the purpose of administering mineral leases. That definition furnishes an appropriate general guideline for interpretation of the same phrase in Article 34.

Although the courts spoke previously of the effect on prescription wrought by the presence of a shut-in well as an "interruption," no case arose requiring a clear determination of whether the effect as one of interruption or suspension. Further, though it seems that under the prior jurisprudence the "interruption" or "suspension", as the case may be, would have continued until the well was placed in production, there were no cases considering the possible effect of discontinuance of the interruption or suspension by an event such as a fire causing loss of the well. Regardless of whether the effect is deemed an interruption or a suspension of prescription, drafting of a provision treating the effect as continuing as long as the well was capable of producing in commercial quantities would have required some definition of the effect of events, such as blowouts, fires, or other occurrences, which would render the well incapable of production in paying quantities. Because it would be extremely difficult for a title examiner to determine the status of a well which remains shut in for an extended length of time, it is provided in Article 34 that the presence of a shut-in well be treated as an interruption of prescription on the date on which production is obtained in the surface production test and that prescription commences anew from the date on which the well is shut in following the test. This will preserve a mineral servitude for ten years, and it is unlikely that a market could not be found or any other condition hindering production be cleared up within that interval.

La.R.S. 30:112 (1958 supp.) (repealed) contained provisions which were difficult if not impossible to construe, but which appeared to contemplate that there was an effect on prescription only in the case of "contracts" providing for shut-in royalty payments. Indeed, some of the .prior .decisions might have been interpreted as making the effect dependent on the existence of such payments. However, the better view of the cases, and the intended principle of Article 34 is that the effect is not dependent on the type of mineral lease involved but only on whether there is a well present on the servitude tract or acreage unitized therewith which is proven to be capable of production in commercial quantities, not on whether shut-in royalties designated as constructive production in a lease are being paid.

Insofar as Article 34 limits the effect of an interruption to unitized acreage, it is harmonious with Article 33 regarding unit drilling operations and Article 37 regarding unit production.

Art. 35. Unitization with tested shut-in well as interruption of prescription

If the land, or part thereof, burdened by a mineral servitude is included in a conventional or compulsory unit on which there is a well located on other land within the unit capable of producing in paying quantities, as required by Article 34, and shut in at the time the unit is created, prescription is interrupted on and commences anew from the effective date of the order or act creating the unit.

Acts 1974, No. 50, §35, eff. Jan. 1, 1975.

Comment

In the vast majority of cases, the principle already stated in Article 34 is of greater significance to mineral royalty owners than to mineral servitude owners because if the well has been drilled on the servitude tract or on a unit after its formation, an interruption of prescription will result from the drilling operations. However, if the unit is formed after drilling, testing, and shutting in of the well, the rule will be of essential value to owners of mineral servitudes since no interruption will have been wrought by the drilling operations. Thus, Article 35 specifies that the effective date of the order or act creating the unit governs the date of interruption and commencement anew of prescription rather than the actual date on which the unit well might previously have been shut in.

47

Art. 36. Production as interruption of prescription

Prescription of nonuse is interrupted by the production of any mineral covered by the act creating the servitude. The interruption occurs on the date on which actual production begins and prescription commences anew from the date of cessation of actual production.

Acts 1974, No. 50, §36, eff. Jan. 1, 1975.

Comment

The rule stated in Article 36 concerning interruption of prescription by production is consonant with prior law. La. R.S. 30:112 (1958 supp.) (repealed); *e.g.*, Mays v. Hansbro, 222 La. 557,64 So. 2d 232 (1953). The prior law regarding the date of commencement of prescription anew after production was unclear. La. R.S. 30:112 (1950)(repealed) indicated that prescription might have commenced anew either after cessation of production or cessation of "production operations." The phrase "production operations" was highly ambiguous, and using the date of cessation of actual production therefore lends desirable certainty to the law.

Art. 37. Unit production as interruption of prescription

Production from a conventional or compulsory unit embracing all or part of the tract burdened by a mineral servitude interrupts prescription, but if the unit well is on land other than that burdened by the servitude, the interruption extends only to that portion of the servitude tract included in the unit.

Acts 1974, No. 50, §37, eff. Jan. 1, 1975.

Comment

As to compulsory units, Article 37 preserves the previous rule concerning production from a compulsory unit well located off the servitude tract. See Jumonville Pipe & Machinery Co. v. Federal

Land Bank, 230 La. 41, 87 So. 2d 721 (1956); Childs v. Washington, 229 La. 869, 87 So.2d 111 (1956); Frey v. Miller, 165 So. 2d 43 (La. App. 3d Cir. 1964), writs denied, 246 La. 844, 167 So.2d 669. For a discussion of these decisions see Hardy, "Ruminations on the Effect of Conservation Laws and Practices on the Louisiana Mineral Servitude and Mineral Royalty," 25 La. L. Rev. 824, 845-853, 858-861 (1965). As to production from compulsory unit wells on the servitude premises, this article is harmonious with Trunkline Gas Co. v. Steen, 249 La. 520, 187 So. 2d 720 (1966). The impact of Article 37 as to conventional units is unclear as the prior jurbprudence was inconsistent. Compare Elson v. Mathewes, 224 La. 417, 69 So. 2d 734 (1953) with Crown Central Petroleum Corp. v. Barousse, 238 La. 1013, 117 So. 2d 575(1960). The principle articulated in Article 37 is chosen to provide a single rule applicable to both conventional and compulsory unit operations. When a deed or other instrument is silent as to the intent of the parties regarding the effect of unit operations or production, the rule provided by law is made uniform. To distinguish the effect of compulsory unit operations from that· of conventional operations would be arbitrary. Parties may, however, contract for a broader rule under the provisions of Article 75.

Art. 38. Good faith production for beneficial purpose required

To interrupt prescription it is not necessary that minerals be produced in paying quantities. It is necessary only that minerals actually be produced in good faith with the intent of saving or otherwise using them for some beneficial purpose.

Acts 1974, No. 50, §38, eff. Jan. 1, 1975.

Comment

Article 38 is in harmony with the jurisprudence. Mars v. Hansbro, 222 La. 557,64 So.2d 232 (1953). The concept of production in paying quantities is peculiar to lease administration and is appropriate to the lessor-lessee relationship. However, the test for use of a servitude should not be that minerals be produced in paying quantities as long as the production is in good faith.

> Economically, it .does not seem that a servitude owner or his lessee would be likely to continue a losing operation for any extended period of time. Therefore, as a matter of fact, it seems that more often than not production continued for any length of time will be in paying quantities. However, it is quite possible that production might be continued for a short period of time in good faith in an attempt to make a particular property pay. Even though unsuccessful, such attempts should be recognized as uses of mineral servitudes as long as they are in good faith and the production is put to beneficial use.

Art. 39.   Attempt to restore or secure new production as interruption of prescription

After production has ceased and prescription has commenced anew, it may be interrupted by good faith operations conducted in accordance with the general principles of Articles 29 through 31 to restore production or to secure new production from the same well or mine, whether from the same geological formation or one different from that previously producing.

Acts 1974, No. 50, §39, eff. Jan. 1, 1975; Acts 2023, No. 88, §1.

Comment

Article 39 treats a situation which has not yet been of importance in the jurisprudence. Nevertheless, it is one which might arise and warrants treatment in the Mineral Code. Once actual production of minerals has ceased operations seeking to restore production or to secure new production from the same site may be conducted. It is felt that as long as such operations are conducted in good faith and in accordance with the basic principles stated in Articles 29 through 31, they should constitute an interruption of prescription.

Insofar as the petroleum industry is concerned, Article 39 should be construed to include any good faith reworking operations or operations for recompletion of the well in another sand that involve use of equipment in the well bore. Mere gathering of geological or geophysical information is not intended to suffice, though gathering such information might properly constitute part of an overall reworking operation interrupting prescription.

Art. 40. Interruption applicable to all minerals and modes of use

An interruption of prescription applies to all types of minerals covered by the act creating the servitude and to all modes of its use.

Acts 1974, No. 50, §40, eff. Jan. 1, 1975.

Comment

Article 796 of the Civil Code [repealed] provides that the mode of servitude is subject to prescription as well as the servitude itself. Article 40 assures that Article 796 of the Civil Code will not be applicable to mineral servitudes unless parties make some express agreement regarding prescription of mode of use. It is unrealistic and inequitable to provide that after conducting drilling and production operations for an extended period of time a servitude owner could not then mine the same or different minerals by a different method.

Article 798 of the Civil Code [now, C.C. art. 759] provides that if a servitude is used less extensively than the right given in the title creating it, the servitude is reduced to that which is preserved by possession during the prescriptive period. This article has not been applied to a mineral servitude except in the case of Ohio Oil Co. v. Ferguson, 213 La. 183, 34 So. 2d 746 (1948), in which the servitude owner sold to another all of his rights in a specified portion of the servitude tract. However, the question of the applicability of this article where only one mineral has been produced during the prescriptive period has not been raised in the jurisprudence. The intent of Article 40 is to assure that Article 798 of the Civil Code will not be applied to limit the extent of an interruption by operations for discovery and production of or

51

actual production of one mineral. Additionally, it is intended that use of one particular method of mining would not exclude other forms. Thus, strip mining would not exclude shaft mining or drilling.

Art. 41. Commencement of prescription anew following attempt to restore or secure new production

When prescription is interrupted, it commences anew from the last day on which operations are conducted in good faith to secure or restore production in paying quantities with reasonable expectation of success.

Acts 1974, No. 50, §41, eff. Jan. 1, 1975.

Comment

Article 41 is in keeping with the other articles regarding commencement of prescription anew following termination of operations and termination of production. See Articles 30 and 36. See also Articles 34 and 35.

SUBPART C. BY WHOM A USE MAY BE MADE

Art. 42. By whom a mineral servitude may be used

Except as provided in Articles 44 through 52, use of a mineral servitude must be by the owner of the servitude, his representative or employee, or some other person acting on his behalf.

Acts 1974, No. 50, §42, eff. Jan. 1, 1975.

Comment

Available Civil Code analogies for Article 42 include Articles 618, 793, 794, and 804 [now C.C. arts. 621, 757, 764]. Article 618 provides that a usufruct is forfeited for nonuse "by the usufructuary or by any person in his name." Article 793 provides that "it is not necessary that it [the servitude] should be exercised exclusively by the owner to whom it is due, or by those who use his rights, or who represent him directly, as the usufructuary, the lessee or tenant, the attorney-in-fact or agent. It suffices if the servitude has been exercised by workmen employed by the owner, or by his friends, or those who come to see him." Article794, however, qualifies 793 by requiring that "the use which anyone, even a stranger makes of" the servitude be one "appertaining to the estate." Article 804 provides that if a plea of prescription of nonuse is asserted, the owner of the estate to which the servitude is due must prove that "he, or some person in his name, has made use of the servitude as appertaining to his estate."

As the mineral servitude is in the nature of a personal servitude less than usufruct, it is reasonable to adopt the concept of Article 618 that a use must be by the servitude owner or someone in his name. Similarly, analogy can be made to Article 793, applicable to predial servitudes, insofar as it requires, that a use must be one "appertaining to" the dominant estate, substituting the servitude owner for the concept of the dominant estate. In practical terms, this boils down to the concept that use of a mineral servitude be by someone acting in behalf of the servitude owner in some fashion.

In policy terms, it is felt that it would be unwise as a basic rule to open the way for drilling or mining operations by one other than the servitude owner or someone acting in his behalf to constitute a use of a mineral servitude. The mineral servitude is not like a servitude of passage, which can easily be used by one other than the servitude owner, as contemplated by the Civil Code. The theory of this and the succeeding articles is that what the mineral servitude owner buys is a right to conduct exploratory and mining activities and to retain all or a share of resultant production. It is incumbent upon him to act within the prescriptive period to avoid extinction of his rights. To constitute a use, he or someone acting in his behalf must conduct the operations. If circumstances arise making it possible and desirable for him to adopt operations by

53

someone else, the rules stated in Articles 44 through 53 govern the procedures for doing so. These articles are structured so as to protect third parties, including the landowner, by the requirements of registry. They also protect the policy inherent in Article 42 that the use must be by the servitude owner or someone acting in his behalf by requiring that the servitude owner act within the prescriptive period of his interest and that he be obligated to pay his share of the cost of investment and operation. The one limited exception to these rules is the case of operations being conducted by a unit operator acting under a compulsory unitization order. In this instance, the operations of the unit operator are deemed to be for the benefit of all persons having an interest in the unit, and the policy underlying the conservation laws should not be disturbed.

Art. 43. When a person is acting on behalf of servitude owner

A person is acting on behalf of the servitude owner only when there is a legal relationship between him and the servitude owner, such as co-ownership or agency, or when there is clear and convincing evidence that he intended to act for the servitude owner. Silence or inaction by the servitude owner will not suffice to establish that a person is acting on behalf of the servitude owner.

Acts 1974, No. 50, §43, eff. Jan. 1, 1975.

Comment

The manner in which Article 43 is phrased leaves room for accommodation of the possibilities that a servitude might be exercised by a co-owner, though acting without direct consent, or even by a *negotiorum gestor*. However, it is the intent of the last sentence of Article 43 to negate the ruling of the Louisiana Supreme Court in Nelson v. Young, 255 La. 1043, 234 So. 2d 54 (1970). In that case, the silence of the servitude owner was utilized to establish a quasi-contractual relationship between the landow.ner who had granted a mineral lease and the servitude owner, with the result that operations conducted by the landowner were said to interrupt prescription in behalf of the servitude owner. This was held despite the fact that the servitude owner did not assert any claim that the operations constitute a use until five or six years after the date on which his rights would otherwise have prescribed. This decision is inimical to, the system of prescription which has been fashioned by the courts.

The reasoning underlying Article 43 and interpretation of Articles 793 and 794 (see comment under Article 42) have been expressed and sustained in Pan American Petroleum Corp. v. O'Bier, 201 So. 2d 280 (La. App. 2d Cir.1967). Included in Article 43 is the concept enunciated in Mire v. Hawkins, 249 La. 278, 186 So. 2d 591 (1966), that insofar as questions of use are concerned, the operator of a unit established by order of the Commissioner of Conservation acts as the "representative" of all those entitled to participate in production from the unit. The effect of the use is wrought by the unit operations regardless whether a particular servitude owner or his lessee or other representative has contributed or is bound to contribute to the cost of the well or wells involved. This idea is expressly set forth in Article 47.

As to the effect of operations under any form of voluntary unitization, a use could only be found if a servitude owner is a party to or otherwise bound by the unitization agreement, declaration, or other instrument establishing the unit.

Art. 44. Adoption of operations by another

A mineral servitude owner may adopt operations or production by a person other than those designated by Article 42 if his servitude includes the right to conduct operations of the kind involved.

Acts 1974, No. 50, §44, eff. Jan. 1, 1975.

Comment

Article 44 deals with a problem that occurs only rarely. See Nelson v. Young, 255 La. 1043,234 So.2d 54 (1970); Sample v. Louisiana Oil & Refining Corp., 162 La. 941, 111 So. 336 (1927); Pan American Petroleum Corp. v. O'Bier, 201 So. 2d 280;(La.; App. 2d Cir. 1967). The Sample case denies to a mineral owner the effect of a use as a result of operations by a corporation of which plaintiff was a stockholder as he was not personally a party to the contract giving rise to the operations and the operations were not conducted in his behalf. Suggested but unanswered is the question whether operations of a stranger could ever be retroactively adopted by a mineral servitude owner. In the O'Bier case the Second Circuit Court of Appeal held that utilization by the landowner of a small amount of gas for domestic purposes could not be considered a use by the servitude owner. However, the recent decision in Nelson v. Young permits a servitude owner to receive the benefit of an interruption of prescription where the landowner executed a lease on mineral rights then outstanding and production was subsequently obtained for a period running beyond the prescriptive date. Five or six years after the prescriptive date, and more than two years after the productive well was plugged and abandoned, the servitude owner claimed that the operations were his own and that an interruption of prescription resulted. Using a theory of quasi-contract based on the silence of the servitude owner during the period production was being obtained as indicating a ratification and adoption of the lease contract, the court held in favor of the servitude owner. This case, as noted in the comment following Article 43, is inimical to the system of prescription fashioned by the courts based on the servitude analogy. The relationship between the landowner and servitude owner requires that the servitude owner or someone in his behalf make a use of the servitude within the prescriptive period. To interpret the silence of the servitude owner as ratifying the actions of the landowner and the lessee is questionable as there are many possible motivations or explanations for the silence. The court expressed some fear of rewarding or encouraging clandestine and unlawful acts of the landowner in situations of this kind. However, as the owner of a real right, the servitude owner has adequate means at his disposal to protect himself. He can bring real actions; he can sue in delict for appropriation of his property rights and of the movables taken when minerals are severed; and he can sue for restitution, based on the theory that the landowner has been enriched by having exercised the servitude owner's rights. All of these things he should be permitted to do, provided he does so within the proper prescriptive period. However, if the prescriptive date of the mineral servitude has passed and neither the servitude owner nor anyone acting in his behalf has done anything to use his rights, either actually or by adoption, the servitude should expire.

Article 44 is applicable to both unsuccessful, or "dry hole," drilling operations and to those resulting in production. Insofar as unsuccessful operations are concerned, Article 44 is based upon the idea that if a mineral servitude owner is willing and able to make the necessary financial contribution to underwrite the cost of unsuccessful operations, he should be permitted to adopt them as his own as long as he meets the conditions stated in Articles 45 through 52, which are intended to assure the reality of the adoption and to give notice to those who may subsequently deal with the property.

As to productive operations, Article 44 reflects established jurisprudence in permitting the servitude owner to claim his share of production and receive benefit of an interruption of prescription when the claim is made while production is still continuing, See, *e.g.*, Huckabay v. Texas Co., 227 La. 191, 78 So. 2d 829 (1955); Arkansas Fuel Oil Corp. v. Weber, 149 So. 2d 101 (La. App. 2d Cir. 1963). In such cases, of course, there is a use immediately upon commencement of participation resulting from the ongoing production if the claim is made within the prescriptive period of the servitude. Thus the problem of retroactivity is usually insignificant. However, the jurisprudence does not treat the situation in which production is commenced and ceases within the prescriptive period. It is intended that the servitude owner be permitted to claim his share of production and to receive benefit of a use if his claim is made in accordance with Articles 45 through 52, one of the principal conditions being that he do so within one year of his knowledge of the operations or in any event prior to the date on which his interest would otherwise prescribe. See Art. 45. If the claim is not timely asserted, no interruption of prescription can be had, but recovery can be made for the share of production attributable to the servitude if the action, whether in delict or for restitution, be brought within the proper time.

Art. 45. Time within which adoption must be made

An adoption must be made within three years of the servitude owner's knowledge of such operations or production and in any event prior to the date on which his rights would otherwise prescribe. This limitation does not affect the prescription applicable to any action that the servitude owner may have against another for the wrongful appropriation of his rights of exploration or of production belonging to him.

Acts 1974, No. 50, §45, eff. Jan. 1, 1975.

Comment

Article 45 seeks to place a reasonable limit on the time that a servitude owner may delay taking action to adopt the operations of another. He must, therefore, do so within three years of his knowledge of the operations, but in any event he must do so prior to the prescriptive date. Thus, if the servitude owner learns of the operations less than three years prior to the prescriptive date of his interest, he may not take the three year period otherwise available. Stated shortly, the servitude owner must act within three years of his knowledge of the operations or prior to the prescriptive date of his servitude, whichever is less.

Article 45 will prohibit a servitude owner from standing by for too great a period, waiting to see if the risk taken by another pays off before deciding to adopt the operations in question and receive benefit of a use of his rights. In viewing this rule, it must be borne in mind that it is not applicable to those situations covered by Article 43, such as operations being conducted by a co-owner, in which one other than the servitude owner conducts operations but is deemed to be acting in his behalf.

Art. 46. Procedure for adoption

Adoption of the operations of another is accomplished when the servitude owner files for registry in the conveyance records of the situs of his servitude an instrument describing the land subject to the servitude, identifying the operations, specifying the date on which the operations commenced, and expressing the intent to adopt them as his own.

Acts 1974, No. 50, §46, eff. Jan. 1, 1975.

Article 46 sets forth the procedure by which the adoption is accomplished. The intent is to require some public signification that can reasonably give notice to the landowner and others that the adoption is being made. The policy of requiring positive action by the servitude owner and the interest of effective notice are both served by this requirement.

Art. 47. Compulsory unit operations; adoption unnecessary

When drilling or mining operations or actual production otherwise sufficient to interrupt prescription takes place on a compulsory unit including all or a part of the land burdened by a mineral servitude, an interruption of prescription takes place without formal adoption by the owner of the servitude.

Acts 1974, No. 50, §47, eff. Jan. 1, 1975.

Comment

The rule stated in Article 47 is implicit in Article 43. The Louisiana Supreme Court has held that operations by the unit operator of a compulsory unit are conducted by him as the "representative" of all persons with interests in the unit. Thus, the unit operator is acting on behalf of a servitude owner in this instance even though he may not have paid or become obligated to pay his share of the costs. Nevertheless, it was deemed desirable to specify this exception in the context of the requirements of Articles 46 and 48 to make it clear that in the case of compulsory unit operations the servitude owner need not file notice or obligate himself to pay costs except as he may be obligated under the terms of the conservation act and the order establishing the unit.

Recognizing that Article 47 will confer a benefit on some servitude owners who have not contributed and might not be required to contribute to a well, it is felt that there are several reasons to justify the rule. This solution is more easily administered by the courts than one that would require determinations of whether an economic contribution has been made or can be required to cover the cost of the unit well. Also, this solution provides a stable, predictable rule that simplifies the task of the title examiner and parties dealing with property subject to mineral servitudes. It should be emphasized that this provision relates only to the right to receive the benefit of an interruption of prescription as between the servitude owner and land owner. It does not relate to or affect any rights of the unit operator to recover costs from other "owners" in the unit as that term is defined in La. R.S. 30:3(8) (1950) or the question whether the unit operator may require payment in cash. See Humble Oil & Refining Co. v. Superior Oil Co., 165 So. 2d 905 (La. App. 4th Cir. 1964).

As noted in the comment following Article 43, the servitude owner's right to benefit by voluntary unit operations is dependent upon whether he is a party to or otherwise bound by the unitization agreement, unit declaration, or other instrument establishing the unit. If the unit well or wells are drilled off the servitude tract, the servitude owner cannot benefit unless he is so bound. If the well or wells are drilled on the servitude tract and the servitude owner is not a party or otherwise bound, his right to claim the operations would be governed by Articles 44 through 53 as the operations are the kind that would require obedience to those rules governing adoption of operations by persons not acting in behalf of the servitude owner in order that the servitude owner receive due benefit of an interruption of prescription.

Art. 48. Obligation of servitude owner to pay costs

Except as provided in this Article, upon filing for registry of the instrument required by Article 46, the servitude owner becomes obligated to pay his proportionate share of the reasonable, actual costs of development and operation of the well or mine. He is not obligated to do so if the operations adopted were conducted by a possessor in legal or moral bad faith and resulted in production to which the servitude owner is entitled.

Acts 1974, No. 50, §48, eff. Jan. 1, 1975.

Comment

It was felt that if a mineral servitude owner is to receive benefit of a use resulting from operations by another, he should, as a basic rule, be required to pay the investment and operating costs involved. It is the intent of Article 48 that the filing of notice results in the establishment of a legally enforceable obligation to pay, and that unless the servitude owner is exempted from payment under the one exception stated in this article, there is not be be argument over whether the debt is owed but only over the amount of reasonable, actual costs. Further, unless the party operating the well agrees, the obligation cannot be satisfied out of production, except to the extent that in accounting for past production, the servitude owner may offset an equal amount of the costs owed by him.

It is established that, absent the question of adoption of operations insofar as a use is concerned, the owner of mineral rights is not obligated to pay costs to a stranger who has unlawfully obtained production and has acted in bad faith in doing so. State v. Jefferson Island Salt Mining Co., 183 La. 304, 163 So. 145 (1935); compare, Wetherbee v. Railroad Lands Co., 153 La. 1059, 97 So. 40 (1923). It was felt that in such a situation, if the servitude owner acts within the time period established by Article 45, he should not be required to forego the meaningful economic advantage of being able to recover the value of the production taken without accounting for costs. The balance here is cast in favor of continuing to impose a real penalty for unethical conduct of this kind and simultaneously conferring a real benefit upon the party wronged as a means of compensating for the wrongful conduct. In cases of this kind, it is important also, that as to future production the servitude owner will become a participant and will become obligated to pay all or his ratable portion of future costs. It was felt, however, that the case is somewhat different when the operations are unsuccessful, and thus Article 49 provides that if the operations are unsuccessful, the servitude owner not only has to pay the costs involved but foregoes any right to recover damages. If this were not the rule, the servitude owner would be able to claim benefit of a use without real obligation to participate in the cost of the operations constituting a use. For a fuller discussion of this distinction, see the comment following Article 49.

It should be observed again, in connection with Article 48, that operations on a compulsory unit do not have to be formally adopted according to Article 47, and therefore the provisions of Article 48 regarding the obligation to pay costs are inapplicable to such operations.

Art. 49.   Unsuccessful operations; waiver of damages when adopted

If the operations adopted were unsuccessful, the servitude owner is not only obligated to pay costs as required by Article 48, he also waives any right to damages against the party conducting the operations.

Acts 1974, No. 50, §49, eff. Jan. 1, 1975.

Comment

As indicated in the comment following Article 48, a distinction has been made as to the obligation to pay costs as between producing wells or mines opened in bad faith and other operations that a servitude owner may seek to adopt. The basis for imposing the obligation to pay costs is the policy idea that if a servitude owner is to receive credit for an interruption of prescription, he should undertake the economic obligations involved. In the normal case, the servitude owner will lease, but in some fashion, if he or a representative conducts the operations, his interest will have to bear the costs of the enterprise, either directly or indirectly by some contractual arrangement shifting the costs to a party with whom the servitude owner has agreed. To receive credit for use resulting from operations of a stranger, the same economic burden should fall upon the servitude owner's interest. In the case of productive wells, the law already requires that the servitude owner account to persons in good faith for costs incurred in drilling and operating wells or mines. *E.g.*, Wetherbee v. Railroad Lands Co., 153 La. 1059, 97 So. 40 (1923). This principle is perpetuated in Article 48. In the case of bad faith operators, an exception has been made, as discussed in the comment following Article 48. The exception is made to prevent allowing a bad faith wrongdoer from, in effect, escaping the full consequences of his wrongful act. In the case of the dry hole, Article 49 necessarily requires that if the servitude owner seeks to benefit by the operations, he must forego his right to damages. If this rule were not adopted, the consequences would be that although under the terms of Article 48 the servitude owner would be obligated to pay the costs involved, he would have a right to turn immediately and sue the wrongdoer for damages for having unlawfully conducted the operations, thus making the requirement of Article 48 meaningless and defeating the stated policy objective of requiring the servitude owner's interest to be subject to the economic burden it would have to bear if he or his representative had conducted the operations and an interruption of prescription had resulted under Articles 42 and 43.

Art. 50. Adoption a matter of right

The servitude owner may adopt the operations of another as a matter of right. Consent of the party conducting them is not required.

Acts 1974, No. 50, §50, eff. Jan. 1, 1975.

Comment

The motive for Article 50 is to make the opportunity to adopt operations of another a reality. If this Article were not adopted, it might be possible for a party drilling a well or opening a mine to attempt to deny the servitude owner the right to adopt the operations or at least to delay his adoption and possibly promote the extinction of the servitude. The servitude owner should not be made vulnerable to such possible conduct.

Art. 51. Adoption when servitude under lease

The owner of a mineral servitude may adopt the operations of another even though his rights are under lease and his lessee is unwilling to share in the costs of development and operation. If the operations have resulted in production to which the servitude owner is entitled and the servitude owner's lessee refuses to participate in the operations after production is first obtained, the lessee is not entitled to participate in production from the operations except by express agreement with the mineral servitude owner. In the absence of agreement, the mineral lease, if otherwise maintained according to its terms, remains in force except as to the well or wells or mine or mines as to which the servitude owner has asserted his claim and in which the lessee has refused to participate.

Acts 1974, No. 50, §51, eff. Jan. 1, 1975.

Comment

When productive operations are being adopted and a servitude owner's lessee refuses to pay the operating costs, the servitude owner should be permitted to complete the adoption himself. It would be unfair in these cases if the lessee could sit idly by after production is obtained, allow the servitude owner to pay costs, and then claim his share of production from the well or wells involved after it becomes clear that the wells will payout. To avoid this, it is required that the lessee make a business decision as to whether he wants to participate in the wells at the time. If he does not do so at the time, he is foreclosed from doing so later. His rights as to the remainder of the lease are protected, however, in that he can maintain the remainder by any means permitted by the lease contract.

Art. 52. Right to claim production in absence of adoption

Although the servitude owner fails to adopt operations by another, he may claim the proportion of production allocable to his interest which was obtained prior to the lapse of three years from his knowledge of the operations resulting in production or the date on which his servitude prescribed, whichever occurs first. If he does so, he is obligated to pay his proportionate share of the cost of development and operation accrued prior to the date on which his servitude prescribed unless the person conducting the operations was in legal or moral bad faith.

Acts 1974, No. 50, §52, eff. Jan. 1, 1975.

Comment

Article 52 seeks to deal with the difficult problem of what disposition is to be made of those cases in which the servitude owner fails to adopt operations of another within the prescriptive period but has been wronged in the sense that production to which he is entitled has been wrongfully taken. The combined principles in Articles 42 through 53 require that a servitude owner act to preserve his servitude within the prescriptive period either by conducting operations himself or through some representative or by adopting the operations of a person who has conducted them but does not fall within the classes named in Article 43. Thus, for the purposes of the relationship between the landowner and servitude owner, action on the latter's part must be taken within the prescriptive period. Yet it is possible that a stranger could obtain production to which the servitude owner is entitled and that the servitude owner might not discover that fact or choose to act on it within the period required by Article 45. In such a case, the articles of the Mineral Code in question distinguish between the landowner-servitude owner relationship and the cause of action to which the wrongful conduct gives rise. The servitude owner is required to act within ten years to preserve his rights. If he has not done so, his rights are terminated. But he may still have his action against the wrongdoer who has appropriated severed minerals. In this regard, such actions may be brought in tort or as quasi contractual actions, and the appropriate prescriptive period would have to be observed in bringing the action to recover for the minerals taken. Liles v. Texas Co., 166 La. 293, 117 So. 229 (1928); Liles v. Producers Oil Co., 155 La. 385, 99 So. 339 (1924); Maron v. Texas Co., 150 La. 556,90 So. 922 (1921); White v. Philips Petroleum Co., 232 So.2d 83 (La.App.3d Cir. 1970). See Note, 31 La. L. Rev 681 (1971). In such actions, of course, the servitude owner would be liable for accounting for his share of costs of development and operation unless the wrongdoer was in legal or moral bad faith.

Art. 53. Adoption possible only as specifically provided

Articles 44 through 52 provide the only means by which the prescription of nonuse may be interrupted by operations conducted by persons other than those designated in Article 42.

Acts 1974, No. 50, §53, eff. Jan. 1, 1975.

Comment

Article 53 is inserted out of an abundance of caution to make certain that the holding in Nelson v. Young, 255 La. 1043,234 So.2d 54 (1970) is negated.

SUBPART D. INTERRUPTION OF PRESCRIPTION BY ACKNOWLEDGMENT

Art. 54. Interruption of prescription by acknowledgment; formal requirements

The prescription of nonuse may be interrupted by a gratuitous or onerous acknowledgment by the owner of the land burdened by a mineral servitude. An acknowledgment must be in writing, and, to affect third parties, must be filed for registry.

Acts 1974, No. 50, §54, eff. Jan. 1, 1975.

Comment

Limitation of the power to acknowledge to the owner of the land burdened is consistent with La. Civil Code art. 770 (1870) and the cases limiting the power to create a servitude to the landowner. See Long-Bell Petroleum Co. v. Tritico, 216 La. 426, 43 Sc.2d 783 (1950); Ohio Oil v. Ferguson, 213 La. 183, 34 So.2d 746 (1947); and Hodges v. Norton, 200 La. 614, 8 So.2d 618 (1942). Clearly the only party who should be entitled to interrupt the running of

66

liberative prescription by acknowledgment should be the holder of the title with which the mineral rights would reunite if terminated.

The holding of James v. Noble, 214 La. 196, 36 So.2d 722 (1948) does not require that there be "consideration" for a valid acknowledgment of a mineral servitude. Thus, Article 54 specifies that an acknowledgment may be onerous or gratuitous. An acknowledgment of a mineral servitude is not the same as an acknowledgment interrupting the ordinary liberative prescription operating as a release of a debt. Public policy supports acknowledgments of ordinary obligations on an informal basis. However, acknowledgment of mineral rights is a step affecting a valuable asset and an exchange of equivalents or "consideration" might legitimately be required. The law has evolved without any such requirement, but it has compensated for this by the development of a rigid set of formal rules intended to assure that a landowner is fully aware of and clearly intends the legal consequences of his act in acknowledging outstanding mineral rights. In function these formal requirements are closely akin to the requirement of certain formalities to support a valid donation of immovables. Observance of these formalities is sufficient to give full evidence of the liberal intent supplying cause for the act and to warrant legal enforcement of it even in the absence of "consideration." In the case of acknowledgments of outstanding mineral servitudes, the formal requirements serve a similar function, that of supplying reliable evidence of a party's serious intent to interrupt the running of liberative prescription. Article 54 and the succeeding articles dealing with acknowledgments are essentially a preservation of the established law.

The requirements of Article 54 that an acknowledgment be written and filed for registry are consistent with those of the established jurisprudence and statutory law. See Haynes v. King, 219 La. 160, 52 So.2d 531 (1951); Goldsmith v. McCoy, 190 La. 320, 182 So. 519 (1938); La. R.S. 9:2124-27 (1950).

Art. 55. Express intent required

An acknowledgment must express the intent of the landowner to interrupt prescription and clearly identify the party making it and the mineral servitude or servitudes acknowledged.

Acts 1974, No. 50, §55, eff. Jan. 1, 1975.

Comment

Article 55 combines rules which have evolved in several cases. James v. Noble, 214 La. 196, 36 So. 2d 722 (1948) sets forth the following requirements for an instrument to interrupt prescription by acknowledgment: (1) the intent must be express and certain; (2) it (the instrument) must have been made for that purpose; and (3) it (the instrument) must adequately describe the property to which it is to apply. Additional requirements grew out of Arkansas-Louisiana Gas Co. v. Thompson, 222 La. 868, 64 So.2d 202 (1953) and Roberts v. Cooper, 127 So. 2d 369 (La.App.2d Cir. 1961), which involved attempted acknowledgments in unitization agreements. The efforts at acknowledgments in these two cases failed, not because the intent to acknowledge was not expressed, but because it was not related to each interest which each landowner intended to affect by execution of the agreement and because of inadequacy in description of the interests in question and the lands burdened. These cases vividly illustrate the difficulty of securing acknowledgments in multilateral transactions involving several tracts of land and multiple mineral servitude interests. Although a less formal approach might be helpful to the draftsman of conveyances and contracts, it was considered needlessly unsettling to the law to change the established standards. The requirements stated in Article 55 are those that presently exist, though restated in simpler form.

It is intended that these rules apply not only to instruments executed for the sole purpose of interrupting prescription but to all other contracts or conveyances intended to effect acknowledgments. The early case of Frost-Johnson Lumber Co. v. Nabors Oil and Gas Co., 149 La. 100, 88 So. 723 (1920) created some doubt concerning the effect of the use of words of reservation in a conveyance of land burdened by an outstanding mineral servitude. Any such doubts have been laid to rest by the Louisiana Supreme Court in Wise v. Watkins, 222 La. 493, 62 So.2d 653 (1953), which held that the earlier decision was unsound insofar as it held words of reservation constituted an acknowledgment interrupting prescription. Similarly, it is intended that a conveyance of a mineral servitude interest to a party already

68

owning such rights would be of no effect as an acknowledgment because of the complete failure to observe the rules set forth in this article. See *e.g.*, Long-Bell Petroleum Co. v. Tritico, 216 La. 426, 43 So.2d 782 (1950). It should be noted that the acknowledgment rules do not mean that parties desiring to create a new servitude, perhaps under circumstances in which they wish to merge two outstanding servitude interests into one and thus decrease the use burden, cannot effectively do so by means of appropriately worded conveyances reflecting the intent of the servitude owner to relinquish outstanding interests and the intent of the landowner to create a new mineral servitude rather than simply acknowledging the outstanding interest or interests. However, as in the case of an acknowledgment, any such transaction would have to be documented to reveal the intent of the parties clearly and expressly. Also, the validity to such a conveyance would have to be determined according to the rules governing original conveyances. Principal among these would be the requirement of cause, supplied either by formalities sufficient to support a donation or some exchange of equivalents.

SUBPART E. CONTRACTUAL EXTENSION OF PRESCRIPTION

Art. 56. Contractual extension of servitude; requirements

A landowner may extend a mineral servitude beyond the prescriptive date for a period less than that which would result from an interruption by an acknowledgment. The extension must meet all of the requirements for an acknowledgment and must specify the period for which the servitude is extended.

Acts 1974, No. 50, §56, eff. Jan. 1, 1975.

Comment

In stating the legal power of the parties to extend a servitude interest for a period less than ten years beyond the original prescription date, this article reflects the prior jurisprudence. See *e.g.*, Armour v. Smith, 247 La. 122, 170 So.2d 347 (1964); Adam v. Johnson, 133 So.2d 175 (La. App 4th Cir. 1961). The requirements concerning the content of an instrument accomplishing such an effect, particularly the intent factor, are, however, changed from the prior rules by the provisions of Articles 56 and 57. The requirements of writing and filing for registry are consistent with the basic article concerning creation of mineral servitudes and with the present law. See Haynes v. King, 219 La. 160, 52 So.2d 531 (1951); Goldsmith v. McCoy, 190 La. 320, 182 So.2d 519 (1938).

Articles 56 and 57 deal only with extensions for periods less than that which would result from interruption of prescription. An attempt to effect an extension for a greater period would have to be given the same effect as creation of a mineral servitude for a period greater than ten years. See Hodges v. Norton, 200 La. 614, 8 So. 2d 618 (1942). Thus, the extension might be given effect subject to the requirement that some use or other event interrupting or suspending the running of prescription occur within ten years. Such an attempted extension would in effect represent a conversion of an ordinary servitude to a fixed term servitude expiring at the end of the period of extension regardless of any use made of it.

If a contractual "extension" were attempted for a period equal to the legal term of ten years, it would, in effect, be an acknowledgment. As the rules for a valid "extension" are the same as those for a proper acknowledgment, the use of the term "extension" in such a situation is inappropriate.

It was one of the anomalies of prior law that the Louisiana Supreme Court required an express intent to acknowledge for the purpose of interrupting prescription but in the case of contractual extensions by joint leases required only an intent to execute a "joint lease." This provided an opening for achieving the effect of an interruption by intentional execution of a "joint lease" with a primary term of ten years. Armour v. Smith, 247 La. 122, 170 So. 2d 347 (1644). This inconsistency is undesirable and provides partial motivation for changing the contractual extension rules, particularly as applies in the joint lease cases, to conform to the rules for acknowledgments.

As is true of acknowledgments, the servitude owner need not give an agreed equivalent, or "consideration," for the extension to be valid. See Article 54 and the comment thereunder. As the same formal rules applicable to acknowledgments are to be applied to extensions, seriousness of intent is adequately shown by observance of the formalities and no exchange of equivalents is necessary.

Considerable difficulty arose in the jurisprudence over the effect of execution by the landowner and a mineral servitude owner of such instruments as joint leases. In Mulhern v. Hayne, 171 La. 1003, 132 So. 659 (1931), the supreme court clearly stated that the execution of a joint lease with a primary term extending beyond the original prescriptive date would have the effect of an acknowledgment. This was in keeping with the early decision of Frost-Johnson Lumber Co. v. Nabors Oil and Gas Co., 149 La. 100, 88 So. 723 (1920), holding that the use of words of reservation in a conveyance of land subject to outstanding mineral servitudes could constitute an acknowledgment interrupting prescription. Both decisions used the judicial technique of finding an implied intent to affect the running of prescription because of the circumstances of the transaction. The retreat from these decisions was lengthy and difficult. In the case of acknowledgments in conveyances, the jurisprudence culminated in rejection of the technique of inference of an implied intent. Wise v. Watkins, 222 La. 493, 62 So.2d 653 (1953). However, the joint lease jurisprudence took a different turn. Rather than infer that the parties intended to acknowledge an outstanding interest for the purpose of interrupting prescription, the court ultimately ruled that intentional execution of a joint lease would "extend" the servitude interest, at least for the life of the lease. Achee v. Caillouet, 197 La. 313, 1 So. 2d 530 (1941). The intent required, however, remained merely an intent to execute a joint lease, not an express intent to affect the running of prescription. See Armour v. Smith, 247 La. 122, 170 So. 2d 347 (1964); Adam v. Johnson, 133 So. 2d 175 (La. App. 4th Cir. 1961). But see, Elkins v. Roseberry, 233 La. 59, 96 So. 2d 41 (1957) and the dissenting opinion of Justice Summers in Armour v. Smith, *supra.* Thus, the intent to affect the running of prescription continued to be based on an inference from the fact that the parties executed a lease for a period running beyond the prescriptive date of the outstanding servitude interest and which both agree would remain in force and effect as to both interests according to the terms of the lease.

The "implied intent" technique is undesirable. The general policy in both the acknowledgment and joint lease extension cases has been to protect the landowner against unintended acts having the effect of lengthening the duration of outstanding mineral interests. In furtherance of this policy, it was felt beneficial to have a single set of rules applicable to all instruments affecting the running of prescription. Thus, Article 56 abandons the "implied intent" approach. Under the new code provisions an affect on the running of prescription can be found only in the presence of an express intent.

Insofar as the joint lease cases provide a limited means by which a mineral operator could acquire a secure lease on land subject to a mineral servitude, the need for retention of the joint lease rule is obviated by Article 144, which now permits a landowner to execute a lease with an after-acquired title clause that will bind not only himself but all subsequent owners of the land. Thus, by taking separate leases from the servitude owner and the landowner, the latter with an after-acquired title clause, the lessee can now be assured of a secure lease even if the servitude should expire.

Art. 57. Extended servitude subject to rules of prescription

An extended mineral servitude is subject to the rules relating to interruption of prescription.

Acts 1974, No. 50, §57, eff. Jan. 1, 1975.

Comment

There was nothing in the established jurisprudence concerning the meaning of the term "extension" as it was utilized in the joint lease cases. Did the term mean that if a use of the servitude occurred within the period of extension, but after the original prescriptive date, such a use would be of no effect in preserving the servitude if the contract working the extension expired? If so, what were the consequences of a use after the transaction resulting in the extension but prior to the original prescriptive date? On the other hand, it was quite possible that the extension was merely a lengthening of the life of the servitude subject to all other normal rules of prescription so that if a use occurred prescription was interrupted as of the date of the use. The question of the meaning of the term "extension" was raised but avoided in Robinson v. Horton, 190 La. 919, 2 So.2d 647 (1941). In avoiding decision of the question, the Supreme Court merely stated that the contract which had given rise to the extension was itself still in force; therefore, the effect of drilling and production as a use was irrelevant to a decision of the case at bar. The decision in Armour v. Smith, 247 La. 122, 170 So.2d 347 (1964) involved a similar factual situation, but the legal effect of operations otherwise sufficient to constitute a use was not determined.

Article 57 clarifies this ambiguity by providing that any contract resulting in an extension of the life of a mineral servitude for a period less than an interruption by acknowledgment would preserve the interest subject to all the normal rules of prescription. Thus, a use at any time would interrupt prescription, and if the contract (e.g., as joint lease) giving rise to the extension expired shortly thereafter, the servitude interest would remain alive independent of the contract for a period of ten years running from the date of use.

Parties to an agreement of the sort in question may alter the presumption concerning the effect of operations sufficient to constitute III use by express stipulation. Freedom of contract to restrict the laws of prescription otherwise applicable is expressly contemplated :by Article 72. See also the general provisions in Article 3.

SUBPART F. SUSPENSION OF PRESCRIPTION

Art. 58. Prescription not affected by minority or other disability

The prescription of nonuse is not suspended by the minority or other legal disability of the owner of a mineral servitude.

Acts 1974, No. 50, §58, eff. Jan. 1, 1975.

Comment

Article 58 perpetuates prior law. La. R.S. 9:5805 (1950). Necessarily included in the rule is the principle that co-ownership of a mineral servitude by a minor or other disabled person will not have any effect on the running of prescription, contrary to the rule applicable to ordinary predial servitudes. La. Civil Code art. 802 (1870) [now C.C. art. 763]. See also La. Acts 1944, No. 232, which preceded the 1950 legislation and abolished the rule of Article 802 as to mineral servitudes. Regarding the retroactive effect of La. R.S. 9:5805, see Mire v. Hawkins, 177 So. 2d 795 (La.App.3d Cir. 1965); Hardy, "Work of the Louisiana Appellate Courts for the 1965-66 Term, Mineral Rights," 27 La. L. Rev. 497-501 (1967).

Art. 59. Suspension of prescription by obstacle

If the owner of a mineral servitude is prevented from using it by an obstacle that he can neither prevent nor remove, the prescription of nonuse does not run as long as the obstacle remains.

Acts 1974, No. 50, §59, eff. Jan. 1, 1975.

Comment

Article 59 adopts a general principle found in Article 792 of the Civil Code [now C.C. art. 755] which has been applied only in rare instances. It is worthwhile to retain the concept. However, the problem is defining those instances in which it should be applied. Most of the jurisprudence is devoted to defining those things that are not obstacles rather than those that are. To make it plain that unless specified in subsequent articles there is no intent to change the present law in this regard, it is worthwhile to cite the principal cases in this area. In Coyle v. North Centrai Texas Oil Co., 187 La. 238, 174 So. 274 (1937), it was held that sale of a mineral servitude subject to a prior recorded mineral lease did not make the lease an obstacle. See also Gaily v. McFarlain, 194 La. 150,193 So. 570 (1940). In Gayoso Co. v. Arkansas Natural Gas Corp., 176

74

La. 333, 145 So. 677 (1933), it was held that the granting of a mineral lease by the landowner prior to the prescriptive date of an outstanding mineral servitude did not constitute an obstacle. In Clark v. Tensas Delta Land Co., 175 La. 913, 136 So. 1 (1931), it was held that the fact that the landowner owned one-half of the mineral rights and another party owned the remaining one-half posed no obstacle to the servitude owner's right to exercise his mineral rights.

In McDonald v. Richard. 203 La. 155, 13 So. 2d 712(1943), it was held that an oversale of mineral rights with bad faith on the part of both parties did not create any present interest in property on which the running of prescription was suspended by reason of an obstacle in the form of the already outstanding mineral servitudes. In this regard, see also White v. Hodges, 201 La. 1, 9 So.2d 433 (1942), in which a good faith oversale was held to have created a present interest in property on which the running of prescription was suspended by obstacle in the form of the outstanding rights. The status of this case as precedent was placed seriously in question as a result of McDonald v. Richard, *supra*; Bates v. Monzingo, 221 La. 479, 59 So. 2d 693 (1952); and Hicks v. Clark, 225 La. 133, 72 So. 2d 322 (1954). Regarding oversales, see Articles 76-77.

In Perkins v. Long-Bell Petroleum Co., 227 La. 1044,81 So. 2d 389 (1955), it was held that the filing of a suit by a landowner contesting title to mineral rights would not suspend the running of liberative prescription. However, it must be noted that the case involved certain special facts in that the landowner had executed a lease in favor of the same company holding lease rights from the servitude owner and had apparently done everything reasonable, in the court's judgment, to facilitate the possibility of development by the servitude owner's lessee during the period of litigation. This has left open the question whether a suit might, in proper circumstances, constitute a sufficient obstacle to warrant finding a suspension of prescription, and the court gave strong indication that under proper circumstances an obstacle would be found to exist.

In Hightower v. Maritzky, 194 La. 998, 195 So. 518 (1940), it was held that reservation by the landowner of executive rights over a mineral servitude interest did not constitute an obstacle suspending the running of prescription.

In Dart v. Breiting, 136 So. 2d 501 (La. App. 1st Cir. 1962), it was held that the landowner's refusal to execute or ratify a lease granted by a fractional mineral servitude owner with executive rights on the entire mineral interest, or even to ratify the mineral servitude owner's power of attorney to execute the lease, did not constitute an obstacle.

In McMurrey v. Gray, 216 La. 904, 45 So. 2d 73 (1949), the facts rather clearly indicate the presence of a physical obstacle (locking of an entrance gate by the landowner). However, the court did not deal with the case in terms of obstacle as no question of suspension of prescription was actually raised. The problem there faced was whether the servitude owner had a right to continue good faith operations which might result in an interruption of prescription even beyond the original prescriptive date.

In Boddie v. Drewett, 229 La. 1017, 87 So. 2d 516 (1956), it was held that the issuance of a compulsory unitization order including the entirety of a servitude tract and excluding the tract from the designated drilling area constituted an obstacle suspending prescription. However, this decision was overruled in Mire v. Hawkins, 249 La. 278, 186 So. 2d 591 (1966), and the *Mire* decision is retained under Article 61.

Art. 60. Suspension effective as to all minerals

An obstacle to drilling or mining operations or to production of any mineral covered by an act creating a mineral servitude suspends the running of prescription as to all minerals covered by the act.

Acts 1974, No. 50, §60, eff. Jan. 1, 1975.

Comment

Article 60 is harmonious with the principle of Article 41, which provides that an interruption wrought by operations for or production of one mineral interrupts prescription as to all minerals covered by the act creating the servitude. The possibility that an obstacle should be deemed to terminate if production of another mineral would be economically feasible and a reasonable operator in the type of industry involved would produce such other mineral was considered. However, it was felt that the substantial uncertainty that would be created by such a rule is undesirable, and the article is therefore promulgated in this form.

Art. 61. Compulsory unitization order not an obstacle; establishment of mining plan is an obstacle

A. Issuance of a compulsory unitization order establishing a unit that includes all or part of a tract burdened by a mineral servitude does not constitute an obstacle to its use.

B. The inclusion of land burdened by a servitude that includes the right to develop lignite or coal in a mining plan to conduct surface lignite or other forms of coal mining and reclamation operations is an obstacle to the use of that servitude with respect to all land included in the mining plan provided the following requirements are satisfied:

(1) Lignite or another form of coal susceptible of being mined has been discovered as a result of acts committed on the land or due to acts providing a reasonable basis of proof of the discovery of the mineral.

(2) A mining plan for the ultimate production of lignite or other forms of coal, together with a permit issued by the appropriate government official, is filed in the conveyance records of the parish or parishes in which the land burdened by the servitude is located.

(3) The mining plan along with any amendments thereto, provides for the ultimate production of the lignite or other forms of coal from the land burdened by the servitude.

(4) Actual mining operations have begun on land included in the plan, although such operations are not being conducted on the land burdened by the servitude.

Prescription shall begin to run again when reclamation operations on the land burdened by the servitude are complete, the land burdened by the servitude is deleted from the mining plan, or there is no longer in effect a permit for lignite or other form of coal mining and reclamation as to any land included in the mining plan, whichever is sooner.

Acts 1974, No. 50, §61, eff. Jan. 1, 1975. Amended by Acts 1982, No. 780, §1.

Comment

Article 61 maintains the ruling of the Supreme Court in Mire v. Hawkins, 249 La. 278, 186 So. 2d 591 (1966). That decision overruled the obstacle concept as articulated in Boddie v. Drewett, 229 La. 1017,87 So. 2d 516 (1956). Adoption of this article, and thus rejection of the obstacle concept, should be viewed as intimately connected with the principles embodied in Articles 33, 34, and 38. Those articles establish the basic rule that unit operations of any kind, if otherwise sufficient to interrupt prescription, will interrupt· prescription only as to the unitized portion of a servitude tract when the operations are conducted off the servitude premises. On-premises operations will interrupt prescription as to the entirety of the servitude tract.

The term "compulsory unitization order" refers to units established by order of the Commissioner of Conservation or any other state or federal agency exercising the police power. It does not include mere spacing regulations or regulations concerning assignment of productive acreage such as those promulgated by the Commissioner of Conservation in Statewide Order No. 29-H, Finding 5, for the purpose of computing allowables.

Comment -1982

This article is to provide treatment for servitude and royalty owners similar to that for leases under Article 115(C). Inclusion of land in a mining plan is, in many respects, similar to inclusion of land in an oil or gas unit. In other respects, the inclusion of land in a mining plan is more analogous to creation of an obstacle to development (or actual production in terms of Articles 98-99) prior to the time the land is scheduled to be mined. Treating the establishment of the mining plan as an obstacle in the manner provided prevents the loss of the servitude or royalty where the owner is unable as a practical matter to interrupt prescription despite the known existence of producible minerals on the land. The obstacle treatment of this article would apply only to an interest included in the mining plan. Thus if there were a separate servitude for oil and gas or other minerals, the mere establishment of the mining plan would not serve to suspend prescription as to it.

PART 5. INDIVISIBILITY OF THE MINERAL SERVITUDE

Art. 62.   Mineral servitude indivisible except as specifically provided

Except as provided in Articles 63 through 71, the rights and obligations of the owner of a mineral servitude are indivisible.

Acts 1974, No. 50, §62, eff. Jan. 1, 1975.

Comment

Article 62 affirms the concept of Article 656 of the Civil Code [now C.C. art. 652] applicable to predial servitudes which has been regarded as theoretically applicable to mineral servitudes but has been functionally circumvented in several instances. See Ohio Oil Co. v. Ferguson, 213 La. 83, 34 So. 2d 746 (1947) (sale of all of a servitude owner's rights on a portion of the servient estate deemed to divide the "advantages" of the servitude, relying on La. Civil Code art. 657 [now, C.C. art. 653]); Jumonville Pipe & Machinery Co. v. Federal Land Bank, 230 La. 41, 87 So. 2d 721 (1956)

79

(unitization); Childs v. Washington, 229 La. 869, 87 So. 2d 111 (1956) (unitization); but see Trunkline Gas Co. v. Steen, 249 La. 520, 187 So. 2d 720 (1966) (unitization); White v. Frank B. Treat & Son, Inc., 230 La. 1017, 89 So. 2d 883 (1956) (unitization).

Art. 63. Presumption arising from separate description of tracts forming continuous body of land

A single mineral servitude is created by an act that affects a continuous body of land although individual tracts or parcels within the whole are separately described.

Acts 1974, No. 50, §63, eff. Jan. 1, 1975.

Comment

Article 63 Sustains established law. Lee v. Giauque, 154 La. 491, 97 So. 669 (1923). Under Articles 3 and 72 parties may alter this rule by express stipulation.

Art. 64. Presumption when servitudes created on noncontiguous tracts

An act creating mineral servitudes on noncontiguous tracts of land creates as many mineral servitudes as there are tracts unless the act provides for more.

Acts 1974, No. 50, §64, eff. Jan. 1, 1975.

Comment

Article 64 sustains established law. Lee v. Giauque, 154 La. 491, 97 So. 669 (1923). It also represents a rule of public policy that cannot be negated by stipulation. See Article 73.

Art. 65. Division of servient estate not division of servitude

The division of a tract burdened by a mineral servitude does not divide the servitude.

Acts 1974, No. 50, §65, eff. Jan. 1, 1975.

Comment

Article 65 incorporates a principle embodied in Article 776 of the Civil Code [now C.C. art. 747) which is generally recognized as being applicable to mineral servitudes.

Art. 66. Right of owners of contiguous tracts to create single servitude

The owners of several contiguous tracts of land may establish a single mineral servitude in favor of one or more of them or of a third party.

Acts 1974, No. 50, §66, eff. Jan. 1, 1975.

Comment

Articles 66 and 67 deal with a question which has not yet been litigated, although the matter has been noted as a problem. See Whitehall Oil Co. v. Heard, 197 So. 2d 672 (La. App.3d Cir. 1967), discussed in Hardy, "Mineral Rights, the Work of the Louisiana Appellate Courts for the 1966-67 Term," 28 La. L. Rev. 355, 366 (1968). The effect of these articles is to permit owners of contiguous land is to join together to form a single servitude even though the result might be that a landowner would thus be owner of an interest covering not only the lands of others but his own as well. This can be viewed as a limited exception to the principle that a landowner may not fractionate his title in favor of himself. This problem has been raised frequently for practitioners in connection with partitions, and the exceptions to normaI rules represented by Articles 66 and 67 originated from this rather commonly encountered situation. Article 66 authorizes landowners generally to create a single servitude in favor of one or more among them or of a third party. The tracts must, however, constitute a continuous body of land. Article 67 is directed specifically toward the partition situation.

Art. 67. Right of co-owners to create single servitude in partition of land

Co-owners of land constituting a continuous whole may partition it and reserve a single mineral servitude in favor of one or more of them.

Acts 1974, No. 50, §67, eff. Jan. 1, 1975.

Comment

See the comment following Article 66.

Art. 68. Effect of limitation of servitude rights to specified horizons or levels

A single mineral servitude is established on a continuous tract of land notwithstanding that certain horizons or levels are excluded or the right to share in production varies as to different portions of the tract or different levels or horizons.

Acts 1974, No. 50, §68, eff. Jan. 1, 1975.

Comment

Article 68 is consistent with the established jurisprudence. Gulf Oil Corp. v. Clement, 239 La. 144, 118 So. 2d 361 (1960) (sale of mineral rights on continuous tract but at varying levels on different portions of the tract nevertheless created but a single servitude); Gunby v. Commercial Solvents Corp., 170 So. 2d 259 (La. App. 2d Cir. 1965) (sale of mineral rights on continuous tract of land subject to a previous outstanding fractional mineral servitude on the central of three tracts making up the whole created a single servitude). Article 68 is applicable even if the original conveyance includes rights to separate strata or defined depth levels as long as the rights conveyed underlie a continuous body of land on which a single servitude is created.

Art. 69. Effect of partial conveyances of servitude rights

The conveyance or reservation by a mineral servitude owner of a portion of his rights does not divide the mineral servitude but creates only a co-ownership, except that if a person other than the servitude owner acquires all of the rights granted by the act creating the servitude in a specific geographical area, the servitude is divided.

Acts 1974, No. 50, §69, eff. Jan. 1, 1975.

Comment

Article 69 sustains the rulings of the Supreme Court in Hodges v. Norton, 200 La. 614, 8 So. 2d 618 (1942) and Ohio Oil Co. v. Ferguson, 213 La. 183, 34 So. 2d 746 (1947). Regarding the latter case, it is to be observed that the Supreme Court rationalized its opinion on the basis of Article 657 of the Civil Code [now C.C. art. 653], which provides that although the right of servitude itself is indivisible, its advantages may be divided in kind if susceptible of such division. Since the functional result of the Ferguson case was to impose separate use requirements on the two portions of a tract when a mineral servitude owner sells all of his rights on one portion and retains all the original rights on the remainder it is better simply to regard this as an actual division of the servitude rather than continue to use the concept of division of the "advantages" of the servitude. In this respect the mineral servitude more strongly resembles the personal servitudes. It is provided in Article 538 of the Civil Code [now C.C. art. 541] that usufruct is divisible. Under Article 69 the concept of divisibility is given limited application. Article 69 also perpetuates the ruling of Arent v. Hunter, 171 La. 1059, 133 So. 157 (1931), insofar as it applies to mineral servitudes. In that case the landowner reacquired all of the servitude rights in certain portions of the tract originally burdened. A division of the servitude was held to result as to the remaining portions, which had been rendered noncontiguous by the landowner's reacquisition.

Art. 70. Effect of contracts for use or development of portion of servitude

Execution of a lease or other contract for use or development of a portion of a tract burdened by a mineral servitude does not divide the servitude.

Acts 1974, No. 50, §70, eff. Jan. 1, 1975.

Comment

Article 70 sustains prior jurisprudence. Levy v. Crawford, Jenkins & Booth, 194 La. 757, 194 So. 772 (1940)(leasing of portions of the servitude tract by the servitude owner does not divide that mineral servitude). Any other rule would unreasonably hamper the servitude owner in making legitimate use of his rights.

Art. 71. Partial unitization not a division

Unitization of a portion of a tract burdened by a mineral servitude does not divide the servitude.

Acts 1974, No. 50, §71, eff. Jan. 1, 1975.

Comment

Insofar as compulsory units are concerned, Article 71 negates the suggestion in Childs v. Washington, 229 La. 869, 87 So.2d 111 (1956) and Jumonville Pipe & Machinery Co. v. Federal Land Bank, 230 La. 41, 87 So. 2d 721 (1956) that the issuance of a conservation order containing only a portion of a servitude tract divides the servitude. The validity of this judicial suggestion brought into question by the decision in Trunkline Gas Co. v. Steen, 249 La. 520, 187 So. 2d 720 (1966). Insofar as conventional units are concerned the impact of the article is doubtful as the jurisprudence is unclear. Compare Elson v. Mathewes, 224 La.

417, 69 So. 2d 734 (1953) with Crown Central Petroleum Corp. v. Barousse, 238 La. 1013, 117 So. 2d 575 (1960). It should be emphasized that the landowner and the servitude owner may contract for a different result than that applicable under this article as long as the agreement in this regard is express. See Articles 3 and 72.

PART 6. CONVENTIONAL ALTERATION OF THE LEGAL INCIDENTS OF CREATION OF A MINERAL SERVITUDE

Art. 72. Parties free to contract except as specifically limited

Parties to an act creating a mineral servitude may alter the applicable legal rules subject to the limitations provided in Articles 73 through 79.

Acts 1974, No. 50, §72, eff. Jan. 1, 1975.

Comment

Article 72, in combination with those which follow, incorporates most of the present jurisprudence regarding the right of contracting parties to alter the legal incidents of creation of mineral servitudes.

The section does not deal with the problem of reversionary rights, though that matter definitely relates to the topic of freedom of contract. In this regard see Articles 76 through 79. Also, the topic of contractual extension of prescription for periods less than ten years, such as by execution of a joint lease, is related but is not treated in this section as it is dealt with in Articles 56 and 57.

Art. 73. Single servitude may not exist on noncontiguous tracts

A single mineral servitude may not be created on two or more noncontiguous tracts of land.

85

Acts 1974, No. 50, §73, eff. Jan. 1, 1975.

Comment

Article 73 articulates the rule of Lee v. Giauque, 154 La. 491, 97 So. 669 (1923) and assures that that rule is not merely one of construction for mineral conveyances but a limitation of contractual freedom springing from public policy considerations inherent in the system of prescription.

Art. 74. Right to fix term or shorten prescriptive period; effect of stipulation for prescriptive period greater than ten years

Parties may either fix the term of a mineral servitude or shorten the applicable period of prescription of nonuse or both. If a period of prescription greater than ten years is stipulated, the period is reduced to ten years.

Acts 1974, No. 50, §74, eff. Jan. 1, 1975.

Comment

Article 74 represents the established jurisprudence. For example, under Hodges v. Norton, 200 La. 614, 8 So. 2d 618 (1942) it is possible to create a mineral servitude for a term greater than ten years. However, the normal rules of prescription are applicable in that if the rights are not used, or prescription otherwise affected, the interest will terminate at the end of ten years even though the stipulated term has not run. Further, the Supreme Court has indicated in Leiter Minerals, Inc. v. California Co., 241 La. 915, 132 So. 2d 845 (1961) that parties may fix a period of prescription by contract which is different from and less than that which would normally be imposed by law if they had been silent. Though the standing of this opinion as precedent is doubtful, there is no reason to doubt the validity of the stated principle and no basis upon which to deny contracting parties this freedom. Several articles of the Civil Code applicable to predial servitudes suggest contractual freedom of the kind herein contemplated. See La. Civil Code arts. 709, 751, 752 (1870) [now C.C. arts. 697, 728, 729].

The limitation that parties cannot contract for a prescriptive period greater than ten years is firmly established in the jurisprudence. *E.g.*, Hodges v. Norton, *supra*; Bodcaw Lumber Co. of La. v. Magnolia Petroleum Co., 167 La. 847,120 So. 389 (1929); LeBleu v. LeBleu, 206 So. 2d 551 (La. App. 3d Cir. 1968); Ober v. McGinty, 66 So. 2d 385 (La. App. 2d Cir. 1953); but see Chicago Mill & Lumber Co. v. Ayer Timber Co., 131 So. 2d 635 (La. App. 2d Cir. 1961). The question of when a contract contrary to this rule has been executed is not solved by Article 74. In this regard, see the discussion of LeBleu v. LeBleu, *supra*, and the discussion of other problems concerning the date of creation of mineral servitudes following Article 28.

Consideration was given to the matter of establishing rules of construction to aid the courts in determining whether parties intend to fix the duration of a mineral servitude or to subject it to a prescriptive period other than that which would be imposed if the parties were silent. However, it was determined merely to state some guidelines for construction in this comment. In the event of silence as to the term of a mineral servitude, the right created is permanent or perpetual, but it is subject to loss by accrual of the prescription of nonuse. Parties to an agreement which does not specify a fixed term or a prescriptive period other than the legal one are, of course, free to limit the duration of the rights created or to alter the prescriptive period by subsequent agreement, subject to the same limitations applicable to the original instrument.

It is established by Hodges v. Norton, *supra*, and Bodcaw Lumber Co. of La. v. Magnolia Petroleum Co., *supra*, that if a term greater than ten years is specified, this fixes the duration of the interest created. It is, however, still subject to the prescription of nonuse and will expire prior to the running of the specified term if not used within the legal prescriptive period.

It is more difficult to construe instruments specifying a period less than ten years. Unless the creation of a mineral servitude is a part of a security transaction, it is rare that a party will, in the ordinary situation, contract for the creation in his favor of an interest with a fixed term less than ten years. Thus, it is suggested that in the absence of some expression to the contrary in the instrument in question, the specification of a period less than ten years for a mineral servitude should be construed as an agreement on a prescriptive period less than ten years, and the interest should be considered subject to the rules of use and thus renewable by exercise of the rights granted or reserved. Parties are, of course, free to specify that the stated number of years is the term of the interest and not a prescriptive period.

Art. 75. Right to contract regarding rules of use

The rules of use regarding interruption of prescription on a mineral servitude may be restricted by agreement but shall not be made less burdensome, except that parties may agree expressly and in writing, either in the act creating a servitude or otherwise, that an interruption of prescription resulting from unit operations or production shall extend to the entirety of the tract burdened by the servitude regardless of the location of the well or whether all or only part of the tract is included in the unit.

Acts 1974, No. 50, §75, eff. Jan. 1, 1975; Acts 2023, No. 88, §1.

Comment

The parties to the transaction which was the subject of litigation in Leiter Minerals, Inc. v. California Co., 241 La. 915, 132 So. 2d 845 (1961) framed an agreement which could be interpreted as altering not only the prescriptive term of the interest created but the rules of use applicable to the interest as well. In that particular instance, if the instrument is so interpreted, the rules of use were made considerably more onerous than those normally applicable. The degree to which parties can change the rules of use has not been thoroughly elaborated in the jurisprudence.

Because the rules of use are so basically intertwined with the policy underlying the Louisiana system of prescriptible mineral interests, it is desirable to limit freedom of contract by generally preventing liberalization of the rules of use. The one instance in which the rules of use may be made less burdensome is that parties may provide that unit operations or production will interrupt prescription as to the entirety of the servitude tract regardless of the location of the unit well. This is contrary to the basic rules applicable under Articles 33, 34, and 37 when the parties are silent as to the effect of unit operations or production. Parties are, of course, free to make the rules of use more onerous than those imposed by positive law.

PART 7. TRANSACTIONS INVOLVING OUTSTANDING MINERAL SERVITUDES

Art. 76. Expectancy of extinction not an article of commerce

The expectancy of a landowner in the extinction of an outstanding mineral servitude cannot be conveyed or reserved directly or indirectly.

Acts 1974, No. 50, §76, eff. Jan. 1, 1975.

Comment

This Article accords with the holding in Hicks v. Clark, 225 La. 133, 72 So. 2d 322 (1954), insofar as it provides that the reversionary interest is not an object of commerce.

Art. 77. Application of after-acquired title doctrine

If a party purports to acquire a mineral servitude from a landowner when the right purportedly acquired is outstanding in another and the landowner either subsequently acquires the outstanding right or is the owner of the land at the time it is extinguished, the after-acquired title doctrine operates to vest the right in the party who purported to acquire it to the full extent of his title.

Acts 1974, No. 50, §77, eff. Jan. 1, 1975.

Comment

Regarding the application of the after-acquired title doctrine, the prior law is not completely clear except as to the fact that under certain circumstances the court has indicated that the doctrine will be applied. See White v. Hodges, 201 La. 1, 9 So.2d 433 (1942); McDonald v. Richard, 203 La. 155, 13 So. 2d 712 (1943); Bates v. Monzingo, 221 La. 479, 59 So. 2d 693 (1952). Whether parties to an oversale of minerals can enter into such a transaction knowingly is not clear in the jurisprudence. An examination of the record in McDonald v. Richard, *supra*, reveals that both parties were aware at the time of the oversale in question that the vendor of the mineral rights did not own sufficient rights at that time to confer a present interest. In White v. Hodges, *supra*, the court found that the overpurchasers were in good faith. Article 77 does not require that either or both parties be acting in good faith. Insofar as this rule might permit some parties deliberately to enter into an oversale, there is no damage to the prescriptive system because the overpurchaser's title cannot be perfected unless the overseller later acquires the rights previously outstanding or remains owner of the land at the time of their extinction. No subsequent owner of the land may be bound by the oversale unless the after-acquired title doctrine has already operated to benefit the overpurchaser at the time the subsequent owner takes title to the land. Thus, permitting deliberate entry into oversale transactions cannot result in the creation of real rights burdening the land for periods greater than ten years, the danger foreseen and obviated by the Supreme Court in preventing dealings with the "reversionary right" in Hicks v. Clark, 225 La. 133, 72 So. 2d 322 (1954). The rules provided in Articles 78 and 79 concerning the running of prescription, if the doctrine operates, are necessary complements to Article 77 in assuring that parties are not free to avoid the system of prescription.

Art. 78. Prescription when after-acquired title doctrine applies; acquisition of outstanding servitude

If the landowner who purported to create the mineral servitude acquires the previously outstanding mineral servitude, after having alienated the land, the party in whose favor the doctrine operates has ten years from the date of the transaction by which he purported to acquire or the remaining period of the rights acquired by his grantor in which to exercise his rights, whichever period is greater.

Acts 1974, No. 50, §78, eff. Jan. 1, 1975.

Comment

There are two conceivable factual situations in which the after acquired title doctrine could operate to benefit the overpurchaser of a mineral servitude. If the party who owned the land at the time of the oversale subsequently alienates the land and, within ten years from the date of the oversale, acquires mineral rights in the land permitting operation of the doctrine, the overpurchaser will be given the benefit of the after-acquired title. The second situation, and the one commonly envisioned by the decided cases, is that the party who owned the land and purported to sell a mineral servitude remains the owner at the time previously outstanding rights are extinguished, thus permitting operation of the doctrine for the benefit of the overpurchaser.

Articles 78 and 79 deal with the problem of the prescriptive period applicable to the title of the overpurchaser once it vests through operation of the doctrine. Article 78 deals specifically with the first factual situation outlined above and solves the problem by providing that the overpurchaser shall have the greater of two possible prescriptive periods: (1) the petiod remaining if prescription were deemed to run from the date of the oversale to him or (2) the period of prescription remaining for the specific mineral servitude acquired by the overseller. It is possible that the overpurchaser can, by application of Article 78, have a period greater than ten years from the date of the oversale to him in which to exercise his rights, but no damage is done to the system of prescription because the landowner, whatever his identity, would have had to create the mineral servitude acquired by the overseller and thus have consented to having that particular servitude outstanding for the legally established prescriptive period.

Art. 79. Prescription when after-acquired title doctrine applies; extinction of outstanding servitude

If the landowner who purported to create the servitude remains the owner of the land at the time of the extinction of the previously outstanding rights, the party in whose favor the doctrine operates has whatever time remains between the date of vesting of title in him and ten years from the date of the transaction by which the party purported to acquire in which to exercise his rights.

Acts 1974, No. 50, §79, eff. Jan. 1, 1975; Acts 2023, No. 88, §1.

Comment

Article 79 deals with the prescriptive period applicable in the common oversale situation, that in which the overseller remains the landowner at the time previously outstanding rights are extinguished, thus permitting operation of the after-acquired title doctrine for the benefit of the overpurchaser. This article in effect utilizes the fiction that if the doctrine operates, the vested title is deemed retroactive to the date of the oversale for the purpose of computing the prescriptive period. Thus, if the doctrine operates seven years after the oversale, the overpurchaser, now the owner of a valid mineral servitude, has three years remaining in which to exercise his servitude.

If the fiction is disregarded, the intended rule is admittedly somewhat illogical. That is, if an oversale does not create a present interest in property, theoretically speaking, prescription should not commence to run until the interest vests by operation of the doctrine. However, if this rule were not adopted, parties entering deliberately into an oversale might be able effectively to burden the land with a mineral servitude for a period greater than ten years.

CHAPTER 5. THE MINERAL ROYALTY
PART 1. THE NATURE OF THE MINERAL ROYALTY

Art. 80. Nature of mineral royalty

A mineral royalty is the right to participate in production of minerals from land owned by another or land subject to a mineral servitude owned by another. Unless expressly qualified by the parties, a royalty is a right to share in gross production free of mining or drilling and production costs.

Acts 1974, No. 50, §80, eff. Jan. 1, 1975.

Comment

This definition accords with that developed. in the jurisprudence. See, *e.g.*, Continental Oil Co. v. Landry, 215 La. 518, 41 So. 2d 73 (1949); Humble Oil & Ref. Co. v. Guillory, 212 La. 646, 33 So.2d 182 (1946). By classical trade usage having the force of binding custom, the royalty is recognized as a non-cost-bearing interest. The second sentence of Article 80 expresses this accepted definition by providing that the royalty is a right to share in production free of investment or operating costs. The parties are free to specify what costs may be imposed on a royalty owner's share of production, but in the absence of express wording, Article 80 would exempt the royalty owner from investment costs and "production" or "mining" costs. The article does not attempt to define what costs fall within these terms, but resort to industrial custom and jurisprudence in Louisiana and other jurisdictions can aid in solving definitional problems.

Determining those things that constitute production costs as compared with processing costs or other costs for which the royalty owner might be liable for his ratable share would have presented insuperable drafting difficulty. Often, this problem is solved by the lease contract entered into by the land or mineral owner. The royalty owner would ordinarily receive the same benefits as to distribution of costs as the lessor. However, in the event the lease contract does not adequately solve this problem, difficulty could arise. The landowner or mineral servitude owner whose interest is burdened by a mineral royalty cannot diminish the sharing rights of the royalty owner without his consent, and the landowner is bound to deal fairly with the interest of his royalty owner in the sense that if he procures economic benefits for himself regarding the bearing of processing or other costs through the execution of a lease, he should procure the same benefits for his royalty owner. The rights and duties of the royalty owner and the landowner as to matters of this kind are specified in Articles 105 through 113, dealing with the relationship between the owner of an executive interest and the owner of a subordinate, nonexecutive interest, into which latter category the mineral royalty falls.

Art. 81. Executive and operating rights not included

The owner of a mineral royalty has no executive rights; nor does he have the right to conduct operations to explore for or produce minerals.

Acts 1974, No. 50, §81, eff. Jan. 1, 1975.

Comment

By definition, since the royalty is only a right to share in production, the owner of such an interest has no right to explore for or produce minerals, and having no such rights, he can neither sell nor lease them. Although Article 81 verges on being superfluous, it was felt desirable to further elaborate the nature of the royalty and clearly state that it does not carry with it any operating rights and consequently no executive rights.

PART 2. WHO MAY CREATE A MINERAL ROYALTY

Art. 82. Who may create mineral royalty

A mineral royalty may be created either by a landowner who owns mineral rights or by the owner of a mineral servitude.

Acts 1974, No. 50, §82, eff. Jan. 1, 1975.

Comment

Although there has been little judicial expression of the basic principle of Article 82 insofar as it concerns the right of a mineral servitude owner to create a mineral royalty, it is certainly implicit in the jurisprudence, particularly in the cases that hold that mineral royalty rights are but an appendage of the mineral rights from which they are carved. Union Oil & Gas Corp. of La. v. Broussard, 237 La. 660, 112 So. 2d 96 (1958); Arkansas Fuel Oil Co. v. Sanders, 224 La. 448, 69 So.2d 745 (1954); Barnwell, Inc. v. Carter, 220 So. 2d 741 (La.App.2d Cir. 1969).

Art. 83. Creation of mineral royalty by conditional owner

A mineral royalty may be created by one whose title terminates at a particular time or upon the occurrence of a certain condition, but it is extinguished at the specified time or on occurrence of the condition divesting the title.

Acts 1974, No. 50, §83, eff. Jan. 1, 1975.

Comment

Article 83 is substantially similar to Article 25, applicable to mineral servitudes. It differs somewhat in that the wording had to be altered to accommodate the fact that a mineral royalty may be created by either the landowner or the owner of a mineral servitude.

95

Art. 84. Creation of mineral royalty by usufructuary

A usufructuary of land whose usufruct includes mineral rights, or the usufructuary of a mineral servitude, may establish a mineral royalty for the period of his usufruct.

Acts 1974, No. 50, §84, eff. Jan. 1, 1975.

Comment

Article 84 differs from Article 26, which prohibits the creation of a mineral servitude by the usufructuary. Functionally, the sale of a mineral royalty for the life of a usufruct is a present realization of income which the usufructuary, under such circumstances, would have a right to in the future. The sale of such a nonoperating right does not pose the same problems as the creation of a mineral servitude. It should be carefully noted that any such interest created by a usufructuary is a mineral royalty and is subject to extinction by prescription under the terms of Articles 13 and 83. Thus, the statement that the usufructuary may create such an interest for the duration of his usufruct is the specification by law of an ultimate term for the interest and should under no circumstances be viewed as permitting creation of an imprescriptible mineral right.

PART 3. MODES OF EXTINCTION OF THE MINERAL ROYALTY

Art. 85. Extinction of mineral royalties

A mineral royalty is extinguished by:

(1) prescription resulting from nonuse for ten years;

(2) confusion with the title out of which it was created;

(3) renunciation of the royalty right on the part of him to whom it is due, or the express remission of his right;

(4) expiration of the time for which the royalty right was granted or happening of the dissolving condition attached to the mineral royalty; or

(5) extinction of the right of him who established the mineral royalty, except that the extinction of a mineral servitude by inheritance or by any act of the servitude owner does not extinguish a royalty burdening the servitude unless the royalty owner is a party to the act or otherwise consents expressly and in writing to become bound by it.

Acts 1974, No. 50, §85, eff. Jan. 1, 1975.

Comment

Article 85 is substantially similar to Article 27 stating the modes by which mineral servitudes are extinguished. It, too, is a partial restatement of Article 783 of the Civil Code [now C.C. arts. 751, 753, 765, 770, 771, 773, 774]. However, it warrants special discussion in three respects: (1) the provision that the royalty is subject to the prescription of nonuse, (2) the provision that extinction by confusion occurs only if the royalty becomes merged with the title out of which it was created, and (3) the provisions of paragraph 5 dealing with the effect of extinction of the underlying title or right out of which a royalty is created.

There is no question that the mineral royalty is subject to the ten-year liberative prescription. See, *e.g.*, Continental Oil Co. v. Landry, 215 La. 518, 41 So. 2d 73 (1949); Humble Oil & Ref. Co. v. Guillory, 212 La. 646, 33 So. 2d 182 (1946); Vincent v. Bullock, 192 La. 1, 187 So. 35 (1939). In some cases, such as Vincent v. Bullock, *supra*, St. Martin Land Co. v. Pinckney, 212 La. 605, 33 So. 2d 169 (1947), and Union Sulphur Co. v. Lognion, 212 La. 632, 33 So. 2d 178 (1947), the court takes pains to say that a mineral royalty is not a servitude and is not subject to the same rules of prescription as the servitude. However, these cases should be taken in the context of their facts and the functional differences between the mineral servitude and the royalty. In most instances, when the courts have used such language, they have been speaking of the fact that the mineral royalty does not carry with it use rights such as those conveyed in the creation of a mineral servitude, and thus the same acts that interrupt prescription of a mineral servitude, short of actual production, do not interrupt prescription accruing against a mineral royalty. Also, in Union Sulphur Co. v. Lognion, *supra*, the court made the distinction as a technique for avoiding the applicability of Article 802 of the Civil Code [now generally, C.C. art. 783], under which ownership of an interest in a predial servitude by a minor suspends the accrual of prescription not only in favor of the minor but also his major co-proprietors. The rule had, of course, been applied to mineral servitudes, and the court was apparently anxious to avoid the complexity in the title system that had resulted from that unhappy application of the Civil Code article.

That the mineral royalty is a real right is established. That real rights less than ownership are subject to the liberative prescription of nonuse is an accepted principle. Therefore, it is proper to say that the mineral royalty is subject to the liberative prescription of nonuse and not the liberative prescription operating as a release from debt. The functional distinctions between the servitude and the royalty remain, of course, and the distinctions carry with them differences in the causes which will interrupt prescription accruing against the two types of mineral rights, as well as other functional distinctions.

Some care should be taken in the reading and application of paragraph 5 of Article 85. The basic rule is applicable only if the royalty is carved out of a mineral servitude. There are instances in which a mineral servitude interest may be burdened by a royalty that is not dependent upon the servitude in terms of its prescriptive life. This is true despite the rules regarding the effect of termination of royalties that were evolved in Arkansas Fuel Oil Co. v. Sanders, 224 La. 448, 69 So. 2d 745 (1954) and Union Oil & Gas Corp. of La. v. Broussard, 237 La. 660, 112 So. 2d 96 (1958). Under those cases, if A creates a mineral royalty in favor of B and then sells a mineral servitude covering one-half of the mineral rights to C, C's interest is charged with the burden of one-half of B's royalty. If B's interest expires while C's mineral servitude is still in existence, C's interest is relieved of that charge. Despite the fact that in this situation C will benefit by the extinction of B's royalty, B's interest is not dependent in the sense required by Article 85, paragraph 5, and extinction of C's servitude prior to extinction of B's royalty would not extinguish B's interest. This can best be illustrated by altering the facts somewhat. For example, assume that X creates a mineral royalty in favor of Y covering a 640 acre tract. Assume also that X subsequently sells a mineral servitude covering all of the mineral rights on the east half of that tract to Z. Production from the west half of the tract would maintain V's royalty as to the entirety of the tract without affecting the life of Z's servitude. If Z's servitude expires, V's royalty rights do not expire with that servitude, despite the fact that if Z had ever produced from his portion of the property, his mineral servitude would have been burdened by V's royalty interest. It is, therefore, important to identify the situations in which the life of a mineral royalty is truly dependent upon the life of a mineral servitude to determine whether the extinction of one will necessarily result in the extinction of the other.

The exceptions in paragraph 5 are necessary to prohibit potential injustice arising from honest or conspiratorial acts of a party or by operation of law. For example, the owner of a mineral servitude who has created a mineral royalty should not be permitted by collusive action, or by arms' length dealing, to extinguish the royalty by a renunciation or remission of his servitude in favor of the landowner. Insertion of the exception in this regard does not inhibit the servitude owner from dealing with his interest as may be of greatest benefit to himself, but it protects the royalty owner appropriately. The other exception contemplates the possibility that a party may, for example, create a mineral servitude in favor of a child, who may in turn create a royalty. Death of the parent with resultant acquisition of the land by the child would extinguish the servitude by confusion. The royalty created by the child, however, should not be extinguished by operation of law in these circumstances.

PART 4. COMMENCEMENT OF PRESCRIPTION

SUBPART A. GENERAL PRINCIPLES

Art. 86. Commencement of prescription of nonuse

Prescription of nonuse of a mineral royalty commences from the date on which it is created.

Acts 1974, No. 50, §86, eff. Jan. 1, 1975.

Comment

Article 86 is identical to Article 28, applicable to mineral servitudes. The jurisprudence regarding mineral royalties does not contain the same discussion of the problem of the date from which prescription commences that is raised by the cases dealing with mineral servitudes. In this regard, see the comment following Article 28. However, there can be no doubt that the same general principles are applicable to both interests.

SUBPART B. INTERRUPTION OF PRESCRIPTION BY USE

Art. 87. Production as interruption of prescription; commencement of prescription anew

Prescription of nonuse running against a mineral royalty is interrupted by the production of any mineral covered by the act creating the royalty. Prescription is interrupted on the date on which actual production begins and commences anew from the date of cessation of actual production.

Acts 1974, No. 50, §87, eff. Jan. 1, 1975.

Comment

The jurisprudence has established that actual production is necessary to interrupt the accrual of prescription against a royalty. Union Sulphur Co. v. Andrau, 217 La. 662, 47 So. 2d 38 (1950); Union Sulphur Co. v. Lognion, 212 La. 632, 33 So. 2d 178 (1947).

There are no cases dealing expressly with the commencement of prescription anew. However, in the decision in Lavergne v. Savoie, 221 So. 2d 71 (La. App. 3d Cir. 1969), this principle is implicit. Also, in the basic cases establishing the rule that production is necessary to interrupt prescription, it is implicit that cessation of actual production will result in the commencement of prescription anew. See, *e.g.*, the cases cited above and La. R.S. 30:112 (1958) (repealed) which was applicable only to mineral servitudes.

Art. 88. Saved production sufficient to interrupt prescription

To interrupt prescription it is not necessary that minerals be produced in paying quantities but only that they actually be produced and saved.

Acts 1974, No. 50, §88, eff. Jan. 1, 1975.

Comment

In Union Sulphur Co. v. Andrau, 217 La. 662, 47 So. 2d 38 (1950), it was established that minor amounts of unsaved production resulting from testing do not constitute an interruption of prescription accruing against a mineral royalty. There is no case definitely stating that production "in paying quantities" is unnecessary to maintain a mineral royalty. However, insofar as mineral servitudes are concerned, the Supreme Court has stated in Mays v. Hansbro, 222 La. 557, 64 So. 2d 232 (1953) that it is "unimportant whether . . . production was in paying quantities so long as there was some production or use of the servitude." This language was adopted by the Second Circuit Court of Appeal in a clarifying per curiam opinion dealing with a mineral royalty. Lee v. Goodwin, 174 So. 2d 651 (La. App. 2d Cir. 1965), writs denied,

248 La. 149, 177 So. 2d 118 (1965). This principle stated in Mays v. Hansbro, *supra*, has been adopted in Article 38 applicable to mineral servitudes. There is, however, a distinction between the rule there stated for servitudes and the rule of this article to be applied to mineral royalties. In Article 38 it is stated that although production in paying quantities is not necessary, it is necessary that minerals be produced "in good faith with the intent of saving the minerals produced, and using, selling, or otherwise disposing of them for some useful purpose." This manner of stating the rule is appropriate to mineral servitudes because the servitude owner has operating rights. The rule for mineral royalties is appropriate because no operating rights accompany the royalty, and the only appropriate test for determining whether an interruption of prescription has occurred is whether there has been production which is actually saved.

Art. 89. Unit production as an interruption of prescription

Production from a conventional or compulsory unit including all or part of the tract burdened by a mineral royalty interrupts prescription, but if the unit well is on land other than that burdened by the royalty, the interruption extends only to that portion of the tract included in the unit.

Acts 1974, No. 50, §89, eff. Jan. 1, 1975.

Comment

This rule is harmonious with that applicable to mineral servitudes under Article 37. The prior jurisprudence regarding the effect of unitization on mineral royalties was unclear. In Frey v. Miller, 165 So.2d 43 (La. App. 3d Cir. 1964), writs denied, 216 La. 844, 167 So. 2d 669 (1964), it was held that if a compulsory unit included only a portion of a royalty tract and the unit well was not located on the royalty tract, the interruption of prescription resulting from production affected only the acreage included within the servitude tract. Article 89 sustains that decision. Inconsistency in the prior law was found, however, in Crown Central Petroleum Corp. v. Barousse, 238 La. 1013, 117 So. 2d 575 (1960), involving a contractual unit. In that case the court reached a result opposite to that in Frey v. Miller, *supra*. Also in Montie v. Sabine Royalty Co., 161 So. 2d 118 (La. App. 3d Cir. 1964), it was held that where a unit including a portion of a royalty tract was formed by exercise of a voluntary pooling power granted by the lessor-landowner whose interest was burdened by the royalty in question, the entirety of the royalty tract was maintained by production from the unit even though the well was not located on the royalty tract. To maintain this inconsistency in the jurisprudence would have been arbitrary particularly since a royalty owner is not even a necessary party to a unitization agreement.

Article 89 thus clarifies the jurisprudence and establishes a uniform rule applicable unless parties contract for a different result either in the instrument creating the mineral royalty or in some subsequent instrument. Contracting in this fashion is permissible. See Articles 3, 72, and 103. For further discussion of the related jurisprudence see the comment following Article 37.

Art. 90. Tested shut-in well as interruption of prescription

When there exists on a tract of land burdened by a mineral royalty, or on a conventional or compulsory unit that includes all or part thereof, a shut-in well proved through testing by surface production to be capable of producing minerals in paying quantities, prescription is interrupted on the date production is obtained by such testing. If only a part of the tract burdened by the royalty is included in a unit and the unit well is on land other than that burdened by the royalty, the interruption of prescription extends only to that portion of the tract burdened by the royalty included in the unit. Prescription commences anew from the date on which the well is shut in after such testing.

Acts 1974, No. 50, §90, eff. Jan. 1, 1975. Amended by Acts 1975, No. 589, §1, eff. July 17, 1975.

Article 90 is identical to Article 34, applicable to mineral servitudes. For discussion, see the comment following Article 34.

Art. 91. Unitization with tested shut-in well; effect as interruption of prescription

If the land or part thereof, burdened by a mineral royalty is included in a conventional or compulsory unit on which there is a well shut in prior to the creation of the unit, located on other land within the unit, and capable of producing in paying quantities as required by Article 90, prescription is interrupted on and commences anew from the effective date of the order or act creating the unit.

Acts 1974, No. 50, §91, eff. Jan. 1, 1975.

Article 91 is identical to Article 35, applicable to mineral servitudes. For discussion, see the comment following Article 35.

Art. 92. Interruption applicable to all minerals

An interruption of prescription applies to all types of minerals covered by the act creating the mineral royalty.

Acts 1974, No. 50, §92, eff. Jan. 1, 1975.

Article 92 is substantially similar to Article 41, applicable to mineral servitudes. It differs only in that there is no reference to modes of use because of the difference in the natures of the servitude and the royalty. With this exception, Article 92 has the same origins and intent as Article 41. For discussion, see the comment following Article 41.

SUBPART C. ACKNOWLEDGMENT AND CONTRACTUAL EXTENSION OF MINERAL ROYALTIES

Art. 93. Application of rules concerning acknowledgment and extension of prescription

Subject to the special rules provided in Articles 94 through 96, the rules applicable to acknowledgments and extensions of prescription running against mineral servitudes are applicable to mineral royalties.

Acts 1974, No. 50, §93, eff. Jan. 1, 1975.

Comment

The provisions made applicable by reference are Articles 54 and 55. The rules applicable to acknowledgment of mineral servitudes have been viewed as applicable to mineral royalties. See, *e.g.*, Crown Central Petroleum Corp. v. Barousse, 238 La. 1013, 117 So. 2d 575 (1960); Union Oil and Gas Corp. of Louisiana v. Broussard, 237 La. 660, 112 So. 2d 96 (1958); Union Oil Co. of California v. Touchet, 229 La. 316, 86 So. 2d 50 (1956); Vincent v. Bullock, 192 La. 1, 187 So. 35 (1939).

Art. 94. Acknowledgment by servitude owner of previously created mineral royalty

When a mineral royalty is created by a landowner who has subsequently created a mineral servitude, the owner of the mineral servitude may acknowledge the previously created royalty for the purpose of interrupting prescription.

Acts 1974, No. 50, §94, eff. Jan. 1, 1975.

It is important to specify that if a mineral royalty is created by the owner of land and the mineral rights covering the land are subsequently sold, the mineral servitude owner can acknowledge the previously created mineral royalty. Union Oil & Gas Corp. of Louisiana v. Broussard, 237 La. 660, 112 So. 2d 96 (1958).

Art. 95. Limited effect of acknowledgment of previously created royalty

When an acknowledgment is made by either the owner of a mineral servitude who takes title subsequent to the creation of a mineral royalty by the landowner or by a co-owner of a mineral servitude who acquires his interest subject to a mineral royalty, the acknowledgment is effective only as to that proportion of the royalty which the interest of the acknowledging party bears to the whole of the mineral rights from which the royalty was originally created.

Acts 1974, No. 50, §95, eff. Jan. 1, 1975.

Comment

Article 95 is intended to deal with situations such as the following hypothetical case. Assume that landowner A creates a mineral royalty in favor of B. A then conveys a mineral servitude covering one-half of the mineral rights to C. C should not be able to acknowledge B's rights except to the extent of one-half of B's royalty rights. A would have to acknowledge the remaining half. This is consistent with the rules established in Arkansas Fuel Oil Co. v. Sanders, 224 La. 448, 69 So. 2d 745 (1954), and Union Oil & Gas Corp. of Louisiana v. Broussard, 237 La. 660, 112 So. 2d 96 (1958) insofar as those cases treat the effect of termination of mineral royalties in a situation of this kind. If, in the hypothetical case just outlined, C were permitted to execute an acknowledgment for the entirety of B's mineral royalty interest, the result would be that C could create a mineral royalty right by means other than title and without an exchange of equivalents, or "consideration." He would not be renewing any portion of B's royalty interest except the half burdening his (C's) mineral servitude by means of the acknowledgment, and he would in effect be creating a new royalty interest in B's favor insofar as the other half would be concerned. It is felt that the rules of acknowledgment should not permit such a result. This clarifies doubt raised by the decision in Union Oil & Gas Corp. of Louisiana v. Broussard, *supra*, in which a co-owner of a mineral servitude attempted to acknowledge an outstanding mineral royalty. Although the facts are not entirely clear, the royalty interest may have been disproportionate to the mineral ownership of the acknowledging party. The court simply indicated that as the acknowledging party's mineral interest was sufficient in size to bear the entire burden of the royalty which he purported to acknowledge, as he was the only party giving up something of value, and as he contended that the interruption was valid, the court would recognize the royalty's existence. Whether the basis for this holding is one of personal liability or a matter of property rights is unclear. As a matter of property rights, a person should not be permitted to create a new mineral royalty by acknowledging an outstanding royalty that only partially burdens his mineral servitude interest. Whether there is a basis for some form of personal liability when a party by judicial admission voluntarily assumes the burden of a royalty is another problem entirely. But an acknowledgment in a situation of this kind should not be permitted to burden the land in the hands of subsequent owners.

Art. 96. Previously created royalty; dependency on mineral servitude when acknowledged

When for the purpose of interrupting prescription the owner of a mineral servitude acknowledges a mineral royalty previously created by the landowner, the royalty thereafter depends upon the continued existence of the servitude.

Acts 1974, No. 50, §96, eff. Jan. 1, 1975.

Comment

Article 96 makes it clear that although a servitude owner can acknowledge a royalty burdening his interest, the royalty becomes dependent on the servitude interest. Thus, if the servitude expires within ten years of the acknowledgment, the royalty expires with it. As observed in the comment following Article 85 a royalty created by the landowner that becomes a charge on a servitude subsequently created is not dependent in the sense that if the servitude is extinguished, the royalty dies with it. Article 96 specifies that if the servitude owner acknowledges the royalty in these circumstances, the royalty thereafter becomes dependent in the sense of Article 85, paragraph 5. That is. if the servitude is extinguished, the royalty dies with it.

SUBPART D. SUSPENSION OF PRESCRIPTION

Art. 97. Prescription not affected by minority or other disability

The prescription of nonuse is not suspended by the minority or other legal disability of the owner of a mineral royalty.

Acts 1974, No. 50, §97, eff. Jan. 1, 1975.

Comment

This Article is identical to Article 58, applicable to mineral servitudes. As noted in the comment following that article, it perpetuates the prior law under La.R.S. 9:5805 (1950).

Art. 98. Suspension of prescription by obstacle

An obstacle to actual production of minerals that would be sufficient to suspend the prescription of nonuse if the owner of a mineral royalty were the owner of a mineral servitude suspends the prescription of nonuse running against the royalty until the obstacle is removed.

Acts 1974, No. 50, §98, eff. Jan. 1, 1975.

Comment

Present jurisprudence recognizes that there is an effect on prescription resulting from circumstances other than actual production. See, *e.g.*, LeBlanc v. Haynesville Mercantile Co., 230 La. 299, 88 So. 2d 377 (1956); Union Oil of California v. Touchet, 229 La. 316, 86 So. 2d 50 (1956). There is no reason why the royalty owner should not receive benefit of a suspension of prescription if there is an obstacle preventing the party holding the operating rights from actually producing when, absent the obstacle, actual production could occur. It is expressly stated in Article 98 that the obstacle must be one to "actual production," and it would not be sufficient if the obstacle were to drilling or reworking operations, for example. For discussion of the obstacle concept as applied to mineral servitudes, see the comment following Article 59.

Art. 99. Obstacle to production from servitude suspends prescription as to dependent royalty

An obstacle to the actual production of minerals that suspends the prescription of nonuse running against a mineral servitude burdened by a mineral royalty also suspends the prescription of nonuse running against the royalty.

Acts 1974, No. 50, §99, eff. Jan. 1, 1975.

Comment

The situations dealt with in Articles 98 and 99 differ slightly. Article 98 presupposes that the royalty is a burden on title to the land and provides relief to the royalty owner where the circumstances are such that actual production cannot be obtained because a fact or condition exists that would constitute an obstacle if the royalty owner owned a mineral servitude instead. Article 99 presupposes that the royalty is a burden on a mineral servitude. If there is an obstacle to actual production benefitting the owner of the underlying servitude interest, the royalty owner is similarly benefitted. See the comment following Article 98.

Art. 100. Suspension effective as to all minerals

An obstacle to production of any mineral covered by an act creating a mineral royalty suspends the running of prescription as to all minerals covered by the act.

Acts 1974, No. 50, §100, eff. Jan. 1, 1975.

Comment

Article 100 is the same as Article 60, except that it applies to obstacles to actual production only, in keeping with the difference between the mineral servitude and the mineral royalty. For relevant discussion, see the comment following Article 60.

PART 5. INDIVISIBILITY OF THE MINERAL ROYALTY

Art. 101.   Mineral royalty indivisible except as specifically provided

Subject to the exceptions provided in Articles 63 through 71 applicable to mineral servitudes, the rights and obligations of the owner of a mineral royalty are indivisible.

Acts 1974, No. 50, §101, eff. Jan. 1, 1975.

Comment

Article 101 is the same as Article 62, applicable to mineral servitudes. For relevant discussion, see the comment following that article. Regarding the exceptions, see the comments following Articles 63 through 71.

Art. 102.   Rule regarding effect of partial conveyance; applicability to mineral royalty

Article 69 is applicable as between the owner of land or of a mineral servitude and the owner of a mineral royalty burdening either.

Acts 1974, No. 50, §102, eff. Jan. 1, 1975.

Comment

Article 102 makes applicable by reference the rule of Article 69 that if a landowner creates a mineral servitude and subsequently reacquires all of the servitude rights as to a specified portion or portions of the land burdened, with the result that the remaining servitude rights burden noncontiguous portions of the original tract, the servitude is divided. Thus the same rule is made applicable to reacquisition of royalty rights. Article 102 further specifies that the rule of Article 69 is also applicable if the owner of a mineral servitude creates a royalty and subsequently reacquires all of the royalty right as to a specified portion or portions of the burdened tract.

PART 6. CONVENTIONAL ALTERATION OF THE LEGAL INCIDENTS OF CREATION OF A MINERAL ROYALTY

Art. 103.   Freedom of contract; application of rules to mineral royalty

Articles 72 through 75 regarding conventional alteration of the legal incidents of creation of mineral servitudes are applicable to mineral royalties.

Acts 1974, No. 50, §103, eff. Jan. 1, 1975.

Article 103 makes Articles 72 through 75, applicable to mineral servitudes, applicable also to mineral royalties. Briefly, the basic rules is one of freedom to contracting parties as provided in Article 72. Article 73 prohibits establishment of one mineral servitude (royalty) on two or more noncontiguous tracts. Article 74 acknowledges the right to fix a term for a servitude (royalty) but prohibits parties from contracting for a prescriptive period greater than ten years. And Article 75 provides that the rules of use applicable to mineral servitudes (royalties) may be made more but not less onerous by contract except that the rules of Articles 89 and 90 may be altered by contract. For further discussion, see the comments following these earlier Articles.

PART 7. TRANSACTIONS INVOLVING OUTSTANDING MINERAL ROYALTIES

Art. 104. Rules applicable to transactions involving outstanding servitudes; applicability to mineral royalties

Articles 76 through 79 concerning transactions involving outstanding mineral servitudes are applicable to mineral royalties, including those created by a mineral servitude owner.

Acts 1974, No. 50, §104, eff. Jan. 1, 1975.

Article 104 prescribes that the rules concerning attempts to deal with the "reversionary right" and operation of the after-acquired title doctrine will also apply to mineral royalties. Briefly recapitulated, Article 76 prohibits dealing with the landowner's expectancy in the extinction of a servitude (royalty) as an object of commerce. Articles 77 through 79 affirm the applicability of the after-acquired title doctrine to oversales of mineral servitudes (royalties) and provide rules concerning the conditions under which the doctrine will operate and the running of prescription in the event of its operation. In the case of mineral royalties, it should be noted that the prohibition against "reversionary right" transactions is operative as to a servitude owner whose interest is burdened by a royalty and that the after-acquired title doctrine can apply to mineral royalties purportedly created by the owner of a mineral servitude.

CHAPTER 6. EXECUTIVE RIGHTS

Art. 105. Nature of executive right

The executive right is the exclusive right to grant mineral leases of specified land or mineral rights. Unless restricted by contract it includes the right to retain bonuses and rentals. The owner of the executive right may lease the land or mineral rights over which he has power to the same extent and on such terms and conditions as if he were the owner of a mineral servitude.

Acts 1974, No. 50, §105, eff. Jan. 1, 1975.

Comment

The problem of the nature of the executive right has not been clarified in the Louisiana jurisprudence. In other jurisdictions if a royalty is created, the right to execute leases and retain the consideration remains united with the mineral estate. If a nonexecutive mineral interest is created, the right to execute mineral leases remains with the mineral estate, but the owner of the mineral interest has a right to share in bonuses, rentals, and other consideration for the making or extension of leases. In neither of these situations is there any dire necessity for defining the executive right. However, if the right is conveyed by itself, it has been variously designated as a power of appointment, a power coupled with an interest, and a statutory power in trust.

The need for definition of the right is perhaps more critical in Louisiana because of the regime of prescription. Thus, it is necessary to know exactly what the executive right includes, whether a conveyance of the executive right alone creates a real right, whether the creation of a mineral royalty accompanied by executive rights creates a mineral servitude or a royalty for purposes of prescription, and, similarly, whether creation of a mineral servitude with a retention by the landowner of the executive right reduces the interest created from a servitude to a royalty for purposes of prescription.

An additional problem is found in the relationship between the holder of the executive right and the owner of a nonexecutive mineral right. In Louisiana, a landowner whose title is subject to a mineral servitude or a mineral servitude owner whose interest is burdened by a royalty has an interest in seeing liberative prescription accrue and having the outstanding right extinguished. He should not be required to act so as to deprive himself of that expectancy. This is not true of other jurisdictions which have no prescriptive system. Thus, in some instances in other jurisdictions the executive has been required to lease for the benefit of the nonexecutive. Although Louisiana should not adopt any position which would be destructive of the system of prescription by requiring a landowner or servitude owner to act contrary to his own legitimate interest in the accrual of prescription, there was no reason not to adopt the overwhelming majority position of other jurisdictions that once the owner of an executive interest undertakes to exercise his right to lease, he must act fairly toward the owner of the nonexecutive right. 2 Williams & Meyers, Oil & Gas Law § 339.2. As there observed, the most difficult question has not been whether a duty exists but the nature of the duty. Articles 105-113 are intended to clarify a very cloudy area of Louisiana law.

The first Louisiana case dealing with the nature of the executive right insofar as it carries a right to income was Mt. Forest Fur Farms of America v. Cockrell, 179 La. 795, 155 So. 228 (934). That case required the court to interpret a deed that created a "perpetual royalty" and also granted the "perpetual and exclusive rights to make and execute mineral leases." Specifically at issue was whether the grantee under the deed had the right to retain bonuses and rentals derived from leases executed by it. The court stated:

> "[A]side from the landowner's exploring his own land for minerals, he has only two possible sources of income or profit in dealing with his land: (1) The cash consideration or bonus which he may receive for the lease, and payments made for renewals of the lease; and (2) the royalty.

> "There is no reason why, in disposing of his land, the landowner may not reserve to himself both of these

116

sources, nor is there any reason why he should not reserve but one of them, or a percentage of one or of both." *Id.* at 798, 155 So. at 229.

Construing the deed the court held that "defendant was ... retaining, with the consent of . . . , [the landowner], the exclusive right to lease, not for the mere privilege of selecting the lessee, or of fixing the terms of the lease, but for the purpose of obtaining from the lease or the granting of it, for himself, his heirs and his assigns, all that the lease might bring, save as therein specified.... The reservation of the right to lease was not reserved to lease as agent, but was reserved for defendant ... his heirs and assigns, which means that the reservation was for their benefit, save as otherwise expressed therein." *Id.* The *Cockrell* decision was followed in Ledoux v. Voorhies, 222 La. 200, 62 So. 2d 273 (1952), which dealt with a deed in which the landowner created a fractional mineral servitude and granted executive rights over his remaining mineral rights.

These decisions are in accord with the results reached by courts in other jurisdictions. See 2 Williams & Meyers, Oil & Gas Law §§ 338 and 339. Based on these cases and the general view with which they are harmonious, Article 105 defines the executive right as the exclusive right to lease, including the right to retain bonuses or other property given for the execution of leases and rentals or other property given for their maintenance, extension, or renewal.

The definitions of the terms "bonus," "royalty," and "rental" found in Article 213 are intended for use in applying Article 105 insofar as it gives the holder of the executive right the right to retain bonuses and rentals.

Art. 106. Executive right a mineral right

The executive right is a mineral right. It may exist independently or as a part of another form of mineral right, such as a mineral servitude.

Acts 1974, No. 50, §106, eff. Jan. 1, 1975.

Comment

Although Mt. Forest Fur Farms v. Cockrell, 179 La. 195, 155 So. 228 (1934) gives definition to the executive right in terms of the right of the holder to retain income, the opinion does nothing in the way of defining its nature as a property right. It was previously unclear whether the executive right, if transferred by itself, would be a real right subject to the prescription of nonuse or merely a personal right. It is important to define the executive right as a type of mineral right and, consequently, according to the generic definition of "mineral rights" in Article 16, an immovable real right. If this were not true, it might be possible for a court, given a factual situation such as that in Mt. Forest Fur Farms v. Cockrell, *supra*, to say that if the landowner who granted the executive right independently as an accompaniment to a royalty subsequently transferred the land to another, the new owner would not be bound by the grant of the executive right as it is merely personal in nature.

It should be observed that the characterization of the executive right in these recommendations does not prevent other forms of contract regarding the execution of leases. Therefore, it is possible to grant a mandate or a power of attorney to execute leases.

Art. 107. Interruption of prescription accruing against executive right

The prescription of nonuse of an executive right existing independently is interrupted by an act or event that would be sufficient to interrupt prescription accruing against a mineral servitude.

Acts 1974, No. 50, §107, eff. Jan. 1, 1975.

Comment

The rule specified in Article 107 is not perhaps the most logical, but the deviation from logic is deliberate and has a purpose. Logic would dictate that the executive right, being subject to the prescription of nonuse, would be subject to being used by its exercise in the obvious sense; that is, by granting a lease. However, it was felt that in view of the general policy underlying the system of prescription of mineral rights generally, permitting an interruption of prescription to occur merely from the act of granting a lease would tend to make it undesirably easy to perpetuate the life of the executive right. Thus, it was felt preferable to provide that prescription accruing against the executive right will be interrupted only by an act or event that would interrupt prescription if the right were a mineral servitude. See Articles 29 through 41 (use); Articles 54 and 55 (acknowledgment). It is important to note that this will incorporate the rule of Article 42 that a use of a mineral servitude must be by "the owner of the servitude, his representative or employee, or some other person acting on his behalf." This would mean that with the possible exception of operations conducted by a unit operator acting under the terms of a compulsory unitization order (see Art. 47), the operations constituting a use would have to be conducted under the terms of lease granted by the executive himself. The provisions of Articles 44-53 regarding adoption of operations conducted by another might, perhaps, be considered theoretically available to the owner of the executive right, but their attractiveness is nullified by the obligation to pay costs if such operations are adopted. See Article 48. The better view of this question would be to consider the provisions of Articles 44-53 as inappropriate to questions of use of the executive right. Article 107 must be read in conjunction with Article 113. The latter provides that if a mineral royalty is created and is accompanied by a grant of the executive right, the executive right is an appendage of the royalty and will expire with it. Given these circumstances, dry hole drilling operations would not interrupt prescription accruing against the executive right.

Art. 108. Nature of executive and nonexecutive interests

An executive interest is a mineral right that includes an executive right. Nonexecutive interests are those that do not include the executive right, such as the mineral royalty, a landowner's interest in minerals the executive right to which has been granted to another, or a mineral servitude the executive right to which has been granted to another.

119

Acts 1974, No. 50, §108, eff. Jan. 1, 1975.

Comment

The concept of the "executive interest" must be articulated because there are so many different ways, some of which are suggested in Article 108, in which the executive right may be created either as a part of or as an appendage to other forms of mineral rights. The concept of the executive interest is also necessary to facilitate statement of the duty owed by the owner of any executive interest to the owner of a nonexecutive interest in granting leases under Article 109. It is also important in that the power to grant mineral leases generally is defined by Article 116 as vested in "a person having an executive interest in the minerals rights on the property leased."

Art. 109. Obligation of owner of executive interest

The owner of an executive interest is not obligated to grant a mineral lease, but in doing so, he must act in good faith and in the same manner as a reasonably prudent landowner or mineral servitude owner whose interest is not burdened by a nonexecutive interest.

Acts 1974, No. 50, §109, eff. Jan. 1, 1975.

Comment

It is the intention of Article 109 to sustain the decisions in Vincent v. Bullock, 192 La. 1, 187 So. 35 (1939) and Humble Oil & Refining Co. v. Guillory, 212 La. 646, 33 So. 2d 182 (1946), insofar as they negate any duty on the part of a landowner or a mineral servitude owner whose interest is burdened by a mineral royalty to lease for the benefit of a mineral royalty owner. No such duty is imposed on the holder of any executive interest under Article 109. The root of these decisions is in the system of prescription. The executive should not be forced to act to the detriment of his expectancy that prescription will accrue against an outstanding mineral right. However, Article 109 intended to reverse the decisions in Whitehall Oil v. Eckart, 252 La. 30, 209

So.2d 11 (1968) and Uzee v. Bollinger, 178 So. 2d 508 (La. App. 1st Cir. 1965) insofar as they hold that the executive owes no duty whatsoever to the nonexecutive. It is the overwhelming majority position in the United States that the owner of an executive minerai interest owes to the owner of a nonexecutive interest some form of duty in exercising the executive right. See 2 Williams & Meyers, Oil & Gas Law § 339.2. The most difficult problem has been to define the duty, not to determine whether it exists. In the cited reference, the authors detail the various appellations that have been used to describe the duty.

As Article 109 states, it is intended to negate the existence of a true fiduciary relationship such as that entailed in agency, or mandate. However, it is also intended that there be a somewhat higher duty than that of ordinary care and good faith. The following passage from 2 Williams & Meyers § 339.2 at 209-210 is explanatory of the intent of Article 109 in this regard:

"Where the interests of the executive and non-executive coincide, the ... improper exercise ... [of the executive right] due to carelessness, inattention, indifference, or bad faith will result in liability. Where the interest of the executive and non-executive diverge, the executive will not be bound to a standard of selfless conduct, such as that imposed on trustees or guardians. He may exercise the executive right with the same self-interest in mind as if there were no outstanding royalty or non-executive mineral interest. But the executive cannot exercise ... the executive right for the purposes of extinguishing the non-executive interest, or for the purpose of benefitting himself at the expense of the nonexecutive. If the conduct of the executive satisfies the ordinary, prudent landowner standard, the fact that the nonexecutive owner has been harmed is not actionable under this view. But if an ordinary, prudent landowner, not burdened by an outstanding non-executive interest, would have acted differently, then the executive's conduct is actionable if it causes harm. We believe this standard fairly effectuates the intent of the parties; it does not require more than can be expected of ordinary landowners and it does not permit less, especially where the 'less' is due to the executive's effort to profit at the expense of the royalty or non-executive mineral owner."

For example, if in the process of executing a mineral lease a landowner whose interest is subject to a mineral royalty negotiates for a specific understanding as to what costs are to be borne by the lessee, whatever benefits he secures for himself he should be bound to secure also for his royalty owner. Absent highly unusual circumstances, the ordinary, prudent landowner would not be likely to negotiate so that three quarters of his royalty interest would be entitled to the economic advantage of the lessee bearing certain costs and the other quarter would be burdened by such costs.

A second example might be found in situations in which the executive has a choice between a high bonus and a small royalty or a low bonus and a large royalty. In these instances, the executive should not be bound to bargain selflessly as a fiduciary but should be free to consider his own economic position in determining which way to structure the lease transaction. However, if the executive is offered a one-fourth royalty, he should not, by the expedient of denominating one-half of that proffered royalty interest as an overriding royalty, be permitted to deprive a mineral royalty owner of the right to share in that additional royalty. This, of course, assumes that the royalty deed in question is of a kind that would permit the royalty owner to share in a stated proportion of royalties, such as "one-half of all royalties accruing from the production of oil, gas, or other minerals" from the tract in question. If the deed limited the royalty owner's right to one sixty-fourth of the whole of all minerals produced, then the executive-lessor would have no motivation to engage in the subterfuge of designating a portion of the royalties as an overriding royalty as the sharing arrangement would be fixed absolutely by the royalty deed which he or his ancestor in title has given.

There are other problem areas. For example, if landowner A grants a mineral servitude covering one-half of the mineral rights to B together with executive rights over A's retained share of mineral rights, can B in negotiating a lease obtain a one-eighth royalty and one-sixteenth overriding royalty? It is the intent of these recommendations to assure that such sleight-of-hand tricks cannot succeed. Under ordinary circumstances a lessor who can obtain a three-sixteenths royalty would not be motivated to secure any part of it as an override but would merely negoitate the full fraction as a lessor's royalty. The standard set forth in Article 109 seeks to foreclose such opportunities for unfair dealing.

Art. 110.   Lease in violation of obligation valid; right of nonexecutive to damages

A mineral lease granted in violation of the standard of conduct required by Article 109 is not invalid for that reason, but the owner of a nonexecutive interest may recover any damages sustained by him by a personal action against the owner of the executive right. The action prescribes one year from the date on which the lease is filed for registry.

Acts 1974, No. 50, §110, eff. Jan. 1, 1975.

Comment

Article 110 seeks to impose proper sanctions for violation of the duty of fair dealing imposed by Article 109 without simultaneously imposing upon mineral lessees the burden of uncertainty in taking leases from owners of executive interests as to whether the executive has violated his duty to the owner of a nonexecutive interest. To these ends, the executive is subject to personal action for violation of his duty, but the lease granted by him in violation of the duty is not invalid. As a further step toward removing uncertainty of lease titles in this regard, Article 110 provides that the action for violation of the duty established in Article 109 must be brought within one year from the date on which the offending lease is filed for registry.

Art. 111. Effect of certain transactions involving executive right

A mineral servitude from which the executive right has been separated is not thereby transformed into a mineral royalty. The creation of a mineral royalty accompanied by a grant of the executive right does not change the royalty right into a mineral servitude.

Acts 1974, No. 50, §111, eff. Jan. 1, 1975.

Comment

Article 111 is essential to solve some vexing problems in the jurisprudence. See Horn v. Skelly Oil Co., 224 La. 709, 70 So. 2d 657 (1954); Standard Oil Co. v. Futral, 204 La. 215, 15 So. 2d 65 (1943); Martel v. A Veeder Co., 199 La. 423, 6 So. 2d 335 (1942); Uzee v. Bollinger, 178 So. 2d 508 (La. App. 1st Cir. 1965); Phillips Petroleum Co. v. Richard, 127 So. 2d 816 (La. App. 3d Cir. 1961); writs denied; Nolen v. Bennett, 119 So. 2d 636 (La. App. 2d Cir. 1960); Cormier v. Ferguson, 92 So. 2d 507 (La. App. 1st Cir. 1957). Detailed discussion of these cases would serve little purpose. It is sufficient to say that there has been no firm basis for prediction as to whether creation of a mineral servitude with a grant to or retention by the landowner of executive rights will reduce the servitude to a royalty. There is even less basis for predicting the interpretation that would be given to a deed creating a mineral royalty together with a grant of the executive right. Certainty is therefore desirable.

Among the questions that arise in this area are the following: does the owner of a nonexecutive mineral servitude have a right to operate in the absence of a lease; in the event of compulsory unitization prior to leasing would he or the holder of the executive right be responsible for drilling costs; who would be liable to third parties for damage resulting from drilling operations on the burdened tract; and, most importantly, what rules of prescription would be applicable? Similar questions arise regarding the position of the holder of an "executive royalty." Although Article 111 does not give specific answers to each of these questions, the general rule that a mineral servitude stripped of executive rights is still a servitude carries with it the application of all legal rules otherwise applicable to the mineral servitude, and the rule that an "executive royalty" is still a mineral royalty similarly imports the application of all legal rules otherwise applicable to royalties.

As noted, the most significant consequence of giving definition to this area of the law is a determination of what rules of prescription will apply. Article 111 certainly gives some flexibility to contracting parties in affording them a functional choice between the servitude and royalty use rules, but there is no real damage to the system of prescription in permitting this. Thus, the owner of a nonexecutive mineral servitude would be entitled to benefit of the dry hole drilling rule and the owner of an "executive royalty" would not. Allowing this degree of freedom to contracting parties does not damage the basic policy underlying the rules of prescription.

Art. 112. Right of nonexecutive to operate

When the executive right is separated from a mineral servitude or ownership of the land, the land or servitude owner has the right, with the consent of the owner of the executive right, to conduct drilling or mining operations on the land.

Acts 1974, No. 50, §112, eff. Jan. 1, 1975.

Comment

Article 112 avoids a possible conflict between the right of the owner of a "stripped down" servitude to operate and the rights of the executive. If the separation of the executive rights does not result in reduction of the interest to a mere royalty, it follows that the servitude owner still has a right to operate individually. Obviously, exercise of this right would cause serious conflict if afterwards the executive determined that he desired to lease. The knot can be effectively cut by subordinating the servitude owner's right to operate to the executive right and prohibiting its exercise without consent of the executive. Specifically stating that the servitude owner retains the right to operate is not, however, engaging in fanciful wordplay. The right to operate has to be fixed in one party or the other. If creation of a "stripped down" servitude does not change the interest into a royalty, the party acquiring the executive rights does not have the right to operate. This, too, is in keeping with the definition of the executive right in Article 105 as being only the exclusive right to lease and to retain bonuses and rentals. Additionally, there are other consequences flowing from placement of the right to operate. If the tract is unitized prior to leasing, for example, the servitude owner is the "owner" of the unleased interest within the meaning of La. R.S. 30:3(8) (1950), the Conservation Act. Therefore, he is responsible for a share of operating costs and drilling costs proportionate to his ownership in the unit. Further, responsibility for damage to third parties flowing from the conduct of operations can be fixed on the "owner" of the unleased interest. Though the economic burden in normally shifted to the operator, the legal relationship between the "owner" and damaged third parties nevertheless exists.

Art. 113. Executive right as appendage of another mineral right

When a mineral right is created and is accompanied by an executive right on the subject land or mineral right, the executive right is an appendage of the mineral right that it accompanies and is extinguished with it.

Acts 1974, No. 50, §113, eff. Jan. 1, 1975.

Comment

Article 113 deals with the nature of a royalty accompanied by a grant of executive rights. If it is determined that such a transaction does not create a servitude, it might be argued that it creates two independent mineral rights each with different prescriptive rules; the executive right, the prescription against which may be interrupted by drilling or mining operations as well as production, and the royalty, which is maintained only by actual production. It is felt, however, that the better view of this transaction is that the executive right should be regarded as dependent upon the royalty. Thus, if the royalty right expires, the executive right expires with it, and prescription accruing against the royalty should not be regarded as interrupted by events other than production. Though rare, this type of transaction has occurred. See Mt. Forest Fur Farms v. Cockrell, 179 La. 795, 155 So. 228 (1934).

CHAPTER 7. THE MINERAL LEASE

PART 1. THE NATURE OF THE MINERAL LEASE

Art. 114. Nature of mineral lease; creation on noncontiguous tracts; effect of unit operations

A mineral lease is a contract by which the lessee is granted the right to explore for and produce minerals. A single lease may be created on two or more noncontiguous tracts of land. Operations on or production from the land burdened by the lease or land unitized therewith sufficient to maintain the lease according to its terms will continue the lease in force as to the entirety of the land burdened.

Acts 1974, No. 50, §114, eff. Jan. 1, 1975, Acts 2023, No. 88, §1.

Comment

The first sentence of Article 114 sets out a functional definition of the mineral lease. This statement should be taken as being the norm and not as excluding contractual, variation of the lease to meet given circumstances. For example, a mineral lease might be granted without the right to conduct operations on the surface of the leased premises, limiting the lessee's right to operating by use of deviated wells or by unitization. The contract would, nevertheless, be a mineral lease. The suggested definition is intended to be consistent with the concepts embodied in Articles 2669 and 2670 of the Civil Code. In the former, it is provided that lease is "a synallagmatic contract, to which consent alone is sufficient, and by which one party gives to the other the enjoyment of a thing ... at a fixed price." The latter states that as in the case of sales, thing, price, and consent are essential.

Article 114 should be read carefully in conjunction with Article 16, providing that the mineral lease falls within the generic term "mineral right" and further providing that all mineral rights are "real rights and are subject either to the prescription of nonuse for ten years or to special rules of law governing the term of their existence." Thus, the running controversy between the courts and the legislature as to the nature of the mineral lease is laid to rest by classification of the interest as a real right. For discussion of the functioning of the mineral lease as a real right, see the comment following Article 16. The mineral lease is not, however, subject to the prescription of nonuse. Article 115 provides the general rule that the mineral lease "may not be continued for a period of more than ten years without mining operations or production." Thus, subject to the exception made for hard mineral leases by Article 115, the parties may stipulate how a lease may be maintained, but it cannot be continued for more than ten years without drilling or mining operations having taken place.

Articles 73 and 103 provide that if a mineral servitude or mineral royalty is granted or reserved on noncontiguous tracts of land in a single deed, there are created as many servitudes or royalties as there are tracts of land. Article 114, in allowing the creation of a single mineral lease on two or more noncontiguous tracts of land, sustains established law. Reagan v. Murphy, 235 La. 529, 105 So. 2d 210 (1958). In that case it was argued that a mineral lease covering noncontiguous tracts was in actuality several leases and that mineral leases are subject to the same rules of prescription of nonuse as are mineral servitudes. The court rejected this proposition, holding that a single mineral lease can be granted on several noncontiguous tracts of land. The landowner in such cases is not without a remedy, for it is the established jurisprudence that the lessee must fully develop the leased property and test every part of land subject to it with reasonable diligence or suffer the lease to be cancelled. See the comment following Article 122.

In providing that operations on the lease premises of land unitized therewith will preserve the lease as to its entirety Article 114 preserves established law based on the concept that the mineral lease is indivisible. In Hunter Co. v. Shell Oil Co., 211 La. 893, 31 So. 2d 10 (1947) part of the lease premises was placed in a unit formed by the Commissioner of Conservation. Production was obtained from a well on land other than that portion of the lease tract within the unit. The court held that the "drilling of a producing well in the unit...within the primary term of the lease complies with the obligation to drill assumed by the lessee under the terms and provisions of the lease and production in paying quantities from such a well constitutes production from all the property described in the lease and maintains the lease in full force and effect." Accord: LeBlanc v. Danciger Oil & Refining Co., 218 La. 462, 49 So. 2d 855 (1950). Under Article 3 parties are free to provide for a result other than that contemplated by Article 114. This is frequently done by the inclusion of a "Pugh clause" in the lease, which effectively reverses the *Hunter* and *LeBlanc* decisions, with the result that if there is a unitization and production is obtained from the unit, the lease is maintained only as to that portion in the unit. The lessee may, however, maintain the lease as to the remainder of the premises by another means permitted by the lease, such as delay rental payments, drilling, or 117 shut-in rentals, provided such options remain open to him. See Odom v. Union Producing Co., 243 La. 48, 141 So. 2d 649 (1962).

Art. 115. Requirement of term; limitation of continuation without drilling or mining operations or production

A. The interest of a mineral lessee is not subject to the prescription of nonuse, but the lease must have a term. Except as provided in this Article, a lease shall not be continued for a period of more than ten years without drilling or mining operations or production. Except as provided in this Article, if a mineral lease permits continuance for a period greater than ten years without drilling or mining operations or production, the period is reduced to ten years.

B. A lease granting the right to explore for and produce solid minerals, except lignite or other forms of coal, may provide for continuation for a period greater than ten years by the payment of rent at least annually if at the time it is extended beyond ten years a hard mineral susceptible of production in paying quantities has been discovered on the land leased, if the lessee has commenced actual mining operations on neighboring land for production of the mineral discovered, and if the plan of development for such mining operations includes the ultimate production of the discovered mineral from the land leased. Such a lease may be maintained by such payments only as long as the operations are continued with the diligence of a reasonably prudent operator without cessation for more than six calendar months but in no event may the lease be maintained by such payments for longer than twenty years.

C.(1) Any lease, granting the right to explore for and produce lignite or another form of coal, which is included within a mining plan and upon which no actual operations have begun, may provide for an extension beyond the initial ten year term for a period of thirty years by the payment of rent, an advance royalty payment or any other form of periodic payment to the lessor, provided the following requirements are satisfied:

(a) Lignite or another form of coal susceptible of being mined has been discovered as a result of acts committed on the land or due to acts providing a reasonable basis of proof of the discovery of the mineral.

(b) A mining plan for the ultimate production of lignite or other forms of coal, together with a permit issued by the commissioner of conservation, is filed in the conveyance records of the parish or parishes in which the leased land is located.

(c) The mining plan, along with any amendments thereto, provides for the ultimate production of the lignite or other forms of coal from the land leased.

(d) Actual mining operations have begun on land included in the plan, although such operations are not being conducted on the lease being extended.

(2) The mining plan may authorize removal of lignite or other forms of coal from different seams, beds or other deposits

and from noncontiguous tracts of land, provided such operations are so integrated as to constitute a single mining plan.

(3) A lease granting the right to explore for and produce lignite or other forms of coal may be extended by payments pursuant to this Subsection as long as mining operations under the plan continue with the diligence of a reasonably prudent operator without cessation for more than five years.

(4) The lease granting the right to explore for and produce lignite or other forms of coal may not be extended for a period greater than forty years unless there have been actual mining operations or production on the land leased or on land unitized therewith.

D. Parties may not contract contrary to the provisions of this Article except to the extent of providing for time periods less than those provided herein or otherwise to increase the obligations of the lessee.

Acts 1974, No. 50, §115, eff. Jan. 1, 1975. Amended by Acts 1976, No. 129, §1; Acts 1980, No. 122, §1; Acts 1982, No. 780, §1.

Comment

Article 115 preserves established law in providing that the interest of the lessee is not subject to prescription. Reagan v. Murphy, 235 La. 529, 105 So. 2d 210 (1958). The same is true of the requirement of a term, a requirement that can be satisfied not only by a term of years but by the standard type of habendum clause providing for a primary term and continuation as long thereafter as there is production in paying quantities or operations are conducted or other conditions for the continuation of the lease are met. It was early established that the mineral lease must have a term. Bristo v. Christine Oil & Gas Co., 139 La. 312, 71 So. 521 (1916). Even six years prior to final disposition of Frost-Johnson

Lumber Co. v. Salling's Heirs, 150 La. 756, 91 So. 207 (1922), the court spoke in terms of public policy in rendering its decision.

The second sentence of Article 115 may be described as new. However, there has always lurked in the background of the law applicable to mineral leases the possibility that the court might hold that although a mineral lease is not subject to the prescription of nonuse, it cannot be granted for a primary term greater than ten years. Customarily, primary terms do not exceed ten years. However, there are some unofficially reported instances in which long term mineral leases have been granted. None of these has ever been litigated. Placing this limitation on the primary term is consistent with the public policy underlying the system of prescription applicable to other mineral rights. The net effect of this limitation in combination with the first sentence is to free the mineral lease of the use rules applicable to servitudes while accomplishing the end of prohibiting all basic forms of mineral rights from remaining outstanding for periods greater than ten years without some form of development. But see Article 149-152 concerning mineral rights on property acquired by the state or federal government. This leaves the matter of what form of drilling or mining operations or production will maintain the mineral lease within the discretion of the contracting parties. Established custom in this regard indicates that there is virtually no danger to the basic philosophy of a system of terminable mineral rights in permitting this freedom. It means also that as held in Reagan v. Murphy, 235 La. 529, 105 So. 2d 210 (1958) and articulated in Article 114 a mineral lease can be granted on more than one tract of land and maintained in its entirety by operations on any of several noncontiguous tracts covered by the lease.

Previously, it was not established that the mineral lease either could or could not be granted for a primary term greater than ten years. The danger of providing expressly that they could be granted for primary terms greater than ten years lay in the possibility that there might be widespread evasion of the public policy embodied in the prescriptive rules applicable to other forms of mineral rights. In selling land, the vendor might reserve a paid up mineral lease with a primary term of thirty years rather than a mineral servitude. Previously, the threat that the court might impose the sort of limitation provided for by Article 115 had a deterrent effect on the widespread granting of long term leases.

The removal of that threat might have resulted in subversion of the entire system of prescription. It is therefore provided that the ten year limitation be imposed. This is viewed as essential to preservation of the mineral property system as a whole.

The very recent advent of the potential for mining low grade coal and ignite in Louisiana together with the potential for mining iron ore and the current production of substances such as bentonite furnish the motivation for the reference to hard mineral leases in Article 115. The nature of hard mineral operations of this kind is that frequently mining operations will be initiated but actual mining will not take place on a particular tract in the project under development until many years after mining is begun. To accommodate this special feature of hard mineral operations of this type, Article 115 legitimates the drawing of leases that have a special brand of what has become known as a "shut-in clause" in oil and gas leases. This option was chosen rather than permitting the granting of leases for terms greater than ten years to preserve the basic structure of the mineral property system and to avoid the chaos that would be wrought in trying to deal with the legitimacy of leases that provide for terms greater than ten years and contemplate development rights to oil, gas, and specified forms of hard minerals as well.

The type of shut-in clause permitted by Article 115 requires three conditions for its operation. First, there must be discovery of minerals that can be produced in paying quantities. This is akin to the same requirement in shut-in clauses in oil and gas leases. Second, actual mining operations must have been commenced, though they need not be on the land burdened by a particular lease. Insofar as discovery is required, there is no great obstacle as in most hard mineral operations the drilling of core holes can prove the existence of the deposits desired to be mined. Without intending to bind courts in dealing with problems of interpretation in this regard, it would seem reasonable to say that the drilling of a core hole on every individual tract in a project would not be required so long as reliable geological and geophysical data show by a preponderance of the evidence that the productive deposits underlie any particular tract subject to lease. Such an interpretation would make the reasonableness of requiring or not requiring core holes on each tract a matter to be determined by the courts according to the circumstances of a particular case. Third, the mining·project in question must include the ultimate withdrawal of minerals from a particular lease in order for the shut-in clause to operate. The mining operations, moreover, must be conducted continuously without interruption of more than six months to permit maintenance of the lease by making the payments authorized by Article 115. Hard mineral leases with clauses of the kind authorized may not be maintained by payments in lieu of production for more than twenty years.

The last sentence of Article 115 is simply to make certain that parties have no basis for contending that they can contract contrary of the limitations of the Article by asserting the right of freedom of contract. This article is a statement of rules involving fundamental public policy.

PART 2. WHO MAY GRANT MINERAL LEASES

Art. 116. Who may grant a mineral lease

A mineral lease may be granted by a person having an executive interest in the mineral rights on the property leased.

Acts 1974, No. 50, §116, eff. Jan. 1, 1975.

Comment

Article 116 contemplates that leases can be granted by the landowner who owns minerals rights, the mineral servitude owner, and by the holder of executive rights over mineral rights which he does not own. Ordinarily, a lessor need not own the thing leased, his warranty being limited to one of peaceful possession and his liability for eviction being for damage and loss "sustained by the interruption of the lease." La. Civil Code arts. 2681, 2682, 2696 (1870). In the case of mineral leases, however, there is a strong functional similarity to the mineral servitude in that time mineral lessee obtains a right to a share of production and operating rights much the same as the owner of a mineral servitude. Thus it is provided that the right to create the mineral lease be limited to those having executive rights. See Articles 105 through 113 concerning executive rights. In Article 120 it is provided that the warranty of the mineral lessee is that of the seller of land. Since this aspect of the law of sale is being applied to determine the responsibility of the lessor, it is proper to require that the mineral lessor be one who is the owner of or has executive rights over the property being leased. In this connection, reference should be made to Article 144 permitting the use of after-acquired title clauses and making such clauses binding on all subsequent owners of the land or mineral rights which are the subject of the lease.

Art. 117. Granting of mineral lease by owner under conditional title

A mineral lease may be granted by the owner of an executive interest whose title is extinguished at a particular time or upon the occurrence of a certain condition, but it terminates at the specified time or on occurrence of the condition divesting the title.

Acts 1974, No. 50, §117, eff. Jan. 1, 1975.

Comment

Article 117 is the same as Articles 25 and 83 applicable respectively to mineral servitudes and mineral royalties. See the comment following Article 25.

Art. 118. Right of usufructuaries to lease

A usufructuary of land may grant a mineral lease on the estate of which he has the usufruct if his usufruct includes mineral rights susceptible to leasing, but any such lease is extinguished with the termination of the usufruct. A usufructuary of a mineral servitude or other executive interest may grant a mineral lease that extends beyond the term of the usufruct and binds the naked owner of the servitude.

Acts 1974, No. 50, §118, eff. Jan. 1, 1975.

Comment

For a full explanation of the rights of usufructuaries, see Articles 188-196. The rule prohibiting a usufructuary of land from executing leases running beyond the termination of his usufruct is consistent with the rules applicable to mineral servitudes and royalties (see Articles 26 and 84) and also with Article 737 of the Civil Code [now C.C. art. 711]. Insofar as Article 118 permits the usufructuary of mineral servitudes or other executive mineral interest to grant leases running beyond the period of his usufruct, it is consistent with the general duty now imposed on the usufructuary by Civil Code art. 567 [now C.C. arts. 539, 576, 628] to keep the thing of which he has the usufruct and to take the "same care of them as a prudent owner does of what belongs to him." The usufructuary could not care for the thing subject to his usufruct properly if in this particular instance he could not lease it for periods running beyond his usufruct because a lessee would be highly unlikely to invest in the development of the land subject to the servitude or other right in question if he could not be assured that his investment would be protected beyond the term of the usufruct. Also, Article 193 purports to give the usufructuary of a mineral servitude the same rights of use and enjoyment as if he were the owner of the servitude. This principle would be left woefully short of having meaning if the usufructuary could not lease the right of which he has the usufruct up to and beyond the term of his usufruct.

PART 3. THE OBLIGATIONS OF THE LESSOR

Art. 119. Obligations of lessor

A mineral lessor is bound to deliver the premises that he has leased for use by the lessee, to refrain from disturbing the lessee's possession, and to perform the contract in good faith.

Acts 1974, No. 50, §119, eff. Jan. 1, 1975.

This Article states established law. Both a vendor and a lessor are bound to make delivery and refrain from interference with possession. La. Civil Code arts. 2475, 2692 (1870). The requirement of good faith performance is inherent in all contracts. La. Civil Code art. 1901 (1870) [now C.C. arts. 1983, 2004, 2014, 2018, 2020, 2022; *cf.* C.C. arts. 1759, 1780, 1951].

Art. 120. Lessor's warranty and limitation of liability for breach thereof

A mineral lessor impliedly warrants title to the interest leased unless such warranty is expressly excluded or limited. The liability of the lessor for breach of warranty is limited to recovery of money paid or other property or its value given to the lessor for execution or maintenance of the lease and any royalties delivered on production from the lease.

Acts 1974, No. 50, §120, eff. Jan. 1, 1975.

Comment

It has been customary for many years to include a warranty of title clause in mineral leases. Thus, Article 120 codifies industrial custom. Further, since it is being provided that insofar as the mineral lease transfers to the lessee operating rights and the right to share in production much the same as those acquired by the owner of a mineral servitude, the warranty of the lessor should logically be that of a vendor. The obligation of the ordinary lessor is only to maintain the lessee in peaceful possession. La. Civil Code arts. 2682, 2692 (1870). The power to exclude or limit warranty is consonant with Article 2402 of the Civil Code [now C.C. arts. 2338, 2339].

Insofar as the lessor's liability in warranty is concerned, Article 2506 of the Civil Code entitles the vendee to restitution of the price, the fruits or revenues when he is obliged to return them to the true owner, the costs occasioned by the suit in warranty by the vendee or that brought by the original plaintiff, and damages, when he has suffered any, besides the price that he has paid. In giving the lessee who has been evicted the right to recover the bonus, rentals, and royalties, Article 120 follows Article 2506 of the Civil Code in giving the right to return of the purchase price and fruits or revenues.

The other items now permitted to the vendee are excluded from this article. It is unclear whether this represents the prior jurisprudence. In Martel v. Hunt, 195 La. 701, 197 So. 402 (1940), it was held that the lessee was not entitled to a proportionate part of drilling costs as damages when there was a partial failure of title; recovery was limited to the bonus. The court relied particularly on the idea that it was obvious from the nature of the lease transaction that the lessee assumed the risk of drilling and had much more to gain than the lessor as well as the fact that it appeared from the record that the lessee had not relied exclusively on the lessor's warranty but had concluded its own title check with full legal advice before committing its funds to drilling. Under the circumstances, the court limited the. recovery. However, in Slack v. Riggs, 177 La. 222, 148 So. 32(1933), distinguished in *Martel*, recovery of drilling costs was permitted. The court in *Martel* interpreted the earlier case as one in which the lessee did rely on the lessor's warranty in committing its money to drilling. Also, the lessee in *Slack* had not paid a cash bonus but had undertaken a drilling obligation. Under the circumstances, it seems that the *Slack* decision is functionally the same as *Martel* in that the drilling obligation was, in effect, the bonus given the lessor for the execution of the lease. In Jefferson Lake Sulphur Co. v. State, 213 La. 1, 34 So.2d 331 (1948), plaintiff sought damages from the State of Louisiana, its lessor. Salt had been removed by a trespasser, and the state had recovered from the trespasser the value of the minerals removed. The plaintiff lessee sought to recover from the state on the same basis as the state had recovered from the trespasser. The court held that damages were not limited to a showing of such profit as the lessee might have made had it mined the salt itself but held the lessee entitled to recovery on the same basis as the state, the value of the salt removed.

In Carter Oil Co. v. King, 134 So.2d 89 (La. App. 2d Cir. 1961) the lessee was permitted to recover the bonus, but the opinion does not reveal any issue as to other possible elements of damages. In Berwick Mud Co. v. Stansbury, 205 So. 2d 147 (La. App. 3d Cir.

138

1967) defendant gave what purported to be a full interest lease. Plaintiff sought recovery of the amount which it had to pay to secure a lease on the unleased interest not covered by defendant's original lease and alternatively for return of a proportionate part of the bonus. The court permitted recovery of the bonus which plaintiff had to pay to secure the unleased interest, which was higher than the corresponding portion of the bonus paid to defendant. This decision was questioned in Harville v. Campbell, 221 So. 2d 273 (La.App.2d Cir. 1969).

The murky jurisprudence suggested a need for clarification in this area. Looking at the economic realities of the situation, the court in Martel v. Hunt, *supra*, seems to have been on sound ground. Mineral exploration and production in general, and petroleum exploration and production in particular, are high risk endeavors. The operator commits funds and conducts business, with certain calculated risks in mind. Sound industrial practice includes the procedure of a thorough title check before major commitments are made. If at the time of the check a defect is found, the normal situation will be that the lessee will be damaged to the extent of loss of the bonus and possibly rentals. Beyond this point, the wise operating practice in the industry, which includes thorough title searches suggests the conclusion that the operator is making his own decision on commitment of funds and is assuming the risk of whatever title defects may exist. If he miscalculates, any loss incurred, beyond bonuses, rentals, and whatever royalties have been paid, has been suffered as much, and probably more, as a result of the operator's own business decision than by virtue of reliance on the lessor's warranty. Economically, it is preferable to place the burden of loss through title failure, beyond the items listed, on mineral operators as a class rather than lessors as a class. To begin with, most landowners would not be able to bear major risk beyond liability for return of bonus, rentals, and royalties, and some would be strained to do that. More importantly, however, title failure should be considered an industrial risk which can be more ably borne by the industry and subsequently spread to consumers as a cost of the mineral products consumed.

It is to be observed that although the recommendation as to damages states a rule to be imposed if the lease contract is silent, parties are free to extend the lessor's liability beyond that which would result from silence on the matter. See also Article 3.

Art. 121. Right of lessee to lease from adverse claimants

A mineral lessee may take leases from persons claiming the leased land or mineral rights or interests therein adversely to his lessor.

Acts 1974, No. 50, §121, eff. Jan. 1, 1975.

Comment

The rule stated in Article 121 is consistent with the rule of Article 120 that the mineral lessor's warranty is that of a seller. Early jurisprudence took a common-sense view of the mineral lease, holding that the rule that a lessee may not contest his lessor's title is inapplicable to mineral leases. Nabors Oil & Gas Co. v. Louisiana Oil & Refining Co., 151 La. 361, 91 So. 765 (1922); Powell v. Rapides Parish Police Jury, 165 La. 490, 115 So. 667 (1928); Gulf Refining Co. of Louisiana v. Hayne, 138 La. 555, 70 So. 509 (1916); Rives v. Gulf Refining Co. of Louisiana, 133 La. 178, 62 So. 623 (1913); Grimm v. Pugh, 197 So. 641 (La. App. 2d Cir. 1940); but see Exchange National Bank v. Head, 155 La. 309, 99 So. 272 (1924), which misinterpreted the *Nabors* decision. However; following the decision in Gulf Refining Co. v. Glassell, 186 La. 190, 171 So. 846 (1936), which held a mineral lease to be like a predial lease and denied lessees the right to bring real actions, the United States Court of Appeals refused to follow the early decisions on this point and held that a lessee cannot deny his lessor's title. Sabine Lumber Co. v. Broderick, 88 F. 2d S88 (5th Cir. 1937). The problems posed by this jurisprudence has usually been met by the inclusion in mineral leases of a clause permitting the lessee to take leases from adverse claimants. Article 121 therefore lays to rest a question existing in the jurisprudence and adopts what has become customary practice in the industry.

PART 4. THE OBLIGATIONS OF THE LESSEE

Art. 122.   Lessee's obligation to act as reasonably prudent operator

A mineral lessee is not under a fiduciary obligation to his lessor, but he is bound to perform the contract in good faith and to develop and operate the property leased as a reasonably prudent operator for the mutual benefit of himself and his lessor. Parties may stipulate what shall constitute reasonably prudent conduct on the part of the lessee.

Acts 1974, No. 50, §122, eff. Jan. 1, 1975.

Comment

The concept of implied covenants or obligations in other jurisdictions resulted from the view of courts that the principal expectation of the parties to a mineral lease is that the property will be developed for the mutual advantage and profit of both parties. Thus, the courts have in various common operating situations imposed upon the lessee the obligation to develop and operate the property in the manner of a reasonable, prudent operator. The general choice of an objective rather than a subjective standard of, say, good faith of the individual operator, is virtually unanimous. In other jurisdictions, this general principle is specified in the form of individual covenants, variously classified by different jurisdictions and different authorities on mineral law. See 5 Williams and Myers, Oil and Gas Law, Ch. 8 (1969). The same authority takes the position that the root of the so-called implied covenants is the general principle of required cooperation among parties to all contracts in the achievement of ·their intended goals.

In Louisiana there is available in the Civil Code a general principle which can serve as a basis for achieving the result of the doctrine of implied covenants in other jurisdictions. Article 2710 requires that the lessee enjoy the thing leased as "a good administrator." This objective standard can aptly be translated into the field of mineral law as the "reasonable, prudent operator" standard which has been consistently applied by Louisiana courts to oil, gas, and mineral leases. See *e.g.,* Williams v. Humble Oil & Ref. Co., 290 F. Supp. 408 (E.D. La. 1968) affirmed, 432 F. 2d 165 (5th Cir. 1970); Carter v. Arkansas-Louisiana Gas Co., 213 La. 1028, 36 So. 2d 26 (1948); Caddo Oil & Mining Co. v. Producers Oil Co., 134 La. 701, 64 So. 684 (1914).

Williams and Meyers divide the specifications of the prudent operator standard into (1) implied drilling covenants, including the covenant to drill exploratory wells, the covenant to reasonably develop the premises after discovery in paying quantities, and the covenant of further exploration; (2) the covenant to market the product; and (3) the covenant to use reasonable care and due diligence in conducting operations on the premises. Other authorities divide these implied covenants differently. In Louisiana, the general obligation to act as a "good administrator" or "prudent operator" has been clearly specified in four situations: (1) the obligation to develop known mineral producing formations in the manner of a reasonable, prudent operator; (2) the obligation to explore and test all portions of the leased premises after discovery of minerals in paying quantities in the manner of a reasonable, prudent operator; (3) the obligation to protect the leased property against drainage by wells located on neighboring property in the manner of a reasonable, prudent operator; and (4) the obligation to produce and market minerals discovered and capable of production in paying quantities in the manner of a reasonable, prudent operator. Additionally, the obligation of the lessee to restore the surface of the lease premises on completion of operations may be viewed as a part of this general standard. Two differences between these observable specifications of the general duty of the lessee can be noted as compared with the division made by Williams and Meyers. One is that the Louisiana cases have not found it necessary to impose an obligation to drill an exploratory well in situations in which other courts did so prior to the more modern "drill or pay" and "unless" types of lease forms. Louisiana courts dealt with this problem through application of articles of the Civil Code dealing with potestative conditions and through the doctrine of serious consideration. See Moses, "Potestative Conditions in Louisiana Oil, Gas and Mineral Leases," 16 Tul. L. Rev. 80 (1941). The second difference is that there is little mention of what Williams and Meyers have termed the covenant to use reasonable care and due diligence in conducting operations. This should not be viewed as negating the existence of any such duty in Louisiana as a specification of the general standard to act as a good administrator. It is simply an indication that as yet there has been little litigation involving situations in which other courts have specified the general duty in that manner. See Louisiana Gas Lands v. Burrow, 197 La. 275, 1 So. 2d 518 (1941), in which plaintiff contended that lessee was failing to produce the full amount of gas permitted by a statute setting maximum production levels for gas wells. The court held that the lessee was not under a duty to produce the maximum amount but indicated that if the statute had been a true proration order issued under an act such as the present conservation act, the lessee might have been duty-bound to produce the full amount permitted by the proration order. This is the only discovered situation in which the facts might be seen as involving an obligation to operate the lease with reasonable care and due diligence.

Article 122 states the general duty of the lessee to act as a reasonable, prudent operator as an adaptation of the obligation of other lessees to act as "good administrators." However, since there is jurisprudence dealing with the common specifications of this duty it is appropriate to discuss the cases briefly.

Reasonable development: There is more jurisprudence relating to development of known mineral producing formations in the manner of a reasonable, prudent operator than in connection with other specifications of the lessee's general duty. Essentially, the relevant cases hold that after production in paying quantities has been obtained from a mineral formation, it is the duty of the lessee to develop the producing formation in the manner of a reasonable, prudent operator taking into consideration both his own interests and those of the lessor. See Gennuso v. Magnolia Petroleum Co., 203 La. 559, 14 So. 2d 445 (1943); Wadkins v. Wilson Oil Corp., 199 La. 656, 6 So. 2d 720 (1942); Coyle v. North American Oil Consolidated, 201 La. 99, 9 So. 2d 473 (1942); Doiron v. Calcasieu Oil Co., 172 La. 553, 134 So. 742(1931); Stubbs v. Imperial Oil & Gas Products, 164 La. 689,114 So. 595 (1927); 131 Caddo Oil & Mining Co. v. Producers Oil Co., 134 La. 701, 64 So. 684 (1914).

The obligation of further development was succinctly summarized by the Supreme Court of Louisiana in Carter v.

Arkansas-Louisiana Gas Co., 213 La. 1028, 1034, 36 So. 2d 26, 28 (l948):

"The law of this state is well settled that the main consideration of a mineral lease is the development of the lease premises for minerals and that the lessee must develop with reasonable diligence or give up the contract; further, that as to what constitutes development and reasonable diligence on the part of the lessee must conform to, and be governed by, what is expected of persons of ordinary prudence under similar circumstances and conditions, having due regard for the interest of both contracting parties ..."

Whether a mineral lessee has complied with his obligation to reasonably develop a known producing formation has been said to be a question of fact determinable by the circumstances of each case. Carter v. Arkansas-Louisiana Gas Co., *supra*. The lessor must prove to the satisfaction of the court that a reasonable, prudent operator would conduct additional drilling operations in the productive formation. If the lessor is able to sustain the burden of proof, he is entitled to cancellation of the lease. Carter v. Arkansas-Louisiana Gas Co., *supra*. See also, Fontenot v. Sumray MidContinent Oil Co., 197 So. 2d 715 (La. App. 3d Cir. 1677); Sellers v. Continental Oil Co., 168 So. 2d 435 (La. App. 3d Cir. 1964). These latter cases develop the concept of partial cancellation as a remedy for nonpayment of royalties. As an equitable device, there does not appear to be any reason why courts could not utilize the remedy of partial cancellation in cases where relief is being granted for nondevelopment. Indeed, in Sohio Petroleum Co., v. Miller, 237 La. 1013, 112 So. 2d 695 (1959), partial cancellation, which was asked as an alternative remedy to complete cancellation, was granted. See, also Romero v. Humble Oil & Refining Co., 93 F. Supp. 117 (E.D. La. 1950) and Nunley v. Shell Oil Co., 76 So. 2d 111 (La. App. 2d Cir. 1954), in which partial cancellation was prayed for by plaintiffs.

No Louisiana court has ever awarded damages for breach of the obligation of reasonable development. The remedy of damages should, however, be regarded as available if proper proof is made. See 5 Williams and Meyers, Oil and Gas Law § 834 (1969). Damage might result from permanent loss of recoverable minerals or from deprivation of present worth of minerals through failure to produce them expeditiously. From a practical standpoint it seems that little in the way of damages can be shown in most cases unless the premises are being drained by wells on adjoining land. In that case, the dispute will be dealt with as a failure to exercise reasonable diligence to protect the property against drainage and damages could be awarded. In this regard see the discussion below of the obligation to protect against drainage.

Further exploration: As noted, Williams and Meyers characterize the covenant of further exploration as being separate from the covenant of reasonable development. This is a defensible view. However, historically in Louisiana the obligation of further exploration can be viewed as an evolutionary off-shoot of the obligation of reasonable development. See Carter v. Arkansas-Louisiana Gas Co., 213 La. 1028, 36 So. 2d 26 (1948). Although the jurisprudence does not make a clear distinction between the obligation of further exploration and the obligation of reasonable development, the distinction nevertheless exists. See Sohio Petroleum Co. v. Miller, 237 La. 1013, 112 So. 2d 695 (1959); Middleton v. California Co., 237 La. 1039, 112 So. 2d 704 (1959); Carter v. Arkansas-Louisiana Gas Co., *supra*; Nunley v. Shell Oil Co., 76 So. 2d 111 (La. App. 2d Cir. 1954).

The obligation to explore and test all portions of the leased premises after discovery of minerals in paying quantities was first announced by the Louisiana Supreme Court in Carter v. Arkansas-Louisiana Gas Co., *supra*. The lessor sued for a cancellation of the lease as to the entire lease premises. A main fault traversed the tract and it was admitted that full development had taken place on one side of the fault. Lessor demanded development on the other side of the fault. Based upon the evidence presented, the court felt the lessor had borne the burden of proving that a reasonable, prudent operator would further explore by drilling wells on the undeveloped side of the fault. Partial cancellation was granted as to the acreage on the undeveloped side of the fault. However, the court noted that had the plaintiff appealed from the judgment of the lower court awarding partial cancellation, he would have been entitled to cancellation of the entirety of the lease. The importance of the Carter case, however, stems from the fact that the court, in its application of the obligation of reasonable development, went further and imposed upon the mineral lessee the duty of further exploration after initial production in paying quantities had been obtained. The court quoted with approval language from the Oklahoma case of Fox Petroleum Co. v. Booker, 123 Okla. 276, 282, 253 P. 33, 38 (1926):

"The principle, as we understand it, is that development of every part of the lease is an implied condition. Therefore, whether the undeveloped portion be a single tract remote from the rest, or a considerable portion of a very large tract ... or the east 100 acres of a tract of 160, it is an implied condition that the lessee will test every part."

The jurisprudence since the *Carter* decision has recognized that the obligation of further exploration is embodied in our law. Middleton v. California Co., *supra*; Sohio Petroleum Co. v. Miller, *supra*; Reagan v. Murphy, 235 La. 529, 105 So. 2d 210 (1958); Wier v. Grubb, 228 La. 254, 82 So. 2d 1 (1955); Eota Realty Co. v. Carter Oil Co., 225 La. 790, 74 So. 2d 30 (1954); Nunley v. Shell Oil Co., *supra*. Federal cases applying Louisiana law are to the same effect. Cutrer v. Humble Oil & Refining Co., 202 F. Supp. 568 (E.D. La.1962); Romero v. Humble Oil & Refining Co., 93 F. Supp. 117 (E.D. La.1950).

The basic similarity between the obligation of reasonable development and the obligation to further explore is that in both instances there must be discovery in paying quantities to make the obligations operative. Some cases have been rather liberal in holding that the lessor has borne the burden of proving that a reasonable, prudent operator would further explore the lease premises. In Nunley v. Shell Oil Co., *supra*, and Romero v. Humble Oil &, Refining Co., *supra*, the courts accepted testimony that lessor had a firm offer from an experienced person to take a lease with a drilling obligation on the unexplored portion of the premises. In both of those cases, it appeared that the defendants had taken the position that even if a well were drilled it would be unsuccessful. The courts seem to have viewed this as tantamount to asserting that the acreage had been condemned. In response to this it was stated that if the acreage had been condemned there was no reason why the lessee should be permitted to sit on the undeveloped acreage in the presence of an offer to drill an exploratory well. Different Circumstances are found in Middleton v. California Co., *supra*, and Saulters v. Sklar, 158 So. 2d 460 (La. App. 2d Cir. 1963). In the *Middleton* case considerable development had taken place, several million dollars in royalties had been paid to the lessor, and lessee presented evidence that it was engaged in a program of seismic exploration of the untested acreage on a 4,600 acre lease. In view of the large size of the lease, the amount of the royalties paid, and the demonstrated plans of the lessee, the court refused to give relief to the plaintiff lessor. In Saulters v. Sklar, *supra*, defendant lessee's response to the plaintiff's demand for further exploration was decidedly evasive. The error committed by the lessee in the *Nunley* case of taking the position that the acreage was condemned was avoided by stating that it felt that the acreage might be valuable for a deep test in the future but that lessee did not deem the present was the time to make such a test. The principal distinction which can be found between Saulters and Nunley is that in one case the lessee took a categorical position that further exploration would be fruitless and in the other the lessee indicated a willingness to consider making a deep test at a future date though that date was undefined. Additionally, the court appears to have given some weight to the fact that the offer to drill on which plaintiff relied was apparently obtained in close proximity to the time of the trial and for that specific purpose.

Protection against drainage: It was established early that a lessor could obtain cancellation for failure to protect the leased premises against drainage through wells on adjoining property. Swope v. Holmes, 169 La. 17, 124 So. 131 (1929). However, it remained unclear for many years thereafter whether a mineral lessor could recover damages for failure to protect the lease premises from drainage. See Billeaud Planters, Inc. v. Union Oil Co. of California, 245 F. 2d 15 (5th Cir. 1957); Coyle v. North American Oil Consolidated, 201 La. 99,9 So. 2d 473 (1942); Louisiana Gas Lands v. Burrow, 197 La. 275, 1 So. 2d 518 (1941); McCoy v. Stateline Oil & Gas Co., 175 La. 231, 143 So. 58 (1932).

However, in Breaux v. Pan American Petroleum Corp., 163 So. 2d 406 (La. App. 3d Cir. 1964), cert. denied, 246 La. 581, 165 So. 2d 481 (1964), it was established that a cause of action for damages for failure to protect the lease premises against drainage does exist in Louisiana. To recover in such an action a lessor must show: (1) the existence of substantial drainage; (2) the quantity of oil or gas that would have been produced from an offset well if drilled at the proper time; (3) the profitability of an offset well in the sense that it would not only meet operating costs but repay investment costs; (4) the lessor's share of the minerals that would have been produced from an offset well had it been drilled at the proper time. This represents the majority view of the elements of a cause of action for damages for failure to protect against drainage. See Williams & Meyers, Oil & Gas·Law §§ 822, 825.2 (1964).

Traditionally, a mineral lessee has been called upon to comply with his obligation to protect the lease premises against drainage by drilling offset wells where economically feasible to do so. However, the court in Breaux added a new dimension to this obligation by suggesting that under certain circumstances a lessee might be under a duty to unitize a portion of the leased premises being drained with the draining well on the neighboring land. See Williams v. Humble Oil & Refining Co., 290 F. Supp. 408 (E.D.La.1968), affirmed, 432 F. 2d 165 (5th Cir. 1970). This means that in those situations where a lessor might not be able to prove that drilling of an offset well would be profitable, he might nevertheless be in a position to allege and prove that a properly formed unit would have protected the premises against drainage. In cases of this kind in which the lessee has no interest in the adjoining well or wells, the basic allegations and required proof would be the same as for the drilling of an offset well, including proof of the economic feasibility of investing in the adjoining well. However, if the lessee of the drained premises is also the operator of the draining well, his money would already have been spent and there should be no requirement that the lessor prove economic feasibility.

Diligence in marketing: A mineral lessee is under a duty to exercise reasonable diligence to secure a market for minerals that have been produced or are capable of being produced in paying quantities. There is rarely a problem in this regard where oil is being produced, as ready markets can usually be found. Most problems arise in connection with the marketing of gas where the magnitude of reserves has not been proved, a market is not readily available, marketing facilities are not available, or administrative delays are involved. The existence of an obligation to exercise reasonable diligence in securing a market is recognized in the Louisiana jurisprudence. See *e.g.* Risinger v. Arkansas-Louisiana Gas Co., 198 La. 101, 3 So. 2d 289 (1941); Hutchinson v. Atlas

Oil Co., 148 La. 540, 87 So. 265 (1921); Lelong v. Richardson, 126 So. 2d 819 (La. App. 2d Cir. 1961).

Restoration of surface: The cases treating the obligation of a mineral lessee to restore the surface of the lease premises as near as is practical to original condition do not specifically include this obligation under the general obligation to act as a prudent administrator. Rather, this obligation has a foundation in Articles 2719 and 2720 of the Civil Code. However, there appears no reason whatsoever to exclude this particular obligation as being a specification of the prudent administrator standard. It is established that the mineral lessee must restore the surface even though the lease contract is silent. Smith v. Schuster, 66 So. 2d 430 (La. App. 2d Cir. 1953). There is apparently an economic balancing process which limits this duty. For example in Rohner v. Austral Oil Exploration Co., 104 So. 2d 253 (La. App. 3d Cir. 1958), the lessee leveled the site on cessation of operations. Among the damages sought by the lessor was the cost of restoring the site of the slush or brine pits to a level of fertility sufficient to grow crops. The court refused to award damages for failure to restore the land to complete fertility, noting that the use of the land was reasonable and the loss of fertility was not due to negligence. Thus, it appears that in effect the obligation to restore the surface is limited by a standard of reasonableness which balances the cost of perfect restoration against the value of the use to which the land is being put. In connection with the obligation to restore the surface, see also Wemple v. Pasadena Petroleum Co., 147 La. 532, 85 So. 230 (1920); Comment, 26 Tul. L. Rev. 522 (1952).

Art. 123. Rent and the obligation to make timely payment thereof

Payments to the lessor for the maintenance of a mineral lease without drilling or mining operations or production or for the maintenance of a lease during the presence on the lease or any land unitized therewith of a well capable of production in paying quantities, and royalties paid to the lessor on production are rent. A mineral lessee is obligated to make timely payment of rent according to the terms of the contract or the custom of the mining industry in question if the contract is silent.

Acts 1974, No. 50, §123, eff. Jan. 1, 1975.

Comment

The obligation of a lessee to pay rent "at the terms agreed on" is stated in Article 2710 of the Civil Code. For purposes of administering the mineral lessor-lessee relationship under the articles of the Civil Code applicable to ordinary leases, courts have long regarded production royalties as "rent." *E.g.*, Milling v. Collector of Revenue, 220 La. 773, 57 So.2d 679 (1952); Roberson v. Pioneer Gas Co., 173 La. 313, 137 So. 46 (1931); Logan v. State Gravel Co., 158 La. 105, 103 So. 526 (1925); Scott v. Hunt Oil Co., 152 So.2d 599 (La. App. 2d Cir. 1963); Hatch v. Morgan, 12 So. 2d 476 (La. App. 2d Cir. 1942). See La. Civil Code art. 2671. Though there is no discoverable direct authority on the matter, it seems equally correct to state that delay rentals and shut-in payments are also rent and must, therefore, be paid timely. The possibility that the parties can, and normally do, make nonpayment of delay rentals an occurrence which automatically terminates the lease, is accommodated by Article 133, providing that a "mineral lease terminates on the expiration of the agreed term or upon the occurence of an express resolutory condition."

The standard "unless" form of mineral lease provides that the lease "shall terminate" unless delay rentals are paid. However, there is often no payment date fixed for production royalties, the timing of such payments being established by individual custom. So-called "shut-in payments" fall into two basic categories. One is the "shut-in royalty" or "lieu royalty" type, upon payment of which there is constructive production within the meaning of the habendum clause of the lease. Although a due date for these payments is normally established, the lease does not usually terminate automatically for nonpayment. The second type of shut-in payment is the shut-in rental. Under this type of clause the shutting in of a well with commercial potential is treated the same as cessation of operations after a dry hole, permitting the commencement or resumption of rental payments. Under this type of clause, the failure to make the shut-in payment usually results in the automatic termination of the lease. The right of contracting parties to provide for automatic termination for nonpayment of any form of rent can be seen as an exercise of the general freedom of

150

contract. See Article 3 of the Mineral Code; La.Civil Code art. 1764 (1870) [now C.C. art. 1933]. However, in the context of the Civil Code articles on leases, the lapse of a delay rental period without payment of rentals might also be regarded as the running of the "certain time," the term, for which the lease is granted. La. Civil Code art. 2674 (1870). Article 2727 of the Civil Code further provides that the "lease ceases, of course, at the expiration of the time agreed on." However, since the standard lease uses the concept of term only in connection with the stated primary term and expiration thereafter for failure to produce or conduct operations in accordance with the lease, the choice of treating the delay rental as rent is preferable, and the exercise of the parties' freedom of contract to provide for automatic termination for nonpayment of such rent represents a contractual variation from the manner in which other rent obligations are stated and their payment is required by the lease. Nonpayment of the delay rental under an "unless" lease is, then, in accordance with Article 133, the occurrence of an express resolutory condition. See also La. Civil Code arts. 2021 and 2026 [now C.C. arts. 1767, 1768]. The obligation of the lessor to deliver the premises and permit the lessee to enjoy the property takes place upon execution of the lease; it is defeated, or terminated, by the failure to pay the rental as required. A suit based on nonpayment of rentals is one for specific enforcement of the express resolutory conditions stated in the contract.

Generally, the courts have displayed a rather strict attitude in administering these resolutory conditions in mineral leases. *E.g.*, Miller v. Kellerman, 228 F. Supp. 446 (W.D.La.1964), aff'd 354 F.2d 46 (5th Cir. 1966), cert. denied 384 U.S. 951 (1966); Broussard v. Phillips Petroleum Co., 160 F. Supp. 905 (W.D.La.1958), aff'd 265 F.2d 221 (5th Cir. 1959); Rushing v. Griffin, 240 La. 31, 121 So. 2d 229 (1960); Johnson v. Smallenberger, 237 La. 11, 110 So. 2d 119 (1959); Atlantic Refining Co. v. Shell Oil Co., 217 La. 576,46 So.2d 907 (950). Thus, as in Johnson v. Smallenberger, *supra*, mere neglect or oversight cannot avoid the enforcement of the express resolutory condition. However, there have been cases in which the lessee has made a good faith effort to pay delay rentals on or before the due date with resultant indulgence on the part of the courts. *E.g.*, Calhoun v. Gulf Refining Co., 235 La. 494, 104 So. 2d 547 (1958) (overpayment well in advance of rental date coupled with silence of lessor); Jones v. Southern Natural Gas Co., 213 La. 1051, 36 So. 2d 34 (1948) (mutual error of parties as to acreage on which rentals based); Baker v. Potter, 223 La. 274, 65 So. 2d 598 (1953) (timely dispatch of payment by Western Union with failure of delivery beyond control and without fault on part of lessee). These cases can be interpreted as establishing that where there is a good faith though erroneous effort to pay which could reasonably have been called to the attention of the lessee by the lessor prior to the rental date, where there is a mutual error as to the amount due, or where nondelivery by a reliable and accepted mode of communication is beyond the control of the lessee, the express resolutory condition will not be enforced. This liberality is at odds with Article 2729 of the Civil Code, which provides that a court cannot permit any delay in dissolution of a lease, that is, it cannot give further time for performance as in the case of ordinary contracts. It is, however, in keeping with a longstanding judicial attitude that the courts have discretion in dissolving mineral leases. One of the most important aspects of characterization of the standard "unless" delay rental clause as an express resolutory condition is that the lessor need not put the lessee in default as a prerequisite to judicial enforcement of the condition.

In the case of a shut-in payment of the kind which is construed as establishing constructive production within the meaning of the habendum clause, it has been held that late payment did not constitute occurrence of an express resolutory condition, and further time for performance was properly allowed. Risinger v. Arkansas-Louisiana Gas Co., 193 La. 101, 3 So. 2d 289 (1941). The court stated that the payment of the shut-in royalty, as contrasted with delay rental payments, was not a "condition precedent" to continuation of the lease. Converting this language to the terminology of Article 133 of the Mineral Code and Article 2021 of the Civil Code [now C.C. art. 1767], it is clear that the "unless" type rental clause is the sort of "condition precedent" which, if not complied with, "defeats" the lessor's obligation to permit continued enjoyment of the thing leased and is therefore a resolutory condition.

Art. 124. Production in paying quantities required; definition

When a mineral lease is being maintained by production of oil or gas, the production must be in paying quantities. It is considered to be in paying quantities when production allocable to the total original right of the lessee to share in production under the lease is sufficient to induce a reasonably prudent operator to continue production in an effort to secure a return on his investment or to minimize any loss.

As to all other minerals, it is sufficient if a reasonably prudent operator would continue production considering the particular circumstances in the light of the nature and customs of the industry involved. In appropriate cases, such as the mining of lignite, a court may consider the total amount of production allocable to the mining plan or project of which a particular lease is a part, rather than merely the amount of production from that lease.

Acts 1974, No. 50, §124, eff. Jan. 1, 1975. Amended by Acts 1976, No. 129, §1.

Comment

This comment is a combined discussion of Articles 124 and 125. As noted herein, these Articles reformulate the existing law rather than working a radical change. Article 125, however, does abolish the old "serious consideration" concept as a legal requirement of a holding that a lease is producing in paying quantities.

The standard mineral lease contemplates that production is one means by which the lease may be maintained during and after the primary term. After the lapse of the primary term, the cessation of production, in the absence of drilling operations or some other means by which the lease is permitted to be maintained, causes an automatic termination of the lease. This termination is clearly a resolutory condition, but it is a term concept. That is, the primary term is the maximum agreed period for which the lease may be maintained without drilling or production attributable to the lease. If the lease is extended beyond the primary term by production, cessation of production results in the expiration of the time, or term, agreed by the parties for the duration of the lease. In this regard, Article 2727 of the Civil Code provides that "the lease ceases, of course, at the expiration of the time agreed on." The jurisprudence is settled that absence of production at the lapse of the primary term results in termination of the lease automatically. Landry v. Flaitz, 245 La. 223, 157 So. 2d 892 (1963); Smith v. Sun Oil Co., 172 La. 655, 135 So. 15 (1931).

It is further settled that even though production continues beyond the primary term, the term of the lease may expire and the contract be automatically dissolved if production is not "in paying quantities." Noel Estate, Inc. v. Murray, 223 La. 387, 65 So. 2d 886 (1953); Vance v. Hurley, 215 La. 805, 41 So. 2d 724 (1949); Stacy v. Midstates Oil Corp., 214 La. 173, 36 So. 2d 714 (1948); Knight v. Blackwell Oil & Gas Co., 197 La. 237,1 So. 2d 89(1941); Parten v. Webb, 197 La. 197, 1 So. 2d 76 (1941); Smith v. Sun Oil Co., *supra*, Logan v. Tholl Oil Co., 189 La. 645, 180 So. 473 (1938); Caldwell v. Alton Oil Co., 161 La. 139, 108 So. 314 (1926). Many leases expressly require that the production be in paying quantities to maintain the lease. However, even though the phrase "in paying quantities" is not present, the courts will read it into the lease with the result that "production" sufficient to maintain a lease must be "in paying quantities." Coyle v. North American Oil Consolidated, 201 La. 99, 9 So. 2d 473 (1942); Brown v. Sugar Creed Syndicate, 195 La. 865, 197 So. 583 (1940); Logan v. Tholl Oil Co., *supra*,' Caldwell v. Alton Oil Co., *supra*.

One of the prime motivations of the requirement that there be production in paying quantities is that the lessee should not be permitted to maintain the lease indefinitely merely for speculative or other selfish purposes. By establishing a primary term beyond which the lease cannot be maintained without drilling or production, the parties have prohibited holding the property merely for speculative purposes. Therefore, it follows that the parties to the normal type of mineral lease do not intend that the lease can be maintained beyond the primary term by an amount of production which does not reasonably hold out the prospect of making a profit on the lessee's total existing investment or of minimizing any loss he might suffer on that investment.

To assure that the lessee is not speculating, Louisiana courts have developed the rule in common with many other states that insofar as the working interest is concerned, the lease must be producing in quantities sufficient to meet current operating expenses and yield a small profit. The amount of the required profit has never been defined. See the authorities cited in the second paragraph of this comment. However, Louisiana has gone further than other jurisdictions and required not only that there be production in paying quantities as to the working interest, but also that there be enough production sufficient to yield royalties sufficient to constitute "serious consideration" to the lessor for maintenance of the lease. See Noel Estate v. Murray, 223 La. 387,. 65 So. 2d 886 (1953); Vance v. Hurley, 217 La. 805, 41 So. 2d 724 (1949); Caldwell v. Alton Oil Co., 161 La. 139, 108 So. 314 (1926). Determinations of what constitutes serious consideration have been made by comparison of the amounts being received in royalties with the amount of the bonus, delay rentals, or shut-in royalties. However, this is shown by analysis of the cases not to be a mere mechanical process. In both Caldwell v. Alton Oil Co., *supra*, and Vance v. Hurley, *supra*, there is extensive discussion of whether the premises had been fully developed. In a suit to have the lease declared terminated by cessation of production in paying quantities, such discussion seems out of place at first glance. However, a close look at the cases reveals the real process at work.

In Caldwell, the lease had been granted for a bonus of $500 for a one year period. Royalties over the eighteen-month period preceding the suit averaged $33.33 per year. The contract of the parties was that a test well was to be drilled within a year and that if that well was dry, a second well would be drilled. The first well produced little, as revealed by the above figures. The defendant contended that he was under no obligation to drill further, having fulfilled the obligation which he originally undertook. The court held, however, that the production from the first well was so small as to render it the same as a dry hole. There having been no drilling of a second well, the contract had expired according to its terms. The implication of this holding is that in an ordinary lease if the lessee has done everything he can reasonably do under the circumstances to develop the lease, the court will not be as deeply concerned with the amount of royalties being paid as compared with the amount of bonuses, rentals, or other payments.

This implication is given substance in Vance v. Hurley, *supra*, in which the entire lease in question had been unitized by order of the Commissioner of Conservation. There being no evidence of other possible developmental steps, the lease was as fully developed as was reasonable under the circumstances. The royalties being received by the lessor amounted to fifty-two cents an acre as compared with a bonus of ten dollar per acre. These figures exclude values attributable to a production payment negotiated by the lessor as additional consideration for the lease which, if included, would still not have altered the unfavorable comparison between current royalties and bonuses. Nevertheless, the court did not declare the lease terminated.

In Noel Estate v. Murray, *supra*, the court declared a lease to be still in force. The lessor was receiving approximately twelve to twenty dollars per acre in royalties annually as compared with a bonus of two dollars and fifty cents per acre. It appeared, also, that the ten acres in contest were as fully developed as was reasonable under the circumstances. However, the court did not conduct any serious inquiry into that matter.

Putting these three cases in perspective, it seems that the amount of the royalties being received as compared with other payments made under the lease is really an evidentiary signal. If the amount is substantial, there will be little further inquiry, as in Noel Estate v. Murray, *supra*. If the amount is small, further inquiry into the status of the development of the lease will be conducted. In Caldwell, though the particular contract was not a standard mineral lease, it can be concluded that the inquiry indicated further drilling in accordance with the contract was required because of the inadequacy of the first well drilled. However, in Vance v. Hurley, *supra*, there was nothing further that the lessee could reasonably do. Therefore, the small amount of the royalties was disregarded. In Noel Estate v. Murray, *supra*, the amount of the royalties was acceptable, and no specific inquiry was conducted into the question of whether the lessee could or should reasonably be expected to do anything further in the way of development. In other words, the role of development or non-development in these cases is an indicator of speculative motive on the part of the lessor. If there is something that he might reasonably do to further develop or explore the lease, his continuing maintenance of the lease by a trifling amount of production is evidence of speculative motive. If he has done all that might reasonably be expected, there is no speculative motive for his continuing maintenance of the lease, and as long as the working interest is making a profit, the lease should be considered as being properly maintained.

Some question might be raised in these cases as to why the matter of development enters the picture at all when the lessor has a remedy for failure to reasonably develop or explore by demanding performance. The advantages to the lessor in proceeding to have the lease declared terminated for failure to produce in paying quantities are obvious. He does not usually have to place the lessee in default, though this is dependent on the terms of the lease. He does not have to bear the heavy burden of proof placed upon him in cases claiming breach of the implied obligation to reasonably develop the premises. On the other hand, the production in paying quantities cases assume situations in which the lease has been maintained by a small amount of production over a substantial time period. This being true, the evidence of speculative motive is strong, and courts apparently feel that the election of the lessor to proceed on the theory that the lease has automatically terminated is one to which he is entitled. A suit seeking damages or dissolution for nonperformance of the obligation of further development is inconsistent with one contending that the lease has terminated for failure to produce in paying quantities. The former must usually be preceded by a demand for performance, thus admitting that the lease is still in force, whereas in the latter, performance is not what is desired by the lessor, his position being based on the contention that the lease has terminated automatically. Thus, the lessor claiming expiration has made a meaningful election.

Viewing the totality of the jurisprudence in this area, it appears that the thrust of the Louisiana cases is that (1) the lease must be producing in such manner as to yield a profit to the working interest over current operating expenses; and (2) the amount of the royalties being paid to the lessor must be sufficient to dispel any notion that the lessee has been holding the lease for speculative purposes and is doing all that might be reasonably expected to maximize his profit on his total investment or minimize any loss thereon.

The articulation of this jurisprudential view is altered as set forth in Article 124 and 125. This change is made by postulating that the production must be sufficient to induce a reasonable, prudent operator to continue producing, not for mere speculation, but in an effort to secure a profit or to minimize the loss on his existing investment from the existing production. There will be no mechanistic test of adequacy of consideration in the form of production royalties as compared with bonuses, rentals, or other sums. However, it will still be possible for the lessor to show that the amount of the royalties is very small as relevant to the issues of the reasonableness of the lessee's conduct or his possible speculative motivation. It is in this sense that the "serious consideration" test has functioned in reality anyway. The requirement of serious or adequate consideration has functioned as an indicator of reasonableness of the lessee's conduct. It should not, however, be elevated to the status of a statutory requirement. The amount of the royalties should be viewed realistically as relevant to reasonableness of the lessee's conduct and without comparison to bonuses, rentals or other sums. The manner in which the test for production in paying quantities is stated in Article 124 is articulated well in the decision of the Texas Supreme Court in Clifton v. Koontz, 325 S.W. 2d 684, 691 (1959):

" ... [T]he standard by which paying quantities is determined is whether or not under all the relevant circumstances a reasonably prudent operator would, for the purpose of making a profit and not merely for speculation, continue to operate a well in the manner in which the well in question was operated.

"In determining paying quantities, in accordance with the above standard, the trial court necessarily must take into consideration all matters which would influence a reasonable and prudent operator. Some of the factors are: The depletion of the reservoir and the price for which the lessee is able to sell his produce, the relative profitableness of other wells in the area, the operating and marketing costs of the lease, his net profit, the lease provisions, a reasonable period of time under the circumstances, and whether or not the lessee is holding the lease merely for speculative purposes.

"The term 'paying quantities' involves not only the amount of production, but also the ability to market the product. . . . Whether there is a reasonable basis for the expectation of profitable returns from the well is the test. If the quantity be sufficient to warrant use of the [product] . . . in the market, and the income therefrom is in excess of the actual marketing cost, and operating costs, the production satisfies the term 'in paying quantities.' "

The test set forth in the Koontz decision is essentially a statement of the manner in which the combined test set out in the Louisiana jurisprudence has functioned and appears preferable to any mechanical test of requiring that as to the working interest there must be only meeting of current operating costs with a "small" but undefined profit left over and that as to the lessor's royalties, there must be "serious" or "adequate" consideration when compared with bonuses, rentals, or other sums paid to the lessor. The courts will be entitled to consider all of the same evidentiary factors which have been of influence previously, but the manner of statement of the legal principle applied will more nearly reflect the true decisional process.

Art. 125. Amount of royalties relevant to reasonableness of lessee's expectation

In applying Article 124, the amount of the royalties being paid may be considered only insofar as it may show the reasonableness of the lessee's expectation in continuing production. The amount need not be a serious or adequate equivalent for continuance of the lease as compared with the amount of the bonus, rentals, or other sums paid to the lessor.

Acts 1974, No. 50, §1, eff. Jan. 1, 1975.

Comment

For a full discussion of the topic of production in paying quantities, see the comment following Article 124. As there noted, Article 125 eliminates the requirement that royalties paid the lessor be "serious consideration" for the continuation of the lease as compared with the amount of bonuses, rentals, or other payments. The discussion points out that this requirement has always functioned as an evidentiary signal rather than a legal requirement; if the royalties are of a satisfactory amount, the courts have made no further inquiry into the status of the development of the lease. If, however, the amount of the royalties has been small as compared with the bonus or some other payment under the lease, the court has inquired further concerning the fullness of the lessee's development of the premises to determine whether the lessee might be holding the property for speculative or other selfish purposes. Article 125 eliminates the "serious consideration" requirement as a legal requirement, but it maintains the relevance of the amount of royalties being paid as a factor for consideration in determining whether the lessee is acting as a reasonable, prudent operator in continuing to produce the property or is acting out of improper motives.

PART 5. TRANSACTIONS INVOLVING THE LESSEE'S INTEREST

Art. 126.   Interests created out of lessee's interest dependent thereon and not prescriptible

An interest created out of the mineral lessee's interest is dependent on the continued existence of the lease and is not subject to the prescription of nonuse.

Acts 1974, No. 50, §126, eff. Jan. 1, 1975.

Comment

It has been held that overriding royalties and similar interests carved out of the working interest are appendages of the working interest and dependent upon it. Fontenot v. Sun Oil Co., 257 La. 642. 243 So. 2d 783 (1971); Arkansas Fuel Oil Co. v. Gary, 227 La. 524, 79 So. 2d 869 (1955); Ascher v. Midstates Oil Corp., 222 La. 812, 64 So.2d 182 (1953); Wier v. Glassell, 216 La. 828, 44 So. 2d 882 (1950). That interests such as overriding royalties created out of the working interest are not subject to the prescription of nonuse in favor of the owner of the working interest is established by Ascher v. Midstates Oil Corp., *supra*. Acts creating overriding royalties, production payments and other similar interests are subject to the registry requirements applicable to mineral leases and other mineral contracts. See Article 18 of the Mineral Code; La. R.S. 9:2721-24 (1950).

Art. 127. Lessee's right to assign or sublease

The lessee's interest in a mineral lease may be assigned or subleased in whole or in part.

Acts 1974, No. 50, §127, eff. Jan. 1, 1975.

Comment

Articles 127 through 132 must be read together. In combination they are an attempt to solve some rather vexing problems existent under the prior jurisprudence. Article 121 leaves undisturbed the developed jurisprudence concerning the distinction between an assignment and a sublease in Louisiana. Consideration was given to altering this distinction. However, it was ultimately determined that it would be simpler to leave that basic law undisturbed and to provide in Articles 128 through 132 that regardless of whether the transaction in question be held to be an assignment or a sublease, there are certain common consequences flowing from the execution of either an assignment or a sublease.

As noted, the jurisprudence firmly establishes the distinction between an assignment and a sublease. In Smith v. Sun Oil Co., 165 La. 907, 116 So. 379 (1928), a conveyance of a mineral lease subject to a reserved overriding royalty and a right to reversion in the event the transferee did not reasonably develop the premises was held to be a sublease. The basic theory was that the lessee had not transferred the entirety of his rights but had retained the override and the right of reversion, the latter of which seemed particularly important to the court in that case. It is not required, however, that there be a retention of any right of reversion or of any right of control on the part of the transferor over the operations of the transferee. It is necessary only that the lessee retain some interest which runs for the life of the lease, such as an overriding royalty or a perpetual or unlimited net profits interest. Broussard v. Hassie Hunt Trust, 231 La. 474, 91 So. 2d 762(1956); Bond v. Midstates Oil Corp., 219 La. 415, 53 So. 2d 149 (151); Roberson v. Pioneer Gas Co., 173 La. 313, 137 So. 46 (1931); Johnson v. Moody, 168 La. 799, 123 So. 330 (1929). This rule has been extended in the holding that when an overriding royalty interest is granted by the transferee of a lease by a separate deed from that by which the lease is assigned to the transferee, the transaction viewed as a whole is still a sublease. Iberian Oil Corp. v. Texas Crude Oil Co., 212 F. Supp. 941 (W.D. La.1963). Also, in Serio v. Chadwick, 66 So. 2d 9 (La. App. 2d Cir. 1953) it was held that a transfer of a 2/64th interest in a lease subject to the right of the transferor to demand a contribution to all wells subsequent to an initial well drilled by the transferor constituted a sublease. However, this latter holding was for the purpose of determining that the parol evidence rule was applicable and does not, therefore, seem to be essential to the result. Its standing as precedent on the criteria for distinguishing a sublease from an assignment is highly questionable.

There are consequences other than those specified in Articles 128 through 132 which will continue to flow from the distinction between sublease and assignment. For example, the security of the assignor is that of vendor, the vendor's lien, whereas the security of the sublessor for payment of the rent and other obligations of the lease is the lessor's right of pledge. See La. Civil Code art. 3249 (vendor's privilege), art. 2705 (lessor's lien)(1870). As to the mineral lessor's privilege see Articles 146-148 of the Mineral Code. There is, therefore, meaning in leaving the jurisprudence concerning the distinction between assignment and sublease undisturbed.

Under the present law, however, questions exist as to the liability of a sublessee to the lessor for performance of the obligations of the original lease, the continuing liability of a sublessor or assignor where the sublease or assignment is without consent of the original lessor, division of the lease, the right of the lessor to refuse performance tendered by a sublessee or assignee, and the effect of notices or demands by a lessor prior or subsequent to an assignment or sublease or recordation thereof. The provisions of Articles 128 through 132 are intended to clarify these specific areas of confusion. For general discussion and criticism of the present jurisprudence on assignment and sublease, see Scott, More on Assignment and Sublease, 12th Institute on Mineral Law 39 (1965); Tucker, Sublease and Assignment: Some of the Problems Resulting from the Distinction, 3rd Institute on Mineral Law 176 (1955).

Art. 128. Responsibility of assignee or sublessee to original lessor

To the extent of the interest acquired, an assignee or sublessee acquires the rights and powers of the lessee and becomes responsible directly to the original lessor for performance of the lessee's obligations.

Acts 1974, No. 50, §128, eff. Jan. 1, 1975.

Comment

Insofar as assignments are concerned, Article 128 represents the present law. Application of Articles 2448 and 2449 to assignments of mineral leases subjects these transactions to the law of sale. One consequence is that the assignee "stands in the shoes" of the assignor. Broussard v. Hassie Hunt Trust, 231 La. 474, 91 So.2d 762 (1956) (dictum); Smith v. Sun Oil Co., 165 La. 907, 116 So. 379 (1928) (dictum); *C.f*, Thomlinson v. Thurmon, 189 La. 959, 181 So. 458 (1938). Application of this principle to subleases is, however, contrary to the theory of the jurisprudence evolved in this area. If a lessee grants a sublease, the sublessee is not in privity with the prime lessor. *E.g.* Berman v. Brown, 224 La. 619, 70 So. 2d 433 (1953). There is a new contract of lease engrafted on the original. Therefore, the prime lessor cannot sue a sublessee for performance of the obligations of the original lease. In Parten v. Webb, 205 La. 799, 18 So. 2d 198 (1944) the prime lessor of a mineral lease sued both sublessor and sublessee without his right to do so being brought into question. The demand for performance was made directly on the sublessee and was considered to be binding on the sublessor. However, in Broussard v. Hassie Hunt Trust, 231 La. 474, 91 So.2d 762 (1956), the Louisiana Supreme Court held that the lessor has no cause of action against a sublessee for breach of any obligation of the original lease as there is no privity of contract between the two.

Nevertheless, the reasons for permitting the lessor to look directly to a sublessee for performance of the obligations of the lease are functional and are very much in keeping with the realities of working interest transactions. For example, it is frequently the case that a lessee will sublease a tract reserving only an overriding royalty, with no right of reversion and no direct control over the manner in which the sublessee conducts operations. As noted, under Louisiana law this is clearly a sublease. Yet the sublessee has assumed all of the obligations of the lease. The intent of his sublessor is effectively to retire from participation in or active and direct control over the conduct of operations. In such cases, there is no reason whatsoever to prohibit the prime lessor from looking to the sublessee for performance. Thus, it is in order to provide that insofar as the sublessee assumes the obligations of the original lease, the prime lessor may demand performance of him directly.

Art. 129. Assignor or sublessor not relieved of obligations or liabilities unless discharged

An assignor or sublessor is not relieved of his obligations or liabilities under a mineral lease unless the lessor has discharged him expressly and in writing.

Acts 1974, No. 50, §129, eff. Jan. 1, 1975.

Comment

Article 129 deals with both the obligations and liabilities of assignors and sublessors for future performance of the obligations of the original lease and the problem of their accrued obligations or liabilities as of the time of an assignment or sublease. It is obvious from the nature of the sublease that the original lessee remains bound to the original lessor and cannot discharge himself by the device of subleasing. The original lease is unaffected by the sublease. It was implicit in such cases as Broussard v. Hassie Hunt Trust, 231 La 474, 91 So. 2d 762 (1956), that if under prior law the lessor could not demand performance from a sublessee, his right to demand fulfillment of the obligations of the original lease against his lessee remained. While it is not the intent of this article to change the rule as to the right of the lessor to demand performance from a sublessee who has assumed obligations of the original lease, it is the intent of this article to retain the concept that the prime lessor can continue to demand performance from his lessee unless he has released him in writing. It is also true of present law that an assignor cannot free himself of the obligations of his contract by assignment without consent of his creditor. The substitution of a new debtor is a form of novation, but it is effective only with the consent of the creditor. La. Civil Code arts. 2189-90 [now C.C. Arts. 1880, 1881, 1882, 1900] (1870). Also, as provided by Civil Code art. 2190 [now C.C. Art. 1900], the intention to make a novation must "clearly result from the terms of the agreement." The substitution of a new lessee has been held to be a form of novation in the case of an ordinary lease. Vignie v. Gouaux, 14 La. Ann. 344 (1859). There is no basis for distinguishing mineral leases from other types of leases in this respect. There are practical reasons for preserving the state of the established law in the case of both subleases and assignments in this particular area. For example, it sometimes happens that a lessor deals with a particular company in preference to others. It should not be possible for a lessee in such a case to unburden himself by either sublease or assignment without the lessor's consent since the lessor may have relied specifically on the solvency and business reputation of the particular lessee. This is clearly the underlying motive for the basic rule that a creditor should not be compelled to accept a new debtor without consent.

Art. 130. Lease not divided by partial assignment or sublease

A partial assignment or partial sublease does not divide a mineral lease.

Acts 1974, No. 50, §130, eff. Jan. 1, 1975.

Comment

There are several cases dealing with partial assignments of leases containing a clause permitting assignment in whole or in part and providing that in the case of a partial assignment failure of an assignee to make payment of his proportionate part of the rentals will not result in termination as to the remainder of the lease. Tyson v. Surf Oil Co., 195 La. 248, 196 So. 336 (1940); Roberson v. Pioneer Gas Co., 173 La. 313, 137 So. 46 (1931); Swope v. Holmes, 169 La. 17, 124 So. 131 (1929). In all of these, the court has held that such a clause makes a lease divisible so that when there is a partial assignment, there are two leases with different sets of rights and obligations between lessor and lessee. Not only will this be true as to the rental obligation, it is true also of the effect of drilling or production on maintenance of the lease. The unarticulated premise of these cases is that in the absence of such provisions the lease would be indivisible in the sense that a partial assignment would not have the effect of creating two leases where but one existed before. It is therefore correct to say that Article 130 reflects established law insofar as assignments are concerned. As to the effect of a partial sublease, it is, again, consonant with the theory concerning the nature of the sublease to conclude that a partial sublease has no divisive effect. This is implicit in decisions such as Roberson v. Pioneer Gas Co., *supra*, in which the court had first to determine whether the transaction in question was an assignment or a sublease. Having concluded that it was an assignment, and taking cognizance of the clause regarding partial assignments, it was held that division resulted. Clearly, if the transaction had been characterized as a sublease, this result would not have followed. This conclusion is reflected in common practice in the petroleum industry. Where a portion of a lease is to be transferred to another operator in return for an obligation well, for example, the lessee will often reserve a 1/1000th overriding royalty. The economic significance of such an interest is negligible. Its purpose is solely to preserve the integrity of the original lease to avoid the effect of an assignment when the lease contains the type of clause treated in the *Tyson, Roberson*, and *Swope* cases. It should be observed that this provision, based on the concept that the lease is indivisible unless otherwise provided by contract, is harmonious with the treatment of mineral servitudes and mineral royalties, which are indivisible in the absence of special agreement to the contrary. It is, therefore, the intent of Article 130 to preserve what is understood to be established law.

Art. 131.   Lessor must accept performance by assignee or sublessee

A mineral lessor must accept performance by an assignee or sublessee whether or not the assignment or sublease is filed for registry.

Acts 1974, No. 50, §131, eff. Jan. 1, 1975.

Comment

Article 131 stems from the belief that the lessor's basic concern is that the obligations of the lease be properly performed. As long as performance is being rendered, he has no major interest in who is rendering it. In the event of a breach, of course, he definitely has an interest in who is responsible to him for that breach. In this respect, he is adequately protected by Article 129, which provides that the lessee is not relieved of his obligations for past or future performance by either an assignment or sublease. Therefore, as long as the lessor is protected from having to accept a debtor on whose solvency and reputation he is not willing to rely without consent, there is no prejudice in providing that he must accept performance from an assignee or sublessee even though the assignment or sublease is not filed for registry. The fact of filing for registry is of no significance in changing the liability of a lessee who assigns or subleases; this is dependent wholly on the consent of the lessor. Thus, filing for registry has no role to play in determining whether the lessor should be bound to accept performance from one other than his lessee. Article 131 may represent a change from the scant authority which exists in this area. In Baird v. Atlas Oil Co., 146 La. 1091, 84 So. 366 (1920), the defendant paid rentals on acreage which had been inadvertently transferred to another party. It was held that since the rentals had not been paid by the record owner of the portion of the lease in question, a person of acquiring a new lease from the landowner had a valid lease. The decision leans heavily on the public records aspect of the situation, concluding that a party seeking to lease the land in question was entitled to rely on the fact disclosed by the records that the lease had been assigned and thus that as the assignee had not paid the rentals, the lease had expired as to the land in question. This seems to be a backward view of the problem. Since a person seeking to lease the property must inquire outside the records to determine whether the lease has been maintained by drilling, production, or payment of rentals, it seems preferable to direct the inquiry to the lessor to determine simply whether performance has been rendered; that is, did the lessor receive the rentals, or were operations conducted under the lease? It should not matter that the check actually came from one other than the record owner as long as any condition or obligation has been satisfied. This view is supportable under the provisions of the Civil Code regarding payment. The term "payment" under Article 2131 [now C.C. Art. 1854] means "not only the delivery of a sum of money, when such is the obligation....but the performance of that which the parties respectively undertook whether it be to give or to do." Thus the term actually means the performance of whatever type of act is necessary to satisfy either an. obligation to give or to do. Article 2134 [now C.C. Art. 1855] provides that an obligation "may be discharged by any person concerned in it. . . ." and that it "may even be discharged by a third person no way concerned in it provided that person act in the name and for the discharge of the debtor, or that, if he act in his own name, he be not subrogated to the rights of the creditor." Without specific reference to these articles the court in *Baird* rejected application of them. It is felt, however, that Article 131 is a sounder view of this matter than that in the *Baird* case. See Tucker, "Sublease and Assignment: Some of the Problems Resulting from the Distinction," 3d Institute on Mineral Law 176 (1955).

Art. 132. Demands by lessor; effect on assignee or sublessee

An assignee or sublessee is bound by any notice or demand by the lessor on the lessee unless the lessor has been given written notice of the assignment or sublease and the assignment or sublease has been filed for registry. If filing and notice have taken place, any subsequent notice or demand by the lessor must be made on the assignee or sublessee.

Acts 1974, No. 50, §132, eff. Jan. 1, 1975.

Comment

The question of the binding effect of notices given by a lessor to assignors and sublessors or assignees and sublessees is not treated in the jurisprudence. It is, however, a matter of practical concern. Article 132 means that a sublessee or assignee, whether or not his interest is filed for registry, takes the lease as he finds it. If there has been a breach of alleged breach of the lease prior to the sublease or assignment, the sublessee or assignee is bound by any demands which the lessor has previously made. If an assignment of sublease is not filed for registry, the lessor is not bound thereby unless he has personally consented. Thus, his demands would be properly made on his lessee and would be binding on holders of interests. If the sublease or assignment has been filed, it is equitable to provide that notices demanding performance be directed to the sublessee or assignee to bind him although a technical argument can be made to the effect that a demand on an assignor or sublessor who has not been released by the lessor is binding on all persons holding interests under the assignor or sublessor. Yet it is quite possible that a lessee might assign his interest and have no concern in making his assignee aware of a demand made upon him. Thus, it does not seem an unfair or intolerable burden to require the lessor to make his demand upon the assignee or sublessee. This does not mean that the lessor will not have to make a demand on his original lessee as a prerequisite to cancellation of a lease which has been subleased, it simply means that if a demand is to be made, it must be made also on the holder of the recorded sublease in order that he be bound by it. In the case of a complete assignment or a partial assignment which divides the lease under its own terms, of course, no demand would have to be made on the assignor as a prerequisite to cancellation as the full lessor-lessee relationship exists between the lessor and the assignee.

PART 6. TERMINATION AND REMEDIES FOR
VIOLATION

Art. 133. Termination of mineral lease

A mineral lease terminates at the expiration of the agreed term or upon the occurrence of an express resolutory condition.

Acts 1974, No. 50, §133, eff. Jan. 1, 1975.

Comment

It is the intent of Articles 133 and 134 to distinguish those situations in which a lease expires by its own terms, either by the running of the primary or extended term or by the occurrence of some express resolutory condition such as failure to pay rentals under the prevalent "unless" type of lease form, from those in which the grievance is nonperformance of the obligations of the lease. Article 2727 of the Civil Code provides that leases cease "of course, at the expiration of the time agreed on." The jurisprudence has embraced this principle. *E.g.*, Taylor v. Kimbell, 219 La. 731, 54 So. 2d. 1(1951); Sittig v. Dalton, 195 La. 765, 197 So. 423(1940); Producers Oil & Gas Co. v. Continental Securities Corp., 188 La. 564, 177 So. 668 (1937); Logan v. Blaxton, 71 So. 2d 675 (La. App. 2d Cir. 1954). The same authorities dearly recognize that when the term of a mineral lease runs, the lessor need not place the lessee in default as a prerequisite to judicial action seeking declaration that the lease has been dissolved by that fact. The jurisprudence also recognizes that there are other types of express resolutory conditions which may occur, such as failure to meet a drilling obligation within the time stated or failure to pay delay rentals, the occurrence of which automatically dissolves the lease. *E.g.* Miller v. Kellerman, 228 F.Supp. 446 (W.D. La. 1964), aff'd 354 F.2d 46 (5th Cir. 1965) (failure to pay delay rentals under "unless" lease); Matheson v. Placid Oil Co., 212 La. 807, 33 So. 2d 527 (1947) (ninety day drilling obligation); Texala Oil & Gas Co. v. Caddo Mineral Lands Co., 152 La. 549,93 So. 788 (1922) (failure to meet one year drilling obligation); Davies v. Texarkana Crude Oil Co., 152 La. 308, 93 So. 104 (1922) (failure to meet one year drilling obligation); Talley v. Lawhon, 150 La. 25, 90 So. 427

170

(1922) (sixty day cessation of operations clause). The same authorities also affirm that when such resolutory conditions occur, no putting in default is necessary as a prerequisite to an action seeking to have the lease declared terminated.

These cases involving expiration of term or occurrence: of express resolutory conditions are distinct from those involving breach by nonperformance not only in the respect that default is not required but also in the different attitude of the courts on the question of whether a lessee should be allowed further time for performance within the discretion of the court. Some leniency has been displayed in special circumstances, such as when a lessee has timely placed a rental payment in the hands of Western Union and it is not delivered for reasons beyond the control of the lessee. Baker v. Potter, 223 La. 274, 65 So. 2d 598 (1953); see also the other cases of leniency concerning rental payments which are discussed in the comment following Article 123. However, it is generally considered that no further time for performance can be allowed. *E.g.*, Taylor v. Kimbell, *supra*. This is logical. In the case of express resolutory conditions such as the typical delay rental clause it is provided that "this lease shall terminate" unless the rental is paid or some other necessary condition for maintenance is met. If this does not occur, the lease goes out of existence. The case is different, however, where the basis for the lessor's complaint is nonperformance. A complaint based upon nonperformance assumes the present existence of the contract, and, unless there has been an active breach of contract, there must usually be a putting in default with further time allowed for performance as a prerequisite to action on the breach. In this connection, see the comment following Article 135. However, if the contract has expired by its own terms, the room for exercise of discretion is slight. Only if there has been some mutual error or a good faith attempt to meet the condition necessary for maintenance of the contract with failure to do so being beyond the control of the lessee or the lessor has in some manner led the lessee to believe that the lease is still in existence and should therefore be prohibited from denying it, should any leniency be exercised. *E.g.*, Calhoun v. Gulf Refining Co., 235 La. 494, 104 So. 2d 547 (1958) (overpayment of rental well in advance of rental date coupled with silence of lessor); Jones v. Southern Natural Gas Co., 213 La. 1051, 36 So. 2d 34 (1948) (mutual error as to acreage on which rentals based); Baker v. Potter, *supra*, (timely dispatch of payment

171

by Western Union with failure of delivery beyond control and
without fault of lessee). When a resolutory condition occurs, the
contract is simply at an end.

Art. 134. Right to relief for violation

If a mineral lease is violated, an aggrieved party is entitled
to any appropriate relief provided by law.

Acts 1974, No. 50, §134, eff. Jan. 1, 1975.

Comment

It is the intent of Article 134 to deal with breaches for
nonperformance where the general law of default applies and to
preserve as remedies for nonperformance of the obligations of a
mineral lease all those forms of relief which have been made
available by the Civil Code, most of which have been utilized in
cases involving mineral leases. Although the remedy of specific
performance has not been granted in Louisiana where the demand
is for compliance with an obligation such as one to drill a well, the
remedy can be appropriate, such as in the case of failure to pay
royalties, if what the lessor desires is payment rather than some
other remedy, or in case of a lessee who seeks to have the lessor
deliver the lease premises to him for his enjoyment.

The award of damages is recognized in a wide variety of cases.
Breach of Implied obligations: Williams v. Humble Oil &
Refining Co., 290 F. Supp. 408 (E.D. La. 1968), aff'd. 432 F. 2d
165 (5th Cir. 1970); Breaux v. Pan American Petroleum Corp., 163
So. 2d 406 (La. App. 3d Cir. 1964). **Breach of obligation to drill
well**: Gillis v. Durbin Bond & Co., 142 F. Supp. 433
(E.D.La.1956), mod. 242 F. 2d 176 (5th Cir. 1957); but see Crane
v. Sun Oil Co., 255 La. 1017, 233 So. 2d 919 (1970). **Surface
damages**: Smith v. Schuster, 66 So.2d 430 (La.App.2d Cir. 1953);
but see Rohner v. Austral Oil Exploration Co., 104 So. 2d 253 (La.
App.1st Cir. 1958).

The remedy of dissolution is the most popularly sought relief
among lessors, for obvious reasons. Under the theory of the Civil
Code, dissolution of a lease or other contract for nonperformance

is an enforcement of the implied resolutory condition which is present in all commutative contracts. La. Civil Code arts. 2729, 2046 [now C.C. Arts. 1876, 2013, 2018] (1870). This remedy, too, has received wide usage. **Breach of implied obligations**: Sohio Petroleum Co. v. Miller, 237 La. 1013, 112 So. 2d 695 (1959); Carter v. Arkansas-Louisiana Gas Co., 213 La. 1028, 36 So. 2d 26 (1948); Wadkins v. Wilson Oil Corp., 199 La. 656, 6 So. 2d 720 (1942); Swope v. Holmes, 169 La. 17, 124 So. 131 (1929); Nunley v. Shell Oil Co., 76 So. 2d 111 (La. App. 2d Cir. 1954). **Breach of obligation to pay royalties**: Melancon v. Texas Co., 230 La. 593, 89 So. 2d 135 (1956); Pierce v. Atlantic Refining Co., 140 So. 2d 19 (La. App. 3d Cir. 1962); Bailey v. Meadows, 130 So. 2d 501 (La. App. 2d Cir. 1961); but see Articles 137-141 limiting the remedy of cancellation for failure to pay royalties. The recent utilization of partial cancellation in cases involving nonpayment of royalties furnished some basis for speculation as to whether this remedy would be judicially extended to other causes of action. Fontenot v. Sunray Mid-Continent Oil Co., 197 So. 2d 715 (La. App. 3d Cir. 1967); Sellers v. Continental Oil Co., 168 So.2d 435 (La.App.3d Cir. 1964). Article 142 specifically permits partial dissolution.

Art. 135. Rules of default applicable except as specified

The provisions of the Louisiana Civil Code concerning putting in default are applicable to mineral leases subject to the following modifications.

Acts 1974, No. 50, §135, eff. Jan. 1, 1975.

Comment

The relevant provisions of the Civil Code are Articles 1931-1933 [now C.C. Arts. 1873, 1874, 1875, 1989, 1990, 1994, 2015]. It has been asserted that default should be a prerequisite to suit only when the party complaining is seeking to recover delay damages and that it should be of evidentiary significance but should not be a prerequisite to an action seeking dissolution of a lease for nonperformance. See Smith, "The Cloudy Concept of Default," 12th Institute on Mineral Law 3 (1965). While this theory has its attractions, it was felt that the established jurisprudence which requires a putting in default, except in certain limited cases, as a prerequisite to a suit seeking dissolution, damages, or both was too well entrenched for radical change to be feasible. It is, therefore, the intent of Article 135 generally to preserve the existing jurisprudence interpreting the Civil Code articles on default in connection with actions for nonperformance of the obligations of a mineral lease.

The division of breaches into active and passive violations now contained in Article 1931 [now C.C. Arts. 1989, 1994] of the Civil Code will be preserved under Article 135. The terminology used in making this distinction in the Civil Code has not been satisfactory, but a change in terminology for purposes of the mineral law would have been difficult without changing the general law. That violations of mineral leases may be either passive or active is established. **Passive breaches, default required**: Brown v. Sugar Creek Syndicate, 195 La. 865,197 So. 583 (1940); Hiller v. Humphrey's Carbon Co., 165 La. 370, 115 So. 623 (1928); Pipes v. Payne, 156 La. 791, 101 So. 144 (1924). **Active breaches, no default required**: Williams v. Humble Oil & Refining Co., 432 F. 2d 165 (5th Cir. 1970); Melancon v. Texas Co., 230 La. 593, 89 So.2d 135 (1956). The Williams decision, treating drainage by a common lessee of adjoining properties as an active breach, is altered by Article 136. The right to secure dissolution for nonpayment of rentals, involved in *Melancon*, is limited by Articles 131-141. However, the decisions still serve to illustrate the vitality of the active-passive breach dichotomy in mineral lease cases.

As noted, the concept of an active breach as defined in Civil Code Article 1931 [now C.C. Arts. 1989,1994] has been applied to mineral leases. The most troublesome area has been the characterization of breach by nonpayment of royalties. Hopefully, however, this difficulty has been cleared up by the provisions of Articles 137-141. For full explanation, see the comments following those articles. The decision in Melancon v. Texas Co., *supra*, involved nonpayment of royalties which were according to the court, being withheld for the purpose of coercing the lessor into authorizing certain pooling agreements. Although the meaning of this case in connection with nonpayment of royalties and the remedies to which a lessor may be entitled therefor has been altered by Articles 137-141, it is still of significance as a statement of the principle that a bad faith refusal to perform an obligation under a mineral lease, particularly if accompanied by a motive to coerce conduct on the part of the lessor, is an active breach of contract. The way is left open by the general incorporation of the Civil Code rules for the courts to characterize conduct of a lessee, or a lessor, as an active breach of contract. In addition to obviating the necessity for a putting in default, another major consequence of characterizing a breach as active is that damages are due from the moment of the breach. Thus, where damages are sought, there is strong motivation to seek characterization of the breach as active.

The rule of Civil Code Article 1933 [now C.C. Arts. 1873 to 1875, 1989, 1990, 2016] that a putting in default is a prerequisite to a judicial demand based on a passive breach of contract is well established. In addition to the authorities already cited see Temple v. Lindsey, 182 La. 22, 161 So. 8 (1935); Pipes v. Payne, 156 La. 791, 101 So. 144 (1924). Damages for passive breach of an obligation of a mineral lease are due only from the time the lessee is placed in default unless the case falls into one of the classes of exceptions discussed below.

Article 1933 of the Civil Code [now C.C. Arts. 1813 to 1875, 1989, 1990, 2016] states the basic rule that damages for a passive breach are due only from the time the debtor is put in default and then lists certain exceptions. Article 1933(1) [now C.C. Arts. 1989, 1990, 2016] deals basically with those instances in which time is of the essence of the obligation, either because of the nature of the obligation and the surrounding circumstances or because the parties have expressly made it so in their contract. As an exception to the default requirement in connection with damage claims for conduct otherwise classifiable as a passive breach, this exception has been little used in mineral lease matters. However, it has been suggested that time is of the essence of contracts for mineral development and that mineral lessees are held to a much higher degree of diligence than in ordinary matters. *E.g.*, Kyle v. Wadley, 24 F.Supp. 884 (W.D.La.1938). This suggestion has broad potential in disputes between mineral lessors and lessees.

Civil Code Article 1933(2) [now C.C. Art. 1873] deals with impossibility of performance by the obligor because of a "fortuitous event or irresistible force." In such cases no damages are recoverable for the inexecution of the contract. This provision has not been utilized in any discoverable mineral lease cases. This is, perhaps, explainable by the presence of elaborate *force majeure* clauses in the standard lease which would obviate necessity for reliance on Article 1933(2) of the Civil Code. This exemption of the obligor from damages is itself subject to exceptions under the terms of Article 1933(3) of the Civil Code. which provides that if the obligor expressly or impliedly undertook the risk of the fortuitous event or if it was preceded by some fault of the obligor without which the loss would not have occurred, damages are nevertheless due.

Civil Code Article 1933(4) [now C.C. Art. 1874] provides: "Although the responsibility of the debtor for the object he was bound to deliver, is incurred from the moment he is put in default, yet if it is lost by some fortuitous event or irresistible force by which it would also have been lost had it been in the hands of the creditor, the debtor is not answerable for the value, but only for the delay. This provision seems more appropriate to sales of movables or to immovables with improvements that are the object of the contract rather than to the law governing mineral leases.

The requirement of a putting in default is also subject to a well recognized exception evolved in the jurisprudence. That is, if a party who has breached a contract and would otherwise be entitled to be placed in default either denies the existence of his obligation or refuses to perform it, the damaged party is not required to place him in default as a prerequisite to an action for dissolution or damages, or both. The expression of the decisions is that to require a putting in default in these circumstances would be requiring "a vain and useless thing." This exception, is specifically recognized as applicable in mineral lease cases. *E.g.* Eota Realty Co. v. Carter Oil Co., 225 La. 790. 14 So. 2d 30 (1954); Wadkins v. Wilson Oil Corp., 199 La. 656, 6 So. 2d 720 (1942). By incorporating the Civil Code rules under Article 135 of the Mineral Code, it is intended that this judicially evolved exception be preserved as well.

Art. 136. Written notice; requirement and effect on claims for damages or dissolution of lease

If a mineral lessor seeks relief from his lessee arising from drainage of the property leased or from any other claim that the lessee has failed to develop and operate the property leased as a prudent operator, he must give his lessee written notice of the asserted breach to perform and allow a reasonable time for performance by the lessee as a prerequisite to a judicial demand for damages or dissolution of the lease. If a lessee is found to have had actual or constructive knowledge of drainage and is held responsible for consequent damages, the damages may be computed from the time a reasonably prudent operator would have protected the leased premises from drainage. In other cases where notice is required by this Article damages may be computed only from the time the written notice was received by the lessee.

Acts 1974, No. 50, §136, eff. Jan. 1, 1975; Acts 1995, No. 1116, §1.

Comment

One of the problems faced by a lessor in obtaining damages for drainage has been that the default requirement virtually emasculates the remedy of damages in many cases. Often the lessor will not discover the drainage and breach until substantial drainage has occurred. A putting in default at that time, establishing the date from which damages can be computed, minimizes the value of the remedy. Some relief from this problem was afforded by Williams v. Humble Oil & Refining Co., 432 F. 2d 165 (5th Cir. 1970), in which drainage by a common lessee of adjoining tracts was regarded as a matter of law as being an active breach of the obligation to protect against drainage. This holding obviated the necessity for default in that case, but if followed, it would also have meant that damages were due from the "moment of the breach," whenever that time could be established. It is the intent of Article 136 to overrule the Williams case insofar as it relieves the lessor of the necessity to put the lessee in default.

However, it is also intended to make the remedy of damages meaningful to the lessor by providing that if the lessee is found to have had actual or constructive knowledge of the drainage and damages are held to be due, they may be computed from the time a reasonably prudent operator would have protected the leased premises. It would be unjust to compute damages from the time of the lessee's knowledge. He should be accorded the fairness of having time within which to react to his actual or constructive knowledge and take such steps as a reasonably prudent operator would take to protect the leased premises, whether by drilling an offset well, forming a unit, or otherwise. Under the circumstances, regarding the breach as passive and requiring the lessor to place the lessee in default is not an unreasonable burden and has no damaging impact on the meaningfulness of damages as a remedy for the lessor. It is to be emphasized that a lessee who is not proven to have had actual or constructive knowledge of drainage is liable in damages only from the time of the putting in default. Further, under Article 136 a putting in default will continue to be a prerequisite to suit for dissolution of the lease on account of a failure to protect against drainage. It should also be noted that nothing in this article alters the burden of proof that must be borne by a plaintiff in securing damages, dissolution, or both, for alleged drainage. See Breaux v. Pan American Petroleum Corp., 163 So. 2d 406 (La. App. 3d Cir. 1964) and the comment following Article 122.

Comments-1995

(a) This Article is new. It fills a gap left by the fact that the 1984 revision of the Obligations articles of the Civil Code eliminated the active and passive breach distinction that existed when Article 135 of the Mineral Code was enacted in 1974 and incorporated the standards of the Civil Code. The comments to Article 1989 (Comment (e)) of the 1984 Obligations revision indicate that it was not the intention of the drafters to change the operation of the Mineral Code. Prior jurisprudence has held that a lessee must be put in default of its implied lease obligations prior to maintaining suit. In Taussig v. Goldlcing Properties Co., 495 So.2d 1008 (La.App. 3d Cir. 1986), the trial court found that the lessees had abandoned the leases because of their failure to undertake additional development. The court treated this as an active breach which obviated the need to put the lessee in default.

The court of appeals held this was error. The attorneys for the lessors made demands for lease cancella-tion, not for development. Thus the demands were not a putting in default. A demand for cancellation is not a substitute for a placing in default, held the court. The tdal court's conclusion that a passive breach had been transformed into an active one obviating the necessity of placing in default under the Civil Code's standards was in error. The court of appeals stated: "Since the duty to develop is an implied obligation, the jurisprudence has consistently held that a breach of this duty is passive, and a formal placing in default is required before judicial intervention may be sought."

(b) An unreported decision, Fina Oil and Chelnical Co. v. Penl1zoil Explora-tion and Production Co., 32nd Judicial District Court, Parish of Terrebonne, No. 95891, Division "D", writ denied, 568 So.2d 1086 (La.1990), has held that this law applicable to mineral leases has now changed with the revision of the Obligations articles. The court ruled that "there is no longer any requirement for a putting in default prior to filing suit for a cancellation of a mineral lease." The court distinguished Taussig on the ground that there was filed in 1983 before the 1984 revision of the Obligations articles of the Civil Code.

(c) The court in Hunt v. Stacy, 632 So.2d 872 (La.App. 2d Cir.1994), came to a different conclusion from the Fina opinion on the analysis of the effect of the 1984 Obligations changes. It held that the Mineral Code continues the ac-tive/passive breach distincLion despite the change in the Civil Code. The court concluded that the legislature intended to retain the distinction between passive and active breaches, as well as the jurisprudence regarding these classifications as to contracts involving oil, gas and other minerals.

(d) The revision of Article 136 to require written notice by a lessor in claims involving drainage, development, or operation of the lease eliminates the discrepancy between the Civil Code and the Mineral Code relative to the active/passive breach distinction arising from the 1984 revision of the Obligations articles of the Civil Code and clarifies the law as reflected in the Taussig v. Goldkillg Properties Co. and the Hunt v. Stacy decisions. The language pertaining to "putting in default" that was found in the prior wording of Article 136 and that remains in Article 135 has been substituted in this revised Article 136 by the requirement of "written notice" of the asserted breach, with the lessee having a reasonable time for performance. This provides consistency with the articles of the Mineral Code on royalty payment and is not intended to limit or otherwise affect the computation of royalties owed or damages arising from breach of the implied obligation to market production as a prudent operator. Frey v. Amoco Production Co., 603 So.2d 166 (La. 1992). The 1984 revision of Article 1991 of the Law of Obligations provides that a putting in default can be by written request for performance, by oral request, or by filing suit for performance. The Civil Code article is not well-suited for the oil and gas industry in matters involving claims of drainage and other breaches of the prudent operator duties found in Article 122 of the Mineral Code because typically the filing of suit for an asserted breach of a prudent operator duty is not for performance of the obligation but for dissolution of the lease. Other Mineral Code Articles and the jurisprudence give guidance as to the circum-stances in which lease dissolution, rather than the remedy of damages, is appropriate.

Art. 137. Nonpayment of royalties; notice prerequisite to judicial demand

If a mineral lessor seeks relief for the failure of his lessee to make timely or proper payment of royalties, he must give his lessee written notice of such failure as a prerequisite to a judicial demand for damages or dissolution of the lease.

Acts 1974, No. 50, §137, eff. Jan. 1, 1975.

Comment

The area of dissolution of mineral leases for nonpayment of production royalties has been one of the most, if not the most, confused and unsatisfactory areas of Louisiana mineral law. Because Articles 137 through 141 constitute a related set of provisions seeking to clarify and improve the law in this area, the background for them and the articles themselves are discussed as a group in this comment.

The story of the law in this area begins with Bollinger v. Texas Co., 232 La. 637, 95 So. 2d 132 (1957) and Melancon v. Texas Co., 230 La.. 593, 89 So. 2d 135 (1956), in which the court found willful, coercive conduct on the part of the lessee, which was withholding royalties to pressure the lessor into giving consent to the formation of certain voluntary production units. This was construed as an active breach of contract, and default was not required. From that point the concept was extended to include situations in which there was no such coercive conduct, such as withholding of royalties because a lessee had not settled a dispute over well costs with the unit operator, Bailey v. Meadows, 130 So. 2d 501 (La. App. 2d Cir. 1961), or failure to pay royalties because of internal reorganization, Pierce v. Atlantic Refining Co., 140 So. 2d 19 (La. App. 3d Cir. 1962). The formula evolved was that if there was a failure to pay for an appreciable length of time without justification, the breach was active in character and no default was required. Conceptually, it has always been difficult to perceive how what is unquestionably a passive breach of contract becomes active merely by the passage of time. The rule could, perhaps, be regarded as a special type of *res ipsa loquitur* device. Thus, the passage of an appreciable length of time without justification apparently of itself warranted an inference that the breach was willful and unjustified, and therefore active, relieving the lessor of the necessity to place the lessee in default. The development gave the courts power to assure timely commencement and payment of royalties in situations in which the remedy provided by Article 1935 of the Civil Code [now C.C. Art. 2000], damages in the form of interest, would not be a sufficient spur to assure diligence on the part of the lessees.

A softening of the courts' attitude emerged as justifications began to be found for failures to pay. These were generally in the form of title difficulties or administrative delays which were beyond the control of the lessee and were basically reasonable. See Broadhead v. Pan American Petroleum Corp., 166 So. 2d 329 (La. App. 3d Cir. 1964); Fawvor v. United States Oil of Louisiana, Inc., 162 So. 2d 602 (La. App. 3d Cir. 1964). Further amelioration of the rule occurred when courts began awarding partial cancellation of leases even though a failure to pay on certain units or portions of the lease had occurred. Fontenot v. Sunray MidContinent Oil Co., 197 So. 2d 715 (La. App.3d Cir. 1967); Sellers v. Continental Oil Co, 168 So. 2d 435 (La. App. 3d Cir. 1964).

The cycle appeared to have returned to very nearly the point at which it began, however, without any court ever having overruled any prior cases. In Hebert v. Sun Oil Co., 223 So. 2d 897 (La. App. 3d Cir. 1969), cancellation was denied on two basic grounds. First, the failure to pay resulted from clerical error in revising tract numbers and distributions following a unit revision. This, the court felt, was justifiable reason for the delay, noting that immediately upon discovery of the error, payment was made. Second, the amount of the royalties in arrears was only $13.54 over a five month period, which the court did not consider a "serious basis for cancelling the lease." This was particularly true in view of the fact that there had been an overpayment on other royalties exceeding the amount in arrears by seven cents.

Insofar as the court accepted the clerical error as an excuse, the decision seemed to be in conflict with Pierce v. Atlantic Refining Co., *supra*, in which the court rejected internal organizational problems as justifying a delay of approximately six months. Also, insofar as the view that the amount of the unpaid royalties coupled with the overpayment of other royalties did not constitute a serious basis for cancellation is concerned, the court did not mention that the supreme court in Bollinger v. Texas Co., *supra*, cancelled a lease where the amount unpaid was very small and an overpayment of shut-in royalties left the lessor without any real economic loss. The only possible distinguishing element is that in *Bollinger*, the court found a willfulness in the lessee's conduct which had coercive motives.

This whole patchwork quilt of jurisprudence required revision. A well-motivated attempt to give lessors some effective remedy besides recovery of interest on royalties due as a means of assuring diligence and promptness in payment of royalties resulted in the evolution of a device which was abused by lessors, and the Hebert case marked the culmination of a reactionary cycle.

The real problem in this area is that lessors are entitled to some meaningful remedy besides recovery of interest which will assure that they will receive timely payment of production royalties. On the other hand, however, the harshness of cancelling a lease which may involve the investment of millions of dollars because of the nonpayment of an insignificant sum of money is obvious. It is the intent of Articles 137-141 to provide lessors with a meaningful

182

remedy while simultaneously giving operators who have made substantial investments in producing properties the security of title which the nature and size of their investment deserves.

Article 137 contemplates that at any time there has been a nonpayment of royalties, the lessor must notify the lessee. It is not intended that this notice be a demand for performance as in the case of the traditional default under the Civil Code. The lessor may not desire performance. The device of notice, then, is merely to inform the lessee that he has not paid royalties deemed by the lessor to be due. Article 138 gives the lessee thirty days within which to respond to the notice either by paying or stating a reasonable cause for nonpayment. Payment or nonpayment or stating or failing to state a reasonable cause for nonpayment in response to the notice has consequences for lessor and lessee as to the remedies available, as provided in Articles 139 through 141.

Article 139 treats the consequences of payment. If the lessee pays royalties in response to the demand, the remedy of dissolution of the lease becomes unavailable to the lessor except in the event of fraud. Thus, even if the lessee has willfully and unreasonably withheld the royalties, the disaster of lease cancellation may be avoided by compliance with the notice. Removal of the remedy or dissolution when the lessee pays, except in the presence of fraud, is compensated for by making an extraordinary remedy available if the original failure to pay the royalties is found to be either fraudulent or willful and without reasonable grounds. This compensating remedy is the award of double the amount due plus interest, as damages, together with a reasonable attorney's fee. If the original failure to pay, though willful, is found to be reasonable or if it resulted from mere oversight or neglect, the only damages due are in the form of interest on the amount found to be due. Attorney's fees may be secured for service in the collection of interest if the lessee fails to pay interest within thirty days of a demand therefor.

Article 140 provides for the consequences of failure by the lessee to respond favorably to the notice required by Article 137. If the lessee fails to pay in response to the notice or to state a reasonable cause for nonpayment within the notice period and if the court finds royalties to be due, the court may award double damages, interest, and attorney's fees regardless of the cause for

183

the original failure to pay, whether it be fraudulent, willful, with or without reasonable grounds, or arises from mere oversight or neglect. Special note should be taken of Article 141 providing that in all cases in which the remedy of dissolution is available, the court should resort to it only if the conduct of the lessee, either in failing to pay royalties originally or in failing to respond favorably to notice as required by Article 137, "is such that the remedy of damages is inadequate to do justice." This is a policy guideline for the courts in administering the remedy of dissolution for failure to pay royalties. The guideline for use of judicial discretion is, however, limited to cases involving failure to pay royalties and should not be extended to other situations in which dissolution is an appropriate remedy.

The total effect of these articles, then, is to provide a spur to timely payment of royalties due while giving lessees a reasonable way in which to avoid the harsh remedy of cancellation. The spur is the special remedy. The means for avoiding cancellation is by responding within the stated period to the notice of failure to pay required by Article 137.

Art. 138. Required response of lessee to notice

The lessee shall have thirty days after receipt of the required notice within which to pay the royalties due or to respond by stating in writing a reasonable cause for nonpayment. The payment or nonpayment of the royalties or stating or failing to state a reasonable cause for nonpayment within this period has the following effect on the remedies of dissolution and damages.

Acts 1974, No. 50, §138, eff. Jan. 1, 1975.

Comment

See the comment following Article 137.

Art. 138.1. Division order; precedence of lease; penalties for failure to pay royalties due

A. For the purposes of this Article, a "division order" is an instrument setting forth the proportional ownership in minerals or other substances, or the value thereof, that is prepared after examination of title and that is executed by the owners of the production or other persons having authority to act on behalf of the owners thereof.

B. A division order shall not alter or amend the terms of the mineral lease. A division order that varies the terms of the mineral lease is invalid to the extent of the variance, and the terms of the mineral lease take precedence.

C. The execution of a division order is not a condition precedent to receiving payment from a lessee. The lessee shall not withhold royalty payments because his lessor has not executed a division order.

D. If the lessee fails to pay royalties solely because his lessor has not executed a division order as defined in this Article, the court shall award as damages double the amount of royalties due, legal interest on that sum from the date due, and reasonable attorney's fees. However, if the lessor fails to supply the name, address, and tax identification number upon written request of the lessee, the lessee's failure to pay royalties shall be deemed reasonable.

Acts 1992, No. 1110, §1; Acts 2023, No. 88, §1.

Comment

See the comment following Article 137.

Art. 139. Effect of payment in response to notice

If the lessee pays the royalties due in response to the required notice, the remedy of dissolution shall be unavailable unless it be found that the original failure to pay was fraudulent. The court may award as damages double the amount of royalties due, interest on that sum from the date due, and a reasonable attorney's fee, provided the original failure to pay royalties was either fraudulent or willful and without reasonable grounds. In all other cases, such as mere oversight or neglect, damages shall be limited to interest on the royalties computed from the date due, and a reasonable attorney's fee if such interest is not paid within thirty days of written demand therefor.

Acts 1974, No. 50, §139, eff. Jan. 1, 1975.

Comment

See the comment following Article 137.

Art. 140. Effect of nonpayment in response to notice or failure to state cause therefor

If the lessee fails to pay royalties due or fails to inform the lessor of a reasonable cause for failure to pay in response to the required notice, the court may award as damages double the amount of royalties due, interest on that sum from the date due, and a reasonable attorney's fee regardless of the cause for the original failure to pay royalties. The court may also dissolve the lease in its discretion.

Acts 1974, No. 50, §140, eff. Jan. 1, 1975.

Comment

See the comment following Article 137.

Art. 141. Dissolution not a favored remedy

In a case where notice of failure to pay royalties is required, dissolution should be granted only if the conduct of the lessee, either in failing to pay originally or in failing to pay in response to the required notice, is such that the remedy of damages is inadequate to do justice.

Acts 1974, No. 50, §141, eff. Jan. 1, 1975.

Comment

See the comment following Article 137.

Art. 142. Dissolution may be partial or entire

A mineral lease may be dissolved partially or in its entirety. A decree of partial dissolution may be made applicable to a specified portion of land, to a particular stratum or strata, or to a particular mineral or minerals.

Acts 1974, No. 50, §142, eff. Jan. 1, 1975.

Comment

Article 142 takes cognizance of and formalizes the remedy which has evolved in the jurisprudence, but about the propriety of which some doubts have remained. Fontenot v. Sunray MidContinent Oil Co., 197 So. 2d 715 (La. App. 3d Cir. 1967); Sellers v. Continental Oil Co., 168 So. 2d 435 (La. App. 3d Cir. 1964). The remedy of partial dissolution developed a means of doing equity and presents great potential for accomplishing that end. See Hardy, "'Mineral Rights -The Work of the Appellate Courts for the 1966-67 Term", 28 La. L. Rev. 355, 363 (1968); Comment 30 La. L. Rev. 84 (1969).

Art. 143. Summary eviction not applicable

A mineral lessee cannot be evicted by summary process.

Acts 1974, No. 50, §143, eff. Jan. 1, 1975.

Comment

> Article 143 makes the summary eviction procedures provided in La. Code of Civil Procedure Arts. 4101-4705 (1960) unavailable to mineral lessors. The remedy is singularly unfit for eviction from mineral leases, and all that is or might be possibly sought in the way of relief can be granted in ordinary proceedings to dissolve a mineral lease.

PART 7. LEASES INVOLVING OUTSTANDING MINERAL RIGHTS

Art. 144. After-acquired title clause may bind lessor and successors in title

A mineral lease may provide that a mineral right that terminates during the existence of the lease and becomes owned by the lessor or his successor in title shall be subject to the lease. If the lease is filed for registry, the provision is binding on all subsequent owners of the land or mineral rights leased.

Acts 1974, No. 50, §144, eff. Jan. 1, 1975.

Comment

> It has been recognized that lessor and lessee may validly execute an after-acquired title clause binding the lessor to subject outstanding mineral rights to the lease if they terminate and become reunited with the landowner's title. Williams v. Arkansas-Louisiana Gas Co., 193 So.2d 78 (La. App. 2d Cir. 1966).

188

However, it was previously the law that such a clause is not binding on the successors and assigns of the landowner who grants a lease containing such a clause. The obligation to subject the outstanding rights to the lease was regarded as "personal" to the lessor and not binding on his successor in title unless expressly assumed by him. Calhoun v. Gulf Refining Co., 235 La. 494, 104 So. 2d 547 (1958). Article 144 changes the law in this respect and permits the execution of leases with after-acquired title clauses which, when filed for registry, will bind the successors in title of the lessor. The principal reason for doing this is that in Louisiana it has been virtually impossible for a lessee to obtain a secure lease at a time when mineral servitude rights were outstanding and on the verge of expiring. In such situations, the servitude owner could not give a lease that would give the lessee security of title, even if the servitude owner had executive rights over the landowner's interest in the minerals. See Dart v. Breitung, 136 So. 2d 501 (La. App. 1st Cir. 1962). The landowner was not ordinarily interested in granting a joint lease as this would have extended the life of the outstanding mineral servitude. E.g., Armour v. Smith, 247 La. 122, 170 So. 2d 347 (1964). As noted above, the landowner could not execute a lease with an after-acquired title clause binding on successors in the title unless the obligation was expressly assumed. This situation has often frustrated efforts at development of land for mineral production. Therefore, the law was changed in this regard.

Insofar as it might be argued that this contravenes the basic policy reflected in the prohibition against dealing with reversionary interests in mineral servitudes and royalties, careful analysis will reveal valid distinctions. First, in the case of servitudes and royalties, permitting commercial dealing in "reversionary rights" would permit one landowner to bind his successor in title to outright alienations of substantial economic interests in the property for periods in excess of ten years. For example, A might sell a mineral servitude to B. Five years later he might sell the reversionary right to C. If A then sold the land to X, X would take title subject to the obligation to recognize an outstanding mineral servitude, in which he has no interest and over the exercise of which he has no direct control, for a period of fifteen years. This is clearly contrary to the public policy. However, the very nature of the mineral lease is different. If A grants a mineral lease to B and then sells the land to X, X takes the land subject to the contract, but contrary to the mineral servitude illustration, the lease is a contract involving mutual benefit to X and B and a complex set of relationships which permit X to exercise control over B to assure that B's operations are conducted for their mutual benefit. Additionally, considering the fact that under Article 115 the primary term of a mineral lease cannot exceed ten years, there is additional protection against violation of the public policy. If A grants a mineral servitude to B and three years later grants to C a mineral lease with a primary term of ten years and containing an after-acquired title clause, his sale of the land to X five years from the creation of B's mineral servitude has different consequences from the sale of the land subject to the prior sale of a reversionary right in a mineral servitude. In this instance, X acquires the land subject to the lease containing the after-acquired title clause. However, none of the mineral rights to which his title is subject can remain outstanding for more than ten years from the date of his acquisition of the land without utilization. The servitude will expire in the absence of use five years from the date he took title. The interest will then simply be subject to the outstanding lease, which cannot remain outstanding for more than eight years from the date of X's acquisition unless there is drilling or production on or attributable to his land or a hard mineral lease is extended under the special provisions of Article 115. Permitting B to acquire a secure lease title under these circumstances promotes the development of the minerals on X's land without subjecting his title to any outstanding rights for a period greater than ten years absent utilization of those rights. Viewed in this light, it is felt that the benefit wrought by permitting lessees to obtain secure leases is desirable and that it is provided at no cost to the general policy of Louisiana's mineral property law.

Art. 145. After-acquired title doctrine; applicability in absence of special clause

If, in the absence of an express provision of the kind contemplated by the preceding Article, a party purports to grant a mineral lease on land or mineral rights that he does not own, any title thereto he subsequently acquires inures to the benefit of the lessee. Successors in title of the original lessor are not bound under this Article unless they agree expressly and in writing to become so bound.

Acts 1974, No. 50, §145, eff. Jan. 1, 1975.

Comment

Article 145 is, paradoxically, both a change in theory in the present law and an accurate reflection of the law as it presently functions. Under prior law the granting of a mineral lease was not a sale. The implied warranty of the lessor was not that of a vendor. However, virtually all standard lease forms contain a warranty of title clause which makes the lessor's warranty the same as that of a vendor of land or real rights in land. In the presence of such a clause, it was held that a lessor who purports to grant a full-interest lease was bound by operation of law to give his lessee the benefit of mineral rights which were outstanding at the time of the lease and which terminated while he was still the owner and lessor of the land. Butler v. Bazemore, 303 F.2d 188 (5th Cir. 1962); but see Bazemore v. Whittington, 245 F.2d 943 (5th Cir. 1957), reversing Whittington v. Bazemore, 133 F. Supp. 163 (W.D.La.1955); see also St. Landry Oil and Gas Co. v. Neal, 166 La. 799, 118 So. 24 (1928), which, however, was decided at a time when it was still generally assumed that the mineral lease was of the same nature as a mineral servitude. There is no question that this was the correct result under these circumstances. Since the lessor's warranty is made that of a vendor by Article 120, Article 145 articulates the logical consequence that the after-acquired title doctrine is applicable when a lessor purports to grant a lease on rights which are outstanding against his title at the time the lease is executed. It further recognizes the general principles of the after-acquired title doctrine in that the lessor must remain the owner of the land at the time the outstanding rights are extinguished in order for the doctrine to operate. Cf. McDonald v. Richard, 203 La. 155, 13 So. 2d 712 (1943). This means that in the absence of an express clause of the kind permitted by Article 144 no successor of the lessor is bound by the lease insofar as it purported to cover an interest greater than that owned by the lessor at the time it was granted.

Concerning application of the after-acquired title doctrine, a lessee cannot be compelled to accept a title acquired by his lessor if he has already filed an action in warranty based on the fact that the lessor did not own all or a part of the rights leased at the time of the transaction. St. Landry Oil and Gas Co. v. Neal, *supra*, (dictum); Brewer v. New Orleans Land Co., 154 La. 446, 97 So. 605 (1923); Hale v. City of New Orleans, 18 La.Ann. 321 (1866). If the lessee in such circumstances discovers that his lessor had no valid title, he has remedies available under Article 120 for breach of the implied warranty of title.

PART 8. THE LESSOR'S PRIVILEGE

Art. 146. Lessor's privilege

The lessor of a mineral lease has, for the payment of his rent, and other obligations of the lease, a right of pledge on all equipment, machinery, and other property of the lessee on or attached to the property leased. The right also extends to property of others on or attached to the property leased by their express or implied consent in connection with or contemplation of operations on the lease or land unitized therewith.

Acts 1974, No. 50, §146, eff. Jan. 1, 1975.

Comment

Articles 146 through 148 are an adaptation of the basic provisions of Article 2705 of the Civil Code establishing the lessor's privilege in the case of ordinary leases. It will be noted that the pledge extends also to property of others on or attached to the property "by their express or implied consent in connection with or contemplation of operations on the lease or land unitized therewith." This serves the function previously performed by the last two paragraphs of Article 2705 and Articles 2706, 2707, and 2708 of the Civil Code, which specify the types of property subject to the lessor's privilege in other instances.

Art. 147. Right to seize property on premises or within fifteen days of removal

The mineral lessor may seize the property subject to his privilege before the lessee removes it from the leased premises, or within fifteen days after it has been removed by the lessee without the consent of the lessor, if it continues to be the property of the lessee, and can be identified.

Acts 1974, No. 50, §147, eff. Jan. 1, 1975.

Comment

The right to follow property after removal from the lease premises is limited to property of the lessee, and in the case of removed property, the privilege must be exercised within fifteen days of removal and is applicable only if the property continues to be owned by the lessee and can be identified. Article 147 is essentially the same as the first paragraph of Article 2709 of the Civil Code.

Art. 148. Manner of enforcement

The mineral lessor may enforce his right of pledge in the same manner as the right of pledge accorded other lessors.

Acts 1974, No. 50, §148, eff. Jan. 1, 1975.

Comment

The lessor's privilege has been enforced against a mineral lessee. Tyson v. Surf Oil Co., 195 La. 248, 196 So. 336 (1940).

CHAPTER 8. MINERAL RIGHTS IN LAND ACQUIRED OR EXPROPRIATED BY GOVERNMENTS ORGOVERNMENTAL AGENCIES

Art. 149. Mineral rights reserved from acquisitions of land by governments or agencies thereof imprescriptible

NOTE: Subsection A eff. until Jan. 10, 2024. See Acts 2023, No. 150.

A. "Acquiring authority" for the purposes of this Section means (1) the United States, the state of Louisiana, and a subdivision, department, or agency of either the United States or the state of Louisiana; (2) any legal entity with authority to expropriate or condemn, except an electric public utility acquiring land without expropriation. An electric public utility acquiring land through expropriation shall be considered as an acquiring authority; and (3) a nonprofit entity, recognized under Sections 501(c)(3) and 170 of the Internal Revenue Code as being organized and operated as a public charitable organization, that is certified by the secretary of the Department of Natural Resources to be a state or national land conservation organization. The certification shall be in writing and shall be a public record. Such certification shall not for that reason alone be construed to authorize the nonprofit entity to exercise expropriation powers. With respect to certifications occurring on and after August 1, 2004, an entity's certification shall require approval by official action of both the Senate Committee on Natural Resources and the House Committee on Natural Resources and Environment.

NOTE: Subsection A as amended by Acts 2023, No. 150, eff. Jan. 10, 2024.

A. "Acquiring authority" for the purposes of this Section means (1) the United States, the state of Louisiana, and a subdivision, department, or agency of either the United States or the state of Louisiana; (2) any legal entity with authority to expropriate or condemn, except an electric public utility acquiring land without expropriation. An electric public utility acquiring land through expropriation shall be considered as an acquiring authority; and (3) a nonprofit entity, recognized under Sections 501(c)(3) and 170 of the Internal Revenue Code as being organized and operated as a public charitable organization, that is certified by the secretary of the Department of Energy and Natural Resources to be a state or national land conservation organization. The certification shall be in writing and shall be a public record. The certification shall not, for that reason alone, be construed to authorize the nonprofit entity to exercise expropriation powers. With respect to certifications occurring on and after August 1, 2004, an entity's certification shall require approval by official action of both the Senate Committee on Natural Resources and the House Committee on Natural Resources and Environment.

B.   When land is acquired from any person by an acquiring authority through act of sale, exchange, donation, or other contract, or by condemnation, appropriation or expropriation, and a mineral right subject to the prescription of nonuse is reserved in the instrument or judgment by which the land is acquired, prescription of the mineral right is interrupted as long as title to the land remains with the acquiring authority, or any successor that is also an acquiring authority. The instrument or judgment shall reflect the intent to reserve or exclude the mineral rights from the acquisition and their imprescriptibility as authorized under the provisions of this Section and shall be recorded in the conveyance records of the parish in which the land is located.

C. If part of the land subject to the mineral right as set forth in Subsection B is divested by the acquiring authority to another who is not an acquiring authority, the mineral right is not divided. However, prescription of the mineral right as to the land divested shall commence and accrue unless it is interrupted by use of the mineral right.

D. If a mineral right subject to prescription has already been established over land at the time it is acquired by an acquiring authority, the mineral right shall continue to be subject to the prescription of nonuse to the same extent as if the acquiring authority had not acquired the land. Upon the prescription or other extinction of such mineral right, the transferor of the land shall without further action or agreement become vested with a mineral right identical to that extinguished, if (1) the instrument or judgment by which the land was acquired expressly reserves or purports to reserve the mineral right to the transferor, whether or not the transferor then actually owns the mineral right that is reserved, and (2) the land is still owned by an acquiring authority at the time of extinguishment.

E. Rights or interests in land originally acquired by an acquiring authority through expropriation and subject to a mineral reservation shall not be transferred by the same or subsequent acquiring authority to another who is not an acquiring authority, unless an exception is provided in R.S. 41:1338 or prior to the transfer:

(1) The acquiring authority first offers to sell or transfer the same right or interest back to the person or entity, or his heirs or successors, from whom such right or interest was originally acquired, if such person or entity still retains the mineral rights reserved.

(2)   The offer shall be in writing and shall be based upon the fair market value of the right or interest.

(3)   The offer shall be delivered by certified mail, return receipt requested, to the last known address of the grantor. The grantor shall have thirty calendar days from the date of receipt to accept or reject the offer in writing. Failure to respond timely shall create a presumption of rejection of the offer.

(4)   If the last known address of the grantor cannot be determined, or if there has been no written response from the grantor to the acquiring authority accepting or rejecting the offer after thirty calendar days from date of receipt, the acquiring authority may institute a civil action by summary proceeding to show cause why the offer should not be considered rejected. A grantor whose last known address cannot be determined shall be treated as an absentee defendant.

F.   The provisions of Subsection E shall not apply to any property acquired or disposed of by the Department of Transportation and Development pursuant to Part XII or Part XVIII of Chapter 1 of Title 48 of the Louisiana Revised Statutes of 1950.

G.   The provisions of this Chapter shall not apply to:

(1)   A transfer to an acquiring authority arising from the nonpayment of ad valorem taxes, or by enforcement of privileges, mortgages, judgments or other obligations for money.

(2)   A transfer in which the acquiring authority neither expressly reserves or excludes nor conveys to the transferor a mineral right otherwise subject to prescription.

(3)   A transfer to an acquiring authority of land with an existing mineral right subject to prescription in which the

instrument or judgment transferring the land does not expressly purport to reserve the mineral right to the transferor or otherwise exclude the mineral right from the acquisition.

(4)   Any lands or mineral rights that are the subject of agreements made pursuant to R.S. 41:1702.

H.(1) Notwithstanding any provision of law to the contrary, when land within the Atchafalaya Basin Floodway is acquired from any person by an acquiring authority by conventional deed, donation, or other contract or by condemnation or expropriation proceedings and by the act of acquisition, order, or judgment, a mineral right otherwise subject to the prescription of nonuse is reserved, the prescription of nonuse shall thereafter not run against the right whether the title to the land remains in the acquiring authority, or is subsequently transferred to a third person, public or private.

(2)   For purposes of this Subsection, "Atchafalaya Basin Floodway" means that area bounded by U.S. Highway 190 on the north, U.S. Highway 90 on the south, the East Atchafalaya Basin Protection levee on the east, and the West Atchafalaya Basin Protection levee on the west.

I. When land is acquired from any person by an acquiring authority or other person, through act of sale, exchange, donation, or other contract, as part of an economic development project pursuant to a cooperative endeavor agreement between the acquiring authority and the state through the Department of Economic Development, as evidenced in a certification by the secretary of the Department of Economic Development attached to the instrument by which the land is acquired, and a mineral right subject to the prescription of nonuse is reserved in the instrument by which the land is acquired, the prescription of nonuse shall be for a period of twenty years from the date of acquisition whether the title to the land remains in the acquiring authority or is subsequently transferred to a third person, public or private.

Acts 1990, No. 37, §1; Acts 1991, No. 745, §1; Acts 2004, No. 919, §1, eff. Aug. 1, 2004; Acts 2008, No. 580, §3; Acts 2013, No. 91, §1, eff. June 4, 2013; Acts 2014, No. 473, §1; Acts 2016, No. 60, §1; Acts 2023, No. 150, §6, eff. Jan. 10, 2024..

Comment-1992

Articles 149 through 152 are a revision of former La. R.S. 9:5806 (1950, as amended 1960). Paragraph A of La. R.S. 9:5806 was in essence Act 315 of 1940, which dealt with situations in which land is deeded to or expropriated by the United States or any of its agencies or subdivisions. Paragraph B was added by Act 278 of 1958, as amended by Act 528 of 1960; it dealt with similar situations where the land is acquired by certain listed categories of state agencies and subdivisions. There were many problems inherent in the prior legislation, and it is the intent of this article to rectify these insofar as possible. These statutes had their origins in the decade between 1930 and 1940 when federal public projects first began to require acquisitions of large amounts of acreage throughout the state. In some instances, landowners alienated their property under the mistaken assumption that it was possible to reserve their rights without those rights being subject to prescription. In others, more knowledgeable owners of large tracts of land were unwilling to part with their lands without being able to reserve the mineral rights free of prescriptive limitation.

Act 315 of 1940, repealing prior legislation on the same subject, was held to be retrospectively applicable in Whitney National Bank v. Little Creek Oil Co., 212 La. 949, 33 So.2d 693 (1947). It was held constitutional in United States v. Nebo Oil Co., 190 F. 2d 1003 (5th Cir. 1951). The retrospective application of the statute has, however, been rejected by the United States Supreme Court in the case of an acquisition deemed by it to arise from and bear heavily on a federal regulatory program. U.S. v. Little Lake Misere Land Co., 412 U.S. 580 (1973). The statute was described as plainly hostile to the interests of the United States, and its future application is cast into deep doubt. The remaining comments on

200

Articles 149-152 are based on the assumption of validity and continued application of the statute at least to conveyances subsequent to 1940.

Act 151 of 1938, had applied both to the state and federal governments, the 1940 act was applicable only to the United States government. Thus, from 1940 until 1958, there was no legislation of this kind applicable to the state or any of its agencies. The enactment of 1958 substantially filled the gap, but there was serious question as to how satisfactorily it did so. Additionally, there were disparities in the express language of the two enactments which gave rise to the possibility that there might be arbitrary distinctions which would give litigants ground for urging a denial of equal protection of the law. Articles 149 through 152 are intended to fill the gaps and eliminate the disparities.

Article 149 treats the effect of acquisitions by the state or federal government or subdivisions or agencies of either. Essentially, if in the act of acquisition mineral rights normally subject to prescription are reserved by the landowner, they become imprescriptible. The nature of the right is not changed; prescription simply does not run so long as the land remains in the hands of the acquiring government or any of its subdivisions or agencies. This would include transfers to subdivisions or agencies other than that which originally made the acquisition. The effect could properly be viewed as a form of suspension of prescription. The fact that the nature of the right reserved is not altered is substantiated in State ex rel. Sabine River Authority v. Salter, 184 So.2d 783 (La.App.3d Cir. 1966), interpreting a similar provision specifically applicable to acquisitions by that project agency. La. Const. Art. 14, § 45 (1921) [continued as a statute by Const.1974, Art. 14, § 16]. The court there held that when mineral rights are reserved by the landowner whose property is expropriated, he has a mineral servitude of the same kind which would be created in an ordinary transaction, the only difference being that prescription does not run. The reservation in instances of this kind does not, therefore, create a separate mineral estate. This is one of the questions which lingered about Act 315 of 1940 applicable to federal acquisitions. What would happen if land acquired by a federal agency were subsequently returned to the stream of private commerce? Hopefully, it would have been decided that rules of prescription would again apply as in the normal case, but the way was open for an argument to the contrary. The 1958 legislation, on the other hand, provided that if the acquisi-tion is by a listed state agency and the property is returned to private com-merce, prescription runs as in the normal case. This was one of the disparities which Article 149 seeks to eliminate by providing that prescription will apply as in the normal case if the land is returned to private commerce, regardless of which government makes the acquisition.

Another change in present law is found in the fact that Article 149 is broadly applicable to the State of Louisiana or any of its agencies or subdivisions. La. R.S. 9:5806(B) (1950) was applicable only to listed categories of state agencies and subdivisions; the State of Louisiana as sovereign was not mentioned. The list of specific and categorized agencies was cumbersome and ambiguous. There is no discernible reason for excluding the state as sovereign. Therefore, the article applies to the state and all of its agencies and subdivi-sions. It is intended to apply to all those governmental organisms previously covered by La. R.S. 9:5806(B) (1950) and to any others not presently listed which might have occasion to acquire lands.

Art. 149.1. Repealed by Acts 2004, No. 919, §2, eff. August 1, 2004.

Repealed Article below is listed for historical purposes

§ 149.1. Mineral rights imprescriptible when reserved in transfers of land to state or national, nonprofit land conservation organization

A. (1) When land is acquired from any person by an organization certified by the secretary of the Department of Natural Resources to be a state or national, nonprofit land conservation organization by conventional deed, dona-tion, or other contract and by the act of acquisition, a mineral right otherwise subject to the prescription of nonuse is reserved, the prescription of nonuse shall not run against the mineral right so long as title to the land remains with the state or national, nonprofit land conservation organization.

(2) The state or national, nonprofit land conservation organization is only authorized to convey the property involved to another state or national, non-profit land conservation organization, to the state, or to the federal government. If the land, or any part thereof, is transferred by the state or national, nonprofit land conservation organization to any other state or national, nonprofit land conservation organization, the state, or the federal government, the prescrip-tion of nonuse shall not apply.

(3)If the nature, purpose, or goal of the state or national, nonprofit land conservation organization changes, such that land conservation is no longer the primary objective, the land that it acquired in its former capacity shall immedi-ately be offered to another state or national, nonprofit land conservation organization, to the state, or to tlle federal government in the same manner and for the same price, if any, as was provided in the original transfer of the land.

B. All lands covered by the provisions of tl1is Section may be open to public use and recreation including but not limited to hunting, fishing, hiking, field trails, trail rides, and picnicking, at the discretion of the state or national, nonprofit land conservation organization depending upon the ecological appro-priateness of such. Such hunting and fishing shall be at the times and in accordance with the state laws establishing licensing and season requirements.

Added by Acts 1983, No. 570, § 1. Amended by Acts 1984, No. 675, § 1; Acts 1986, No. 304, § 1; Acts 1998, 1st Ex. Sess., No. 53, § 1. Repealed by Acts 2004, No. 919, §2, eff. August 1, 2004.

Art. 149.2. Repealed by Acts 2004, No. 919, §2, eff. August 1, 2004.

Repealed Article below is listed for historical purposes

§ 149.2. Mineral rights imprescriptible; natural areas

When land is acquired from any person by the Department of Wildlife and Fisheries pursuant to the Louisiana Natural Areas Registry law, R.S. 56:1861 et seq., by conventional deed, donation, or other contract and by the act of acquisition a mineral right otherwise subject to the prescription of nonuse is reserved, the prescription of nonuse shall not run against the mineral right so long as title to the land remains with the Department of Wildlife and Fisheries.

Added by Acts 1987, No. 324, § 2, eff. July 6, 1987. Repealed by Acts 2004, No. 919, §2, eff. August 1, 2004.

Art. 149.3. Repealed by Acts 2004, No. 919, §2, eff. August 1, 2004.

Repealed Article below is listed for historical purposes

§ 149.3. Mineral rights imprescriptible; nonprofit corporations

When land is acquired from any person by a charitable, nonprofit corpora-tion organized under the laws of the state of Louisiana and qualified under the

U.S. Internal Revenue Code Section 501(C)(3) by conventional deed, donation, or other contract and by the act of acquisition a mineral right otherwise subject to the prescription of nonuse is reserved, the prescription of nonuse shall not run against the mineral right so long as title to the land remains with a charitable, nonprofit corporation as provided herein.

Added by Acts 1990, No. 978, § 1, eff. July 25, 1990. Repealed by Acts 2004, No. 919, §2, eff. August 1, 2004.

Art. 150. Repealed by Acts 2004, No. 919, §2, eff. August 1, 2004.

Repealed Article below is listed for historical purposes

§ 150. Application of prescription to rights outstanding when land acquired

When land is acquired in the manner prescribed in Article 149, the prescrip-tion of nonuse shall continue to run against any then outstanding mineral rights subject to such prescription and shall accrue in favor of the owner from whom the land was acquired. Thereafter, the prescription of nonuse shall not run against such rights except as provided in Article 151.

Added by Acts 1974, No. 50, § 1, eff. Jan. 1, 1975. Amended by Acts 1976, No. 550, § 1.

Comment-1992

Another disparity between the provisions of La.R.S. 9:5806(A) and (B) [re-pealed; see, now, R.S. 31: 149 et seq.] was in their respective treatments of prescriptible mineral rights outstanding at the time of the governmental acquisi-tion. If A sold land to the United States subject to a Yl6 royalty created three years previously in favor of B, the royalty would have become imprescriptible in the hands of B. Franks Petroleum v. Martin, 234 So.2d 268 (La.App.2d Cir. 1970); Franks Petroleum v. Hobbs, 200 So.2d 708 (La.App.2d Cir. 1967). If, however, the acquisition had been by the State Department of Highways, prescription would have continued to run against B and would accrue in favor of A seven years after the acquisition by the state agency. What would have happened if in the intervening seven years the Department of Highways alienat-ed the property to a private owner was not completely clear, but the general intent of the prior statute would have supported a conclusion that prescription would run and accrue as in the normal case, i.e., in favor of the new private owner. This result is contemplated by Articles 150 and 151. It is thus the intent of Articles 150 and 151 to make it clear that if the acquisition is by either" a state or a federal agency, the normal rules of prescription will apply when the property is returned to the stream of private commerce.

Art. 151. Repealed by Acts 2004, No. 919, §2, eff. August 1, 2004.

Repealed Article below is listed for historical purposes

§ 151. Sale to private owner; effect on prescription of outstanding right

Article 150 is applicable only if the government, governmental subdivision, agency, or legal entity with expropriation authority remains the owner of the land at the time the mineral right is extinguished. If the land, 01" a part thereof, is transferred by the government, subdivision, agency, or legal entity with expropriation authority to a private owner, the prescription of nonuse shall commence or resume as to the whole or the part in question from the date on which the act of acquisition by the private owner is filed for registry and shall accrue in his favor.

Added by Acts 1974, No. 50, § 1, eff. Jan. 1, 1975. Amended by Acts 1980, No. 348, § 1. Repealed by Acts 2004, No. 919, §2, eff. August 1, 2004.

Comment

Article 151 is discussed in the comment following Article 150.
388

Art. 152.   Repealed by Acts 2004, No. 919, §2, eff. August 1, 2004.

Repealed Article below is listed for historical purposes

§ 152. Tax titles not affected

Articles 149 through 151 are not applicable to land adjudicated to the State of Louisiana for unpaid ad valorem taxes.

Added by Acts 1974, No. 50, § I. eff. Jan. 1, 1975. Repealed by Acts 2004, No. 919, §2, eff. August 1, 2004.

Comment

As was the case under prior law, Articles 149 through 152 have no effect on the operation of statutes concerning tax sales and the vesting of tax tides.

CHAPTER 9. POSSESSION AND ACQUISITIVE PRESCRIPTION

PART 1. POSSESSION OF MINERAL RIGHTS

Art. 153. How mineral rights are possessed

Mineral rights are possessed by their use or exercise according to their nature.

Acts 1974, No. 50, §153, eff. Jan. 1, 1975.

Comment

The concept of possession strictly applies only to corporeal things. La. Civil Code art. 3432 (1870) [see, now, C.C. art. 3421]. The same Article also provides that possession of incorporeal things, into which class mineral rights fall, is exercised "by the species of possession of which these rights are susceptible." Thus, Article 153 of the Mineral Code is an adaptation or extension of Article 3432 of the Civil Code recognizing that possession of a mineral right is had by exercise of the right according to its nature. A mineral servitude or mineral lease is possessed by conducting drilling or mining operations or producing according to the character of the rights granted. A mineral royalty is being possessed if production attributable to the royalty is taking place. The jurisprudence has recognized the validity of the concept of Article 153. *E.g.*, Lenard v. Shell Oil Co., 211 La. 265, 29 So. 2d 844 (1947).

This and the following articles concerning possession of mineral rights are important in two connections. One is the running and accrual of acquisitive prescription. In this regard see Articles 159 through 163. The other is the relationship between possession and the right to bring the real actions. New Articles have been added to the Code of Civil Procedure to clarify previously cloudy areas of the law applicable to real actions involving mineral rights.

For full explanation of these new provisions, the already existing articles of the Code of Civil Procedure, Articles 3651 through 3664, should be read in conjunction with the new articles, Articles 3666 through 3670, and the comments thereon.

PART 2. POSSESSION OF LAND AS INCLUDING MINERAL RIGHTS

Art. 154. Possession under title as including mineral rights

One who establishes corporeal possession of land as owner under an act translative of title is in possession of the rights in minerals inherent in perfect ownership of land except to the extent mineral rights are reserved in the act or the act is expressly made subject to outstanding mineral rights. This Article does not apply to a mineral lessee of the possessor or any of his ancestors.

Acts 1974, No. 50, §154, eff. Jan. 1, 1975.

Comment

The concept of ownership as contemplated by the Civil Code in Articles 488, 490, 491, and 492 [see, now, C.C. arts. 15, 477, 478] presupposes that a person owns all of the rights included in the bundle making up ownership unless, in the case of imperfect ownership, certain portions of the bundle have been alienated in some fashion. Article 3437 of the Civil Code [see, now, C.C. art. 3426] applies this notion quantitatively to the concept of possession. It is there provided that one possessing under color of title is deemed to possess all property included in the boundaries set forth in his title so long as he intends to do so and even though his physical or corporeal possession includes only a portion of the estate in question. For interpretive cases see, *e.g.*, Marks v. Collier, 216 La. 1, 43 So.2d 16 (1950); Tremont Lumber Co. v. Powers & Critchett Lumber Co., 173 La. 937, 139 So. 12 (1932); Haas v. Currie, 169 La. 1041, 126 So. 547 (1930).

The concept of ownership and the principle set forth in Article 3437 [see, now, C.C. art. 3426] regarding the quantitative effect of partial possession under title lend a firm basis for the assertion that, in the absence of an adverse possession, possession as owner qualitatively includes all of those elements of ownership which the possessor's title purported to convey to him. Thus it can be said that one who possesses according to his title possesses not only quantitatively to the full geographic extent of the boundaries according to his title but also qualitatively to the full extent of the rights which the conveyance by which he acquired the property in question purported to transfer to him.

Viewed in this light, Article 154 provides that one entering into possession under title possesses mineral rights adversely to those owning outstanding mineral rights to which his title is subject to the extent that this title purports to convey mineral rights to him. This is in accord with existing jurisprudence. Lenard v. Shell Oil Co., 211 La. 265,29 So.2d 844 (1947); Goree v. Sanders, 203 La. 859, 14 So.2d 744 (1943); International Paper Co. v. Louisiana Central Lumber Co., 202 La. 621, 12 So.2d 659 (1943); Childs v. Porter-Wadley Lumber Co., 190 La. 308, 182 So. 516 (1938); Connell v. Muslow Oil Co., 186 La. 491,172 So. 763 (1937); Palmer Corp. of Louisiana v. Moore, 171 La. 774, 132 So. 229 (1930). Thus, if A sells a mineral servitude to B and then sells the land to C, excluding from C's deed the servitude previously granted to B, C's possession of the surface does not include the mineral rights. But if the deed fails to mention B's servitude, C's possession includes that element of ownership.

Note should be taken of the fact that this Article does not affect title contests as between a possessor with title and claimants under different chains of title. If title to the land is being litigated as between such claimants, whoever is vindicated as the owner of the land acquires full title, subject only to outstanding rights that might burden his own title. If the opposing title falls, it and all interests derivative from the same chain fall.

The last sentence of Article 154 recognizes an important difference between the mineral lease and other mineral rights. The mineral lease, though it creates a real right in the hands of the lessee is still an elaborate contractual relationship. If a party takes possession of land under title subject to a mineral lease, whether

211

the title discloses the lease or not, the possessor functionally becomes lessor. He is, in that capacity, in a much different position from that of the possessor of land subject to a mineral servitude, a right in which he has no interest and over the exercise of which he has no control. In the latter case, it makes sense to say that the possessor's possession of land is adverse to the servitude owner in those instances in which the possessor's title did not exclude the outstanding mineral rights. However, where the possessor occupies the status of lessor, he is part of a relationship in which there is a mutual interest in the development of the land for production of minerals, part of a type of common undertaking. In this situation it would not be logical or just to construe his possession of the surface as being adverse to his lessee. This will also have procedural consequences in that one possessing land under title subject to a mineral lease will not be able to bring the real actions to secure judgment clearing his title of the lease. He will be relegated to actions seeking judgment that the lease has expired by running of the agreed term or occurrence of some express resolutory condition. See the comments following Articles 133 and 134.

Art. 155. Possession without title as including mineral rights

A possessor of land as owner without title possesses the mineral rights inherent in perfect ownership of land.

Acts 1974, No. 50, §155, eff. Jan. 1, 1975.

Comment

Article 155 deals with possession by one who has no title but possesses as owner. Here, the possessor is occupying the land in the face of the public records. He, in fact, defies all recorded mineral rights as well as the record title to the land. Thus, his possession should be viewed as including all of the mineral rights inherent in perfect ownership as he does not acknowledge to anyone that there are valid, outstanding rights affecting his land. Although decided in a procedural context, this view is supported by Dixon v. American Liberty Oil Co., 226 La. 911, 77 So.2d 533 (1954). Careful note should be taken of the fact that despite the principle of Article 155, one who owns a valid mineral right may interrupt the possession of the adverse possessor of the land without title as to that particular mineral right. Thus, if record owner A conveys a mineral servitude to B, B's exercise of the mineral servitude prior to the accrual of the thirty year prescription in favor of X, a possessor of a portion of the servitude tract without title, will interrupt X's possession of the mineral rights even if the operations are not conducted on the portion of the burdened tract being adversely possessed by X. X may perfect his title to the land as against A, but B's mineral right will burden the perfected prescriptive title. If, of course, B's operations are on the portion of the tract being adversely possessed by X, X's possession may not only be interrupted as to the mineral right but as to the surface as well provided the requisites for a natural interruption of corporeal possession are met. La. Civil Code art. 3517 [see, now, C.C. arts. 3434, 3465]. It is recognized that construction of the law in this manner constitutes somewhat of a contradiction to the full logical extension of Article 155. However, it was felt that to place upon the owner of a mineral servitude or other mineral right the same burden as the law places upon the landowner to patrol his property to discover and evict squatters would be unreasonable.

PART 3. INTERRUPTION OF POSSESSION OF MINERAL RIGHTS BY POSSESSION OF LAND

Art. 156. Interruption of possession by use or exercise of mineral rights

Possession of mineral rights under Article 154 or 155 is lost by adverse use or exercise of them according to their nature. Loss of possession occurs although the production or operations constituting the adverse use or exercise are not on the land being possessed. It is sufficient that the production or operations constitute a use of the mineral rights according to the title of the owner thereof. In the case of a mineral lease, the use or exercise must be such that it would interrupt the prescription of nonuse if the lessee had been the owner of a mineral servitude.

Acts 1974, No. 50, §156, eff. Jan. 1, 1975; Acts 2023, No. 88, §1.

Comment

The first three sentences of Article 156 embody basis concepts recognized by established law. La. Civil Code arts. 3516, 3517, 3520, 3432, 3551 (1870) [see, now, C.C. arts. 3421, 3434, 3462 to 3466]. Lenard v. Shell Oil Co., 211 La. 265, 29 So.2d 844 (1947); Goree v. Sanders, 203 La. 859, 14 So.2d 744 (1943); International Paper Co. v. Louisiana Central Lumber Co., 202 La. 621, 12 So.2d 659 (1943); Childs v. Porter-Wadley Lumber Co., 190 La. 308, 182 So. 516 (1938); Connell v. Muslow Oil Co., 186 La. 491, 172 So. 763 (1937); Palmer Corp. of Louisiana v. Moore, 171 La. 774, 132 So. 229 (1930). In one respect, however, Article 156 either changes or clarifies the law depending on one's view of what the prior law was. Article 3517 [see, now, C.C. arts. 3434, 3465] provides that a natural interruption of acquisitive prescription takes place "when the possessor is deprived of possession of the thing during more than a year, either by the ancient proprietor or even by a third person." This article was, of course, written with particular regard for possession and consequent acquisitive prescription of corporeal things. The jurisprudence has never specifically treated the question of whether possession of a mineral servitude or other mineral right according to its nature by a use sufficient to interrupt liberative prescription would oust an adverse surface possessor from possession of that element of ownership when the use required less than one year. The Civil Code does not treat the question of adverse possession of real rights of any kind as fictitiously included in possession of the corporeal thing in question. However, it is provided in Article 3551 [see, now, C.C. arts. 3462 to 3466] that those causes which interrupt acquisitive prescription will also interrupt liberative prescription operating as a release from debt. Turning this provision around and applying it in reverse, it can be argued that the code embraces the general notion that if there is a use of a mineral right or other real right which would interrupt the prescription of nonuse, this should be sufficient to oust an adverse possessor of the surface whose possession fictitiously included the mineral right in question from possession of that element of ownership even though the use might take place within a span of less than one year. Article 156 accordingly provides that whenever there is a use of mineral rights according to their specific nature the possession of an adverse possessor of the surface can be interrupted and thus acquisitive prescription can also be interrupted by such a use even though the exercise constituting the use requires a period of less than one year. The provision that such an interruption can take place even though not actually on the property being adversely possessed is a statement of established law. See the cases cited in the beginning of this paragraph.

The last sentence of Article 156 treats a hitherto unlitigated problem. The effect of perfection of an acquisitive title to land on an outstanding mineral lease under prior law was problematical. See Hardy, "Some Problems of Possession for Procedural Purposes," Fifteenth Annual Inst. on Mineral Law 120 (1968). The last sentence of this article stems from the concept that a mineral lease is a mineral right and, therefore, a real right, and that its exercise according to its nature will oust an adverse possessor of land whose possession includes the mineral lease in question insofar as the lease is concerned. Some provision must be made for what will constitute "use or exercise" of a lease. Since leases vary and since the standards of conduct that will interrupt liberative prescription accruing against a mineral servitude are established by this Code, the functional similarity of the mineral lease to the mineral servitude makes it reasonable to provide that to interrupt possession by an adverse possessor of the land insofar as it may include a mineral lease, there must be an act or event that would interrupt liberative prescription if the interest were a mineral servitude rather than a lease.

Art. 157. Interruption of possession by acknowledgment

If a person possessing mineral rights under Article 154 or 155 acknowledges the title to mineral rights of the person against whom he is possessing, his possession of the mineral rights ceases on the date of the acknowledgment.

Acts 1974, No. 50, §157, eff. Jan. 1, 1975.

Comment

Article 157 incorporates the principle of Article 3520 of the Civil Code [see, now, C.C. art. 3464]. It is important, however, to observe that only the acknowledgment of the adverse possessor himself will have an effect on his possession and, therefore, acquisitive prescription. Thus, an acknowledgment by the record owner of land may interrupt liberative prescription, but it will have no effect on the possession of an adverse possessor of the surface whose possession includes mineral rights.

Art. 158. Interruption of possession by judicial demand

If a person possessing mineral rights under Article 154 or 155 is made a party defendant in any action involving the possession or ownership of the mineral rights by the owner thereof, his possession of the mineral rights ceases on the date on which the action was filed in a court of competent jurisdiction or on the date of service of citation upon the possessor if the action is not filed in a court of competent jurisdiction. If the action is abandoned, voluntarily dismissed, or not prosecuted at the trial, it is considered that possession never ceased.

Acts 1974, No. 50, §158, eff. Jan. 1, 1975.

Comment

Article 158 reflects previously established law. La. Civil Code art. 3519 (1870) [see, now, C.C. art. 3463]. Allison v. Wideman, 210 La. 314, 26 So.2d 826 (1946). Regarding abandonment, see La. Code of Civil Procedure art. 561 (1960, as amended 1966).

PART 4. THE EFFECT OF ACQUISITIVE PRESCRIPTION ON MINERAL RIGHTS

Art. 159.   Mineral rights not established by acquisitive prescription

Mineral rights may not be established by acquisitive prescription.

Acts 1974, No. 50, §159, eff. Jan. 1, 1975.

Comment

Article 159 articulates the holding of Savage v. Packard, 218 La. 637, 50 So.2d 298 (1950). It is also reflective of Article 766 of the Civil Code [see, now, C.C. art. 739], which provides that "continuous nonapparent servitudes, and discontinuous servitudes, whether apparent or not, can be established only by a title," adding that "immemorial possession itself is not sufficient to acquire such servitudes."

Art. 160. Perfection of title by prescription as including mineral rights

When title to land is perfected by a possessor on the basis of acquisitive prescription, the title includes mineral rights to the extent that his possession included mineral rights for the required prescriptive period.

Acts 1974, No. 50, §160, eff. Jan. 1, 1975.

Comment

Article 160 affirms prior jurisprudence. Goree v. Sanders, 203 La. 859, 14 So.2d 744 (1943); Childs v. Porter-Wadley Lumber Co., 190 La. 308, 182 So. 516 (1938); Connell v. Muslow Oil Co., 186 La. 491, 172 So. 763 (1937); Sample v. Whitaker, 171 La. 949, 132 So. 511 (1930); Palmer Corp. of Louisiana v. Moore, 171 La. 774, 132 So. 229 (1930). It is important in considering this Article to note that where one possessing under title is attempting to clear his own title of an interest by acquisitive prescription, he can usually do so only if his title on its face includes the mineral interest he is trying to clear from his title to the land. However, as to those claiming under different chains of title or by bad faith prescription without title, there are no such restrictions, and if the possessor perfects his title to the land, he extinguishes all mineral rights created by the party against whom he has possessed or that party's ancestors in title unless there is an interruption of his possession as far as the mineral rights are concerned under Articles 156 through 158. For example, this means that if X is possessing land as owner without title against the record owner, A, who has created a mineral servitude covering the land being adversely possessed in the twenty-eighth year of X's possession, the running of acquisitive prescription in favor of X includes title to the land itself and the mineral rights owned by B. This, of course, is subject to the provisions of Articles 156 through 158 concerning possible interruption of possession as to the mineral rights.

Art. 161. Interruption of acquisitive prescription

Acquisitive prescription affecting mineral rights under Article 160 is interrupted by an act or event that results in the loss or cessation of or ouster from possession under Articles 156 through 158.

Acts 1974, No. 50, §161, eff. Jan. 1, 1975.

Comment

The structure of the Articles dealing with possession and acquisitive prescription is to discuss possession first and then prescribe the relationship between possession and acquisitive prescription. Possession is essential to the accrual of acquisitive prescription. Thus, if possession is lost, acquisitive prescription is interrupted.

Art. 162. Suspension of acquisitive prescription

A cause that suspends the running of the prescription of nonuse applicable to mineral rights has no effect on the accrual of acquisitive prescription in favor of one possessing the surface of the land as owner insofar as his possession may include mineral rights. However, if an obstacle to use of a mineral right is created by an adverse possessor, the accrual of acquisitive prescription as to the right is suspended in the same manner as the prescription of nonuse.

Acts 1974, No. 50, §162, eff. Jan. 1, 1975.

Comment

There has been no litigation of this particular problem. Article 792 of the Civil Code [see, now, C.C. art. 755], dealing with the obstacle concept is in that portion of the code dealing with predial servitudes, and the portions dealing with possession and acquisitive prescription make no mention of the possibility that the obstacle concept may in any way relate to acquisitive prescription. As a basic rule, the concept of obstacle is inappropriate to acquisitive prescription. However, it is reasonable to provide that if the possessor himself creates an obstacle, the running of acquisitive prescription in his favor will be suspended in the same manner as the running of liberative prescription. Interpretation and application of this article should be limited to those circumstances in which the obstacle is created with knowledge of the outstanding mineral right or, if innocently created, which actually frustrate an attempt to use the right in question. A possessor in good faith, or even one in bad faith and without title, might be ignorant of the existence of an outstanding mineral right on the land being possessed, and obstacles created innocently should have some effect on the running of acquisitive prescription only if they actually frustrate an attempt to make use of the mineral right in question.

Art. 163. Acquisitive prescription; unavailability to mineral servitude owner

The owner of a mineral servitude cannot by any form of possession perfect an acquisitive title against the owner of a mineral royalty burdening his servitude.

Acts 1974, No. 50, §163, eff. Jan. 1, 1975.

Comment

In view of the fact that under Article 159 mineral servitudes cannot be established by acquisitive prescription, the concept of perfection of title to a mineral servitude by possession is inappropriate. Therefore, the owner of a mineral servitude should not be allowed to "extinguish" a mineral royalty burdening his servitude interest by any form of possession. This is a situation that is highly unlikely ever to occur, because the conduct of operations sufficient to constitute possession over a period of ten years would almost certainly have to include production, the occurrence of which would interrupt prescription accruing against the royalty interest anyway. Nevertheless, as a matter of analytical thoroughness, the statement of this principle in Article 163 is desirable.

CHAPTER 10. CO-OWNERSHIP

PART 1. CREATION OF MINERAL RIGHTS BY CO-OWNERS OF LAND

Art. 164. Creation of mineral servitude by co-owner of land

A co-owner of land may create a mineral servitude out of his undivided interest in the land, and prescription commences from the date of its creation. One who acquires a mineral servitude from a co-owner of land shall not exercise his right without the consent of co-owners owning at least an undivided seventy-five percent interest in the land, provided that the servitude owner has made every effort to contact the co-owners and, if contacted, has offered to contract with them on substantially the same basis that the servitude owner has contracted with another co-owner. A co-owner of the land who does not consent to the exercise of the rights has no liability for the costs of development and operations, except out of his share of production.

Acts 1974, No. 50, §164, eff. Jan. 1, 1975; Acts 1986, No. 1047, §1; Acts 1988, No. 647, §1; Acts 2019, No. 350, §1; Acts 2023, No. 88, §1.

Comment to 1986 Amendment

Articles 164 and 167 are a partial affirmation of analogous articles of the Civil Code and a partial rejection of those articles. Civil Code Article 714 provides that the co-owner of an undivided estate cannot impose a servitude on it without the consent of his coproprietor. In such a case the execution of the servitude is suspended until consent of the other co-owners is given, but prescription commences and continues to run on a servitude so created. Civil Code Article 716 further provides that where the co-owner establishes the servitude on his part of the estate only, consent of the other owners is not necessary, but exercise of the servitude is suspended pending a partition of the land. Except as hereinafter noted, Mineral Code Articles 164 and 167 would reach functional results similar to those which would be reached by application of the articles of the Civil Code. Under Article 167 the owner of a mineral servitude acquired from a co-owner of land will be denied the right to force partition of the servient estate. The effect of Article 164 is to permit the acquisition of servitudes from co-owners of land but to deny to the party acquiring such a servitude a right of use without the consent of co-owners owning at least an undivided ninety percent interest in the land. Thus, the situation is simply one in which the party acquiring the servitude under such circumstances should be aware of the legal consequences of his act.

A further result of Article 164 is that one acquiring a lease of a mineral servitude will be subject to the same restriction on his right to operate as his lessor.

The 1986 amendments to Articles 164, 166, and 175 continue to preserve the principle in the Mineral Code that one co-owner may not conduct operations without the consent of his co-owner, but limit this principle so that a small minority of co-owners cannot prevent mineral operations desired by other owners of rights in the land or mineral rights. Partition remains an alternative in some situations, but the jurisprudence reflects that it often is an inadequate remedy, and it is one which is denied in certain circumstances; i.e., the servitude owner or lessee who acquires his mineral right from a co-owner of the land cannot compel partition.

These amendments are intended to be read broadly in favor of allowing the majority of owners to develop where they so desire. Thus the ninety percent is to be calculated such that it includes the interest of the owner seeking to gain the consent of the others. It is intended that "co-owner" mean any owner without the consent of whom development could not be undertaken.

Art. 165. Creation of mineral royalty by co-owner of land

A co-owner of land may create a mineral royalty out of his undivided interest in the land, and the prescription of nonuse commences from the date of its creation. The consent of the co-owner of the party creating the royalty right is not necessary to entitle the royalty owner to receive his proportionate part of production.

Acts 1974, No. 50, §165, eff. Jan. 1, 1975.

Comment

Article 165 is contrary to that applicable to mineral servitudes under Article 164 in that a co-owner of land, though he may validly create a mineral servitude in proportion to his ownership rights in the land, cannot confer upon the grantee of such a mineral servitude the power to exercise his right except by consent of the other co-owners of the land subject to the servitude. The rationale for that rule is, of course, that a new utilization of land which is the subject of co-ownership requires the consent of the co-owners, and no single co-owner can confer the right to utilize the land without the consent of his co-owner or co-owners unless it be for the purpose of preventing waste or destruction of the co-owned property. However, since the creation of a mineral royalty does not confer an active use right in the same sense that a mineral servitude confers such rights, there is no reason to require the consent of co-owners to the creation of such an interest or to the participation by the owner of such an interest in production. Permitting such sales and actual participation in production without the consent of all co-owners does no violence to the basic rule requiring unanimous consent; for there to be production there will have had to be consent to the exercise of a servitude or the granting of a lease.

Art. 166. Granting of mineral lease by co-owner of land

A co-owner of land may grant a valid mineral lease or a valid lease or permit for geological surveys, by means of a torsion balance, seismographic explosions, mechanical device, or any other method, as to his undivided interest in the land, but the lessee or permittee shall not exercise his rights thereunder without consent of co-owners owning at least an undivided seventy-five percent interest in the land, provided that the lessee or permittee has made every effort to contact the co-owners and, if contacted, has offered to contract with them on substantially the same basis that the lessee or permittee has contracted with another co-owner. A co-owner of the land who does not consent to the exercise of the rights has no liability for the costs of development and operations, except out of his share of production.

Acts 1974, No. 50, §166, eff. Jan. 1, 1975; Acts 1986, No. 1047, §1; Acts 1988, No. 647, §1; Acts 1995, No. 479, §1, eff. June 17, 1995; Acts 2019, No. 350, §1; Acts 2023, No. 88, §1.

Comment to 1986 Amendment

As originally enacted, Article 166 reflected established law in permitting a co-owner of land to lease as to his interest but suspending the right to operate until consent was obtained from the remaining co-owners of the land. Sun Oil Co. v. State Mineral Board, 231 La. 689, 92 So.2d 583 (1957); Gulf Refining Co. v. Carroll, 145 La. 299, 82 So. 277 (1919). For discussion of the effect of the 1986 amendment to Article 166, see comment under Article 164.

Art. 167. Mineral right owner may not compel partition of land

The owner of a mineral right acquired from a co-owner of land cannot compel partition of the land.

Acts 1974, No. 50, §167, eff. Jan. 1, 1975.

Comment

Article 167 is partially discussed in the comment following Article 164. As there noted, it is a rejection of Civil Code Article 740 [see, now, C.C. arts. 716, 717], which permits the owner of a predial servitude acquired from a co-owner of land to compel a partition of the surface to establish that portion of the servient estate on which his right will be applicable. It is singularly inappropriate in the case of mineral rights to allow one acquiring a mineral right to compel partition of the surface. Thus, if one acquiring a right from a co-owner of land cannot secure the consent of the remaining co-owners, the result of this article is that he has simply made a bed in which he must lie. Note should be taken that whereas Article 164 is applicable to mineral servitudes, Article 167 uses the generic term "mineral rights" and is thus applicable whether the right acquired from the co-owner is a servitude, royalty, lease, or other form of mineral right.

PART 2. CO-OWNERSHIP OF MINERAL RIGHTS

SUBPART A. WHEN CO-OWNERSHIP EXISTS

Art. 168. Mineral rights susceptible of undivided ownership

Mineral rights are susceptible of ownership in indivision.

Acts 1974, No. 50, §168, eff. Jan. 1, 1975.

Comment

In Starr Davis Oil Co., Inc. v. Webber, 218 La. 231, 48 So.2d 906 (1950), it was held that the owner of land who retains title to a portion of the mineral rights is not a co-owner with one to whom he has conveyed a mineral servitude. The court, however, indicates that mineral servitudes are susceptible of ownership in indivision, stating that the landowner and servitude owner in that particular instance were not joint owners of a "single right" but rather of "two absolute rights, independent of each other." By implication, then, two or more persons may own a single right or servitude in indivision. This language appears equally applicable to mineral royalties.

The necessity that there be a "single right" is worthy of special note insofar as servitudes are concerned in view of the common practice in Louisiana by which a purchaser of a fractional mineral servitude is referred to as the owner of an "undivided" interest in the minerals. This misleading terminology is attributable to the fact that the Louisiana mineral conveyancing system is similar to those of many Anglo-American jurisdictions in which an ownership system prevails.

The concept that mineral servitudes and royalties are susceptible of owner-ship in indivision is also supported by Articles 494 [see, now, C.C. art. 480]. 1289, 1290, 1308, and 1309 of the Civil Code. The latter four articles are concerned with the right to demand a partition of things held in common. Article 1309 specifically states that usufructuaries of the same estate can institute among themselves the action of partition. Thus, it is clear that such rights are susceptible to ownership in indivision. It is to be noted that under Article 172 co-owners of a mineral servitude or royalty cannot compel partition of their rights. This represents a change of the rule suggested by the Civil Code articles cited above. However, reference to them is appropriate insofar as they support the concept that mineral rights may be co-owned.

Insofar as mineral leases are concerned, the lessee's interest in a mineral lease, like any other "thing", is susceptible of co-ownership. For co-ownership of a mineral lease to exist, it must be established that two or more mineral lessees own undivided fractional interests in the same mineral lease. See La. Civil Code art. 494 [see, now, C.C. art. 480] providing that "it is of the essence of the right of ownership that it can not exist in two persons for the whole of the same thing; but they may be the owners of the same thing in common, and each for the part which he may have therein." Co-ownership of working interests in mineral leases is common. This principle would not be applicable, however, if a partial assignment is made in the presence of a lease clause which is interpreted as importing a division of the lease when a partial assignment is made. See the comment following Article 130. Note should be taken of the fact that unlike mineral servitudes and royalties, mineral leases may be judicially partitioned. Article 173.

Art. 169. Those who are not co-owners of mineral rights

Co-ownership does not exist between the owner of a mineral right and the owner of the land subject to the right or between the owners of separate mineral rights.

Acts 1974, No. 50, §169, eff. Jan. 1, 1975.

Comment

Article 169 accords with established law. Starr Davis Oil Co., Inv. v. Webber, 218 La. 231, 48 So.2d 906 (1950); Clark v. Tensas Delta Land Co., 172 La. 913, 136 So. 1 (1931).

SUBPART B. CREATION OF DEPENDENT MINERAL RIGHTS BY CO-OWNERS OF MINERAL RIGHTS

Art. 170. Right of co-owner of mineral servitude to create mineral royalties

A co-owner of a mineral servitude may create a mineral royalty out of his undivided interest in the servitude and prescription of nonuse commences from the date of its creation. The consent of the co-owner of the party creating the royalty is not necessary to entitle the royalty owner to receive his proportionate part of production.

Acts 1974, No. 50, §170, eff. Jan. 1, 1975.

Comment

The right of the owner of a mineral servitude to create a mineral royalty is recognized by Article 82. The rationale for permitting the co-owner of a mineral servitude to create a royalty is similar though not identical to that for permitting co-owners of land to create royalties. See the comment following Article 165. In the case of mineral servitudes subject to co-ownership, however, there is additional reason to permit creation of royalties. Co-owners of mineral servitudes are given independent rights of operation under Article 175. Thus, unanimous consent to utilize the servitude is not required as in the case of consent by co-owners of land to the exercise of a servitude or mineral lease. See Articles 164 and 166. In light of this fact, there is all the more reason to permit the co-owner of a mineral servitude to convey a passive right to share in production.

Art. 171. Right of co-owner of mineral lease to create dependent rights

A co-owner of the lessee's interest in a mineral lease may create a dependent right such as an overriding royalty, production payment, net profits interest, or other non-operating interest out of his undivided interest without the consent of his co-owner. He may also transfer all or part of his undivided interest.

Acts 1974, No. 50, §171, eff. Jan. 1, 1975.

Comment

Article 171 permits a co-owner of a mineral lease to create nonoperating interests such as those listed to the extent of his ownership in the lease without the consent of the remaining co-owner or co-owners. In so doing, it reflects the accepted industry practice. Nonoperating interests of this kind are passive income interests, and allowing their creation does not conflict with the principle stated in Article 177, which prohibits one co-owner of a lease from operating without consent of the other. The thrust of Article 177 is that management decisions concerning operations must be made by all of the co-owners. However, insofar as one co-owner has a right to share in production, there is no reason why he should be prohibited from dealing with the income stream from his undivided interest as he sees fit. It is true that an argument might be made that permitting a co-owner to alienate portions of the income stream flowing from the lease, even though limited to his own fractional interest, permits him to lessen the value of the co-owned property. However, there has never been any question of this nature raised by those commonly dealing with mineral leases, and it is clear that to prohibit continuation of this custom of dealing would have caused great difficulty.

Insofar as Article 171 permits transfers of all or part of a co-owner's undivided interest, it also reflects established law and practice. See Article 127.

Insofar as royalties are concerned, there are no management or use problems among co-owners of a royalty. In final form the owner of a royalty shares in the income stream from gross production. Partition in effect results from sharing of income among co-owners of the right. If further division is desired, the co-owner of a royalty may dispose of all or any portion of his interest freely and without consent of his co-owners.

SUBPART C. PARTITION OF MINERAL RIGHTS WHICH ARE THE SUBJECT OF CO-OWNERSHIP

Art. 172. Mineral servitudes and royalties subject to partition

Mineral servitudes and royalties are subject to partition.

Acts 1974, No. 50, §172, eff. Jan. 1, 1975.

Comment

Article 172 preserves the principles contained in Articles 1289, 1290, 1308, and 1309 of the Civil Code, which assure for the owner in indivision of any "thing" the right to demand a partition.

Art. 173. Mineral lessee's interest subject to partition; susceptibility of dependent rights to partition

Co-owners of the lessee's interest in a mineral lease may compel partition of their rights. Co-owners of a dependent right created by fewer than all of the co-owners of the lessee's interest cannot be compelled to partition their right.

Acts 1974, No. 50, §173, eff. Jan. 1, 1975.

Comment

Article 173 permits co-owners of the working interest in a mineral lease to compel partition of their respective rights. This, too, is in keeping with the principles in Articles 1289, 1290, 1308, and 1309 of the Civil Code. The availability of partition is especially appropriate for mineral leases. A mineral lease by nature contemplates development and often entails obligations to develop as a condition to maintenance. If a dispute arises among co-owners of a mineral lease, in order for the purpose of the lease to be fulfilled there must be some means of settling the dispute. Otherwise, one co-owner might deprive the others of their present interest by refusing to develop or operate, resulting in the termination of the lease. Permitting co-owners of a lease to operate independently would be unsuitable. Therefore, to protect the other co-owners it is essential that they be permitted some means for settling the dispute by either deriving the present economic worth of their interests from a sale or by acquiring the entire lease in order to be able to exercise the rights and meet the obligations created by it. Partition is the only available device.

Overriding royalties, production payments, and net profits interests are merely passive interests in the economic benefits flowing from operation of a mineral lease. A division actually takes place when production or profits are distributed according to ownership fractions. There is no active use right involved and no need for a right to compel partition of the interest in question. The co-owner of an overriding royalty can achieve the benefit of a partition by selling all or part of his interest.

SUBPART D. RIGHTS AND CONSEQUENCES ARISING FROM CO-OWNERSHIP OF MINERAL RIGHTS

Art. 174. Use by one co-owner inures to benefit of all

A use or possession of a mineral right inures to the benefit of all co-owners of the right.

Acts 1974, No. 50, §174, eff. Jan. 1, 1975.

Comment

Insofar as mineral servitudes are concerned, Article 174 is a restatement of established law. See *e.g.*, Hodges v. Norton, 200 La.

614,8 So.2d 618 (1942). But see Ohio Oil Co. v. Ferguson, 213 La. 183, 24 So.2d 746 (1946). Insofar as mineral royalties are concerned, it is difficult to imagine a situation arising in which a "use" would be made by one co-owner without the other simultaneously "using" his interest by receiving income. Perhaps the only conceivable situation would be if one co-owner received all of the production or its value attributable to the royalty, such as by representing himself to be sole owner of the interest. As to the application of this article to mineral leases, there will be no significance insofar as prescription is concerned since the interest of the mineral lessee is not prescriptible. However, it will have significance in the context of the right to bring real actions. Thus, possession by one co-owner will be construed as possession by the other for purposes of determining the right to bring the possessory action.

Art. 175. Co-owner of mineral servitude may not operate independently

A co-owner of a mineral servitude shall not conduct operations on the property subject to the servitude without the consent of co-owners owning at least an undivided seventy-five percent interest in the servitude, provided that the co-owner has made every effort to contact the other co-owners and, if contacted, has offered to contract with them on substantially the same basis that the co-owner has contracted with another co-owner. "Operations" as used in this Article shall include geological surveys, by means of a torsion balance, seismographic explosions, mechanical device, or any other method. A co-owner of the servitude who does not consent to the operations has no liability for the costs of development and operations, except out of his share of production.

Acts 1974, No. 50, §175, eff. Jan. 1, 1975; Acts 1986, No. 1047, §1; Acts 1988, No. 647, §1; Acts 1995, No. 479, §1, eff. June 17, 1995; Acts 2019, No. 350, §1; Acts 2023, No. 88, §1.

Comment to 1986 Amendment

As originally enacted, Article 175 preserved what was understood to be the then-existing law. The 1986 amendment to this Article allows a co-owner of a mineral servitude to conduct operations in those circumstances where co-owners owning at least an undivided ninety percent interest in the servitude consent thereto. In the event that a co-owner acts without the consent of another, the operations nevertheless will inure to the benefit of all co-owners. Further, the nonconsenting co-owner can claim his share of production subject to the obligation to account for his share of development and operating costs. Cf. Huckabay v. Texas Co., 277 La. 191, 78 So.2d 829 (1955). Although the Huckabay decision was rendered in the context of a demand by the owner of a fractional mineral servitude for his share of production from the lessee of the owners of the remaining share of the mineral rights, there has never been any doubt of its applicability as between co-owners of the same interest.

Comment

This article preserves what is understood to be the present law. If it should happen that one co-owner acts without consent of theother, the operations nevertheless will inure to the benefit of both under Article 174. Further, the nonoperator can claim his share of production subject to the obligation to account for his share of investment and operating cost. Cf. Huckabay v. Texas Co., 277 La. 191, 78 So. 2d 829 (1955). Although that decision was rendered incontext of a demand by the owner of a fractional mineral servitudefor his share of production from the lessee of the owners of the remaining share of the mineral rights, there has never been any doubt of its applicability as between co-owners of the same interest.

Art. 176. Co-owner of mineral servitude may act to prevent waste or destruction or extinction of servitude

A co-owner of a mineral servitude may act to prevent waste or the destruction or extinction of the servitude, but he cannot impose upon his co-owner liability for any costs of development or operation or other costs except out of production. He may lease or otherwise contract regarding the full ownership of the servitude but must act at all times in good faith and as a reasonably prudent mineral servitude owner whose interest is not subject to co-ownership.

Acts 1974, No. 50, §176, eff. Jan. 1, 1975.

Comment

Article 176 applies to mineral servitudes which are subjects of co-ownership the rule applied to co-owners of land by United Gas Public Service Co. v. Arkansas-Louisiana Pipeline Co., 176 La. 1024,147 So. 66 (1933), in which it was held that a co-owner of land was not entitled to enjoin other co-owners from drilling when the property was in danger of being drained by wells on adjacent property. It was there observed that the only means by which the operating co-owner could preserve his interest from destruction was by drilling. This principle is an exception to the rule applicable to co-owners of land stated in Gulf Refining Co. v. Carroll, 145 La. 299,82 So. 277 (1919), in which it was held that a co-owner was without right to exploit the common property for oil or gas, and, consequently, could not grant a lease. However, subsequent cases indicate that a co-owner of land may grant a valid lease, but it may not be exercised without consent of the remammg co-owners. Sun Oil v. State Mineral Board, 231 La. 689, 92 So.2d 583 (1957); Ree Corp. v. Shaffer, 246 So.2d 313 (La. App. 1st Cir. 1971). This latter rule will not be applicable to mineral servitudes under Article 175, which gives an independent right of operation to each co-owner of a mineral servitude.

No attempt is made to give precise definition to the meaning of the term "waste or destruction." Certainly, the threat of drainage recognized in the United Gas Public Service case is a prime example of that possibility. However, others might occur, and it was thought best to leave some nexibility for the courts in dealing with problems of this kind.

Article 176 disposes of several problems which have not been treated in the jurisprudence, such as the liability of non-operating co-owners for costs, which is limited to recovery out of production, and the obligation of the operating or contracting co-owner to deal fairly with the interest of the remaining co-owners. As to the matter of costs, it was felt that non-consenting co-owners should not be burdened by the business judgment of the operating co-owner in situations of this kind except out of production. The strict limitation of recovery of costs to an offset against production should be viewed as limited to those situations in which the acting co-owner makes a demand for costs. If the non-operating co-owner himself makes the demand, courts should be viewed as having some discretion in allowing recovery of costs. See Humble Oil & Refining Co. v. Superior Oil Co., 165 So.2d 905 (La. App. 4th Cir. 1964). Concerning the matter of execution of contracts and the duty of acting as a reasonable, prudent mineral servitude owner whose interest is not subject to co-ownership, two observations are pertinent. First, Article 176 contemplates that the co-owner acting to prevent waste or destruction can contract as to the entire servitude interest. Thus, he can lease the whole of the servitude. In doing so, however, he must act according to the stated standard toward the remaining co-owners. It is not contemplated that this relationship be a full fiduciary relationship. For discussion of this standard, see the comment following Article 109 concerning the duty of the executive to the owner of a non-executive interest.

Art. 177.   Co-owner of mineral lease may not operate independently except to prevent waste, destruction, or termination

A co-owner of the lessee's interest in a mineral lease may not independently conduct operations or, except as provided in this article and Article 171, deal with the interest without the consent of his co-owner. He may act to prevent waste, destruction, or termination of the lease and to protect the interest of all, but cannot impose upon his co-owner liability for any costs or expenses except out of production. In so acting he must act in good faith and must deal with the interest of the remaining owner or owners in the manner of a reasonably prudent lessee whose interest is not subject to co-ownership.

Acts 1974, No. 50, §177, eff. Jan. 1, 1975.

Comment

In prohibiting operation without consent of all co-owners of a mineral lease, Article 177 applies the established rule applicable to co-owners of land. Sun Oil Co. v. State Mineral Board, 231 La. 689, 92 So.2d 583 (1956); Gulf Refining Co. of Louisiana v. Carroll, 145 La. 299,82 So. 277 (1919). This rule has not been applied to mineral servitudes for reasons set forth in the comment following Article 175; nor has it been applied to mineral royalties for the reason that the royalty is not an operating interest. Application of the rule to the mineral lease is desirable in that leases are taken in contemplation of development, and to permit one co-owner to make a business decision which binds or has an effect on the value of the interest of the other co-owner is unwise. If dispute develops concerning utilization of the lease and it cannot be resolved informally, the remedy is the right to compel a partition provided in Article 173.

The right of a co-owner of a lease to act to prevent waste or destruction of the property is the same as that of a co-owner of land. United Gas Public Service Co. v. Arkansas-Louisiana Pipeline Co., 176 La. 1024, 147 So. 66 (1933). This right is also permitted in the case of co-ownership of a mineral servitude. See Article 176. In cases of this kind, the co-owner acts not only for his own interest but for the interest of all other co-owners. To avoid the undesirable effects of binding one co-owner to commit his general assets by the decision of another co-owner, the right of the co-owner who acts to recover costs and expenses is limited to the production attributable to the other co-owners. Additionally, he must be able to prove that he acted in the presence of a threat of waste, destruction, or termination. The strict limitation of recovery of costs to an offset against production should be viewed as limited to those situations in which the acting co-owner makes a demand for costs. If the non-operating co-owner himself makes the demand, some of the same considerations motivating the decision in Humble Oil & Refining Co. v. Superior Oil Co., 165 So.2d 905 (La. App. 4th Cir. 1964), might appropriately permit a court, in exercising its discretion, to allow recovery of costs other than out of production, particularly as between two lessees both engaged in the business of mineral extraction. As is the case with Article 176, applicable to mineral servitudes, the co-owner who acts in protection of the co-owned property must act prudently and in the manner that he would act if he were the owner of the entire property. Essentially, this standard requires that the acting co-owner refrain from discriminatory action detrimental to his co-owners. Any benefits which he secures for his own interest in the property he must also secure for those of his co-owners. For further discussion of this standard see the comment following Article 109 concerning the duty of the executive to the owner of a nonexecutive interest.

PART 3. PARTITION OF LAND AND ITS EFFECT ON MINERAL RIGHTS

Art. 178. When land burdened by mineral right may be judicially partitioned in kind

If land burdened by a mineral right or rights created by fewer than all of the co-owners of the land is judicially partitioned, a partition in kind may not be ordered unless it can be accomplished in such fashion that the allocation of tracts to the co-owners assures that both surface and mineral values of each tract are in the same proportion to the total value of the surface and the mineral rights respectively as each co-owner's interest bears to the whole of the surface and mineral rights respectively and that partition in kind will not significantly impair the ability of any owner subject to the partition to develop the minerals on his own tract.

Acts 1974, No. 50, §178, eff. Jan. 1, 1975. Amended by Acts 1982, No. 780, §1.

Comment

In reality, the overwhelming majority of partitions of land burdened by mineral rights will have to be by licitation. However, it was felt that the possibility of partition in kind should be left open and that a proper definition of the circumstances in which it would take place should be rendered. Article 178 seeks to accomplish these ends. First, it is implicit in Article 188 that if the land to be partitioned is burdened by a mineral right or rights acquired from all of the co-owners, a partition in kind of the surface can be achieved without affecting the outstanding right. In this regard, see Article 186, providing that in such a case if the partition is by licitation, the mineral right is not affected. Thus, if A and B are co-owners in equal portions of a tract of land and X has acquired separate leases from them, each of his respective interest, the surface may be divided in kind without effect on X's leases. If the partition was by licitation, the sale would have no effect on X's lease rights under Article 186.

Article 188 deals more specifically with the situation of a partition of land burdened by a mineral right acquired from fewer than all of the co-owners. For example, in the above factual situation, assume that X had a lease from B only. Assume further that the value of the land was placed at $100,000 and the mineral rights were valued at $50,000. Article 186 would require that a partition in kind would assure to A and B, each, a tract on which the mineral values were equal to his interest, or $25,000, and the surface value was equal to his interest, or $50,000.

Comment-1982

The 1982 amendment to Article 178 is made to take into consideration the fact that for coal and lignite properties it may be preferable to have partition by licitation even if the test for partition in kind of the article could otherwise be established. This is because the owner of one tract could block development by his former co-owner by his own refusal to permit development. The amendment simply returns to the principles of the Civil Code which establish that land is not to be partitioned in kind when loss or inconvenience to one of its co-owners would be the consequence of dividing it; the Mineral Code does not depart from this principle.

Art. 179. Mineral right owner as party to partition of land

If the owner of a mineral right or interest therein is not made a party to an action for partition of the land subject to his right or interest, the partition is not invalid, but the right or interest therein is not extinguished or otherwise affected.

Acts 1990, No. 971, §1.

Comment

Because Articles 179 through 187 are an integrated set of provisions redrafting Article 741 [see, now, C.C. art. 718] of the Civil Code, they will be discussed together in this comment. Article 741 [see, now, C.C. art. 718] in its present form resulted from an amendment adopted in 1940 as a result of the decision in Amerada Petroleum Corp. v. Reese, 195 La. 359, 196 So. 558 (1940). As redrafted, Articles 179-187 do not purport to deal with the impact of partition sales on real rights other than mineral rights or on ordinary leases.

Article 179 of this recommendation has procedural impact in characterizing owners of mineral rights in land being partitioned as necessary parties to an action for partition. This means that although an action may proceed to a partition without an owner of mineral rights being present, upon timely objection he must be made a party if he is subject to the court's jurisdiction. La. Code of Civil Procedure art. 642 (1960). The principle that a partition sale made without joinder of an owner of mineral rights is not invalid is thus in keeping with characterization as a necessary party. If an owner of mineral rights is not joined, his right is simply not affected by the sale.

Articles 180 through 182 provide procedures for appraisal of the property to be sold, for service of that appraisal on all parties, and for an opportunity to oppose the appraisal. The court is required to assure that there will be an equitable distribution of the proceeds. If a mineral right is not appraised, the effect of the sale is the same as if the owner had not been made a party to the action. The sale is valid, but the right in question survives the sale. Article 185. The appraisal required by Article 180 may differ somewhat from that previously required in Article 741 of the Civil Code, which seems to contemplate that there must be an appraisal of the land, meaning the land in full ownership, as well as of the mineral interests being affected by the sale. In view of the fact that it is possible that some interests constituting the value of the whole of the land may not be included in the sale, it is possible that the proportion between the value of a mineral right and the value of the land may be a distorted percentage of the total proceeds. Thus, under Article 180 the appraisal must be of each interest being affected or subject to being affected by the sale and of the aggregate value of all of these individual interests. The proportion of the proceeds to which a mineral right owner is entitled will, therefore, according to Article 183, be matched against the total value of the rights being affected by the sale and not the total value of full ownership of the land. This is deemed more equitable than what appears to be the present law.

The basic rule established by Article 185 is that if a mineral right owner is joined and his interest properly appraised, he participates in the proceeds and his interest is extinguished by the sale. There are, however, some exceptions provided in Articles 186 and 187.

Under Article 186, if the rights of a mineral right owner are derived from the total ownership of the land, his right should not be extinguished, for all co-owners of the land have given their consent to a particular utilization of the land. This would be true even though a party has, for example, secured separate mineral leases or mineral servitudes from each of two co-owners. If the property is partitioned by licitation, the leases or servitudes should remain unaffected. The dispute between the co-owners as to utilization of the land has not centered on its use for mineral development as they have both consented to that particular use, even though by separate acts creating separate property interests. An additional practical reason for this is that if this were not the rule, co-owners could "sell out" a mineral lessee or mineral servitude owner who has already developed the property or is on the verge of doing so.

Under Article 187, if the whole of the land is adjudicated to one who created a mineral right or to his successor or assign, it is only logical to require that he remain bound by the interest he created or to which his interest was subject when he took title. Provision is made for a credit on the purchase price equivalent to the value assigned to the interest which survives the sale.

It should be observed that these articles do not include one of the previously existing exceptions to the rule that interests of parties to the sale are extinguished by it. Article 741 of the Civil Code [see, now, C.C. art. 718] appeared to contemplate that if one who created a mineral right became an owner of part of the property as a result of the sale, the right was perfected and survived as to that part. This would create substantial problems in the case of mineral rights. If a person has taken a mineral lease on a particular property which is partitioned, his interest was in the entire property, not a specified part. Therefore, if his right survived as to a part, he would lose the value represented by loss of his right to explore the remainder. In view of this type of problem, it was thought best not to include that exception under Article 741 in the Mineral Code [see, now, C.C. art. 718].

Art. 180. Appraisal of land to be partitioned required

If the owner of a mineral right or interest therein is made a party to an action for partition of the land subject to his right and it is determined that the partition is to be by licitation, the court shall appoint two appraisers who shall separately value the interest in the land or the mineral rights of each party to the action who is or may be entitled to participate in the proceeds of the sale.

Acts 1974, No. 50, §180, eff. Jan. 1, 1975.

Comment

This Article is discussed in the comment following Article 179 as a part of the commentary on Articles 179 through 187.

Art. 181. Service of appraisal required

A copy of the appraisal shall be served upon each party to the action together with a notice that the appraisal may be homologated after the expiration of fifteen days from the date of service.

Acts 1974, No. 50, §181, eff. Jan. 1, 1975.

Art. 182. Opposition to appraisal permitted

An opposition to the appraisal may be filed by any party to the action at any time before homologation and shall be tried as a summary proceeding.

Acts 1974, No. 50, §182, eff. Jan. 1, 1975.

Art. 183. Distribution of proceeds of partition sale

When the owner of a mineral right or interest therein is entitled to participate in the proceeds of the licitation, the court shall order that the proceeds be distributed in the proportion that the homologated value of the interest of each party who is entitled to participate in the sale bears to the total homologated value of all of the interests of all of the parties.

Acts 1974, No. 50, §183, eff. Jan. 1, 1975.

Art. 184. Effect of failure to appraise mineral right or interest therein

If an appraisal of any mineral right or interest therein is not made as herein required, the partition is not invalid, but the right or any interest therein is not extinguished or otherwise affected.

Acts 1974, No. 50, §184, eff. Jan. 1, 1975.

Comment

This Article is discussed in the comment following Article 179
as a part of the commentary on Articles 179 through 187.

Art. 185. Owner of appraised mineral right entitled to participate in proceeds of sale

Except as provided in Articles 186 and 187, the owner of a mineral right or an interest therein appraised in accordance with these articles is entitled to participate proportionally in the proceeds of the licitation, and his interest is extinguished by the sale.

Acts 1974, No. 50, §185, eff. Jan. 1, 1975.

Comment

This Article is discussed in the comment following Article 179
as a part of the commentary on Articles 179 through 187.

Art. 186. Owner of right derived from all co-owners of land unaffected by licitation

If the rights of an owner of a mineral right or rights or interest or interests therein derive from all of the co-owners of the land, whether by single or separate acts, his rights are unaffected by the licitation, and he has no interest in the proceeds of the sale.

242

Acts 1974, No. 50, §186, eff. Jan. 1, 1975.

Comment

This Article is discussed in the comment following Article 179
as a part of the commentary on Articles 179 through 187.

Art. 187.   Mineral right created by party acquiring land not
affected by sale

If the whole of the land is adjudicated to the party who
created a mineral right or to his successor, the right is not
extinguished or otherwise affected and the mineral right owner has
no interest in the proceeds of the sale. In such cases, the party to
whom the land is adjudicated is entitled to a credit on the total
purchase price equal to the proportionate value of the mineral right
or interest therein.

Acts 1974, No. 50, §187, eff. Jan. 1, 1975.

Comment

This Article is discussed in the comment following Article 179
as a part of the commentary on Articles 179 through 187.

CHAPTER 11. RIGHTS OF USUFRUCTUARIES
IN MINERALS

Art. 188. Mineral rights not included in usufruct of land except as specifically provided

Except as specially provided in Articles 189 through 191, the usufruct of land does not include the landowner's rights in minerals.

Acts 1974, No. 50, §188, eff. Jan. 1, 1975.

Comment

Articles 188 through 196 seek to solve the many problems presented by the judicial interpretations of Article 552 of the Civil Code [see, now, C.C. art. 561 and R.S. 31: 190], which sets forth the so-called "open mine doctrine." See King v. Buffington, 240 La. 955, 126 So.2d326 (1961); Gueno v. Medlenka, 238 La. 1081, 117 So.2d 817 (1960). For discussions see Comment, 34 Tul.L.Rev. 784 (1960); Note, 20 La.L.Rev. 773 (1960). Those decisions applied Article 552 of the Civil Code in a logical manner. The usufructuary of land is not entitled to any of the economic benefits flowing from execution of mineral leases or production thereunder where the leases were executed and the production secured subsequent to the creation of the usufruct. However, these cases did not answer many questions such as: when has a well or mine been "actually worked" within the meaning of the code; if one well has been drilled at the time the usufruct is created what is the right of the usufructuary to production from multiple sands within the well, from deeper sands subsequently penetrated, or from other wells; what are the rights of the usufructuary of a mineral right; what are the rights of a naked owner to use the surface for mineral operations; what are his obligations and liabilities for surface use? Articles 188 through 196 provide solutions to these and other problems.

Article 188 states the basic rule that unless some specific exception is made elsewhere, a usufruct of land does not include the mineral rights inherent in perfect ownership of land.

Art. 189. Conventional usufruct may include enjoyment of mineral rights

A conventional usufruct, including one created by a donation inter vivos or mortis causa, may by express provision include the use and enjoyment of all or a specified portion of the landowner's rights in minerals.

Acts 1974, No. 50, §189, eff. Jan. 1, 1975.

Comment

The right of those creating conventional usufructs to include use and enjoyment of mineral rights is in keeping with the basic concept of freedom of contract and is not violative of any element of public policy.

Art. 190. Usufructuary of land entitled to enjoyment of mines or quarries worked; exception

A. If a usufruct of land is that of parents during marriage, or any other legal usufruct, or if there is no provision including the use and enjoyment of mineral rights in a conventional usufruct, the usufructuary is entitled to the use and enjoyment of the landowner's rights in minerals as to mines or quarries actually worked at the time the usufruct was created.

B. If a usufruct of land is that of a surviving spouse, whether legal or conventional, and there is no contrary provision in the instrument creating the usufruct, the usufructuary is entitled to the use and enjoyment of the landowner's rights in minerals, whether or not mines or quarries were actually worked at the time the usufruct was created. However, the rights to which the usufructuary is thus entitled shall not include the right to execute a mineral lease without the consent of the naked owner.

Acts 1974, No. 50, §190, eff. Jan. 1, 1975; Acts 1986, No. 245, §1.

Art. 191.   When oil and gas wells and lignite operations considered open mines

A. As applied to oil and gas, the principle stated in Article 190 means that if at the time a usufruct is created minerals are being produced from the land or other land unitized therewith, or if there is present on the land or other land unitized therewith, a well shown by surface production test to be capable of producing in paying quantities, the usufructuary is entitled to the use and enjoyment of the landowner's rights in minerals as to all pools penetrated by the well or wells in question.

B.   As applied to lignite or another form of coal, the principle stated in Article 190 means that if at the time a usufruct is created the land has been included in a mining plan, the usufructuary is entitled to the use and enjoyment of the landowner's rights in minerals as to all seams proposed to be developed in the mining plan provided the following requirements are   satisfied:
(1) Lignite or another form of coal has been discovered as a result of acts committed on the land or due to acts providing a reasonable basis of proof of the discovery of the mineral.

(2) A mining plan for the ultimate production of lignite or other forms of coal, together with a permit issued by the responsible government official, is filed in the conveyance records of the parish or parishes in which the land is located.

(3) Actual mining operations have begun on land included in the plan, although such operations need not be conducted on the land subject to the usufruct.

Acts 1974, No. 50, §191, eff. Jan. 1, 1975. Amended by Acts 1982, No. 780, §1.

Comment

Article 191 deals with one of the difficult problems in the area of the rights of usufructuaries in minerals insofar as oil and gas production is concerned. The basic concept is that if minerals are being produced or if there is a proven shut-in well at the time the usufruct is created, the usufructuary is entitled to the use and enjoyment of the "rights in minerals as to all pools penetrated by the well or wells in question." The term "pool" is defined in Article 213(4) [now 213(3)]. The idea that the usufructuary in such circumstances is entitled to full use and enjoyment of the landowner's rights in minerals is somewhat qualified by the provisions of Article 192, and this article should be read carefully in connection with Article 192.

Article 191 does not, perhaps, provide a perfect solution to the problem of what constitutes a "mine or quarry actually worked" in the case of oil and gas, but it is felt to be equitable and administrable. One thought to be borne in mind in this area is that the overwhelming majority of cases in which this question of interpretation arises involve the usufruct of the surviving spouse. La. Civil Code art. 916 (1870) [repealed; see, now, C.C. art. 890]. In such cases, the survivor will usually be participating in half of the income stream from mineral production by virtue of the status of the land as community property. By limiting the right of the usufructuary in the manner provided, the children of the deceased spouse are also given an opportunity to participate in income from mineral production. Definition of an open mine in the case of oil and gas wells starts from the premise that the well must be actually producing or shown by testing to be capable of producing in commercial quantities at the time the usufruct is created. This would include a producing well which has been temporarily taken off production but which remains capable of production in

248

commercial quantities. It excludes wells which are being drilled at the time the usufruct is created, as well as those which are being deepened at that time. All pools penetrated by a well at the time the usufruct is created are included in the rights of the usufructuary. Thus, the naked owner will have rights only as to newly discovered pools.

Comment-1982

The 1982 amendment to Article 191 is to define what is an "open mine" for lignite or another form of coal for purposes of Article 190. When the requirements of this amendment have been met, it is the functional equivalent of inclusion of an oil or gas pool in a unit capable of production in paying quantities. Hence it is given the same treatment as oil or gas under article 191(A).

Art. 192. Right of usufructuary of land to grant lease

If the land subject to the usufruct, or any part thereof, is subject to a lease granted by the landowner prior to the creation of the usufruct, the usufructuary is entitled only to royalties on actual or constructive production allocable to him under Article 191. If such a lease terminates, or if the land or any part thereof is not under lease at the time the usufruct is created, the usufructuary's right of use and enjoyment includes the right to execute leases as to any rights to which the usufructuary is entitled under Article 190 and, accordingly, to retain bonuses, rentals, or other payments, or the proportionate part thereof, allocable to his interest under Article 191. Such a lease executed by the usufructuary shall not extend beyond the period of his usufruct.

Acts 1974, No. 50, §192, eff. Jan. 1, 1975; Acts 2023, No. 88, §1.

Comment

Article 192 begins from the premise that if production on the land subject to the usufruct is being had under leases in existence

249

at the time the usufruct was created, the usufructuary is entitled only to participate in production royalties or payments for constructive production. In the latter circumstances, some attention should be paid to the fact that shut-in clauses in mineral leases vary. Those most commonly in use in north Louisiana provide for payments regarded as the constructive equivalent of production when there is a shut-in well. Those commonly in use in south Louisiana treat a shut-in well as the equivalent of a dry hole, and the lease may be maintained thereafter by the commencement or resumption of delay rentals. In the first instance, the usufructuary entitled to benefit under Article 191 should share in shut-in payments, and in the second instance, he should not, as the parties to the lease have not classified the payments as constructive production for the purpose of administering the lease.

Article 192 also contemplates the possibility that the land subject to the usufruct may not be subject to lease at the time of creation of the usufruct or if it was, that the lease may expire as to all or a portion of the land after creation of the usufruct. The concept of Article 191 that the usufructuary entitled to benefit of the open mine doctrine, and thus to the use and enjoyment of the landowner's rights in minerals as to mines or quarries actually worked at the time the usufruct was created, logically dictates that if the land is not subject to lease or if a lease expires, the usufructuary and not the naked owner will have the right to execute leases as to the rights of which he has the use and enjoyment. It should be carefully noted that under Article 191, the concept of a "mine or quarry" is articulated as the equivalent of a "pool" as defined in Article 213(4) [see, now 213(3)]. Thus, if the situation contemplated by Article 192 should arise, the usufructuary's right to execute leases would be limited to the "pool" or "pools" of which he has the use and enjoyment. As to other extractive industries, Article 190 does not define the term "mine or quarry," and the courts will be left to determine the extent of the usufructuary's right of use and enjoyment and, under Article 192, his right to lease.

Some question might be raised as to how a mine or quarry could be opened at the time of creation of the usufruct without there having been a lease. Two situations present themselves as obvious. First, if the owner of the land at the time of creation of the usufruct was himself extracting minerals at that time, the article might apply. Second, in the case of oil and gas, it might be that an unleased interest had been included in a unit at the time the usufruct was established. In both situations, the usufructuary would be entitled to execute leases.

Article 192 further provides that if a usufructuary of land benefitting under Article 190 or 191 is entitled to lease, he is entitled to retain the bonuses and rentals from leasing. This is in keeping with the concept that if a "mine or quarry" has been actually worked at the time of creation of the usufruct, the usufructary is entitled to the "use and enjoyment of the landowner's rights in minerals as to" such mines or quarries. Leases executed by a usufructuary under Article 192 may not extend beyond the period of his usufruct.

Art. 193. Nature of usufruct of a mineral right

One who has the usufruct of a mineral right, as distinguished from the usufruct of land, is entitled to all of the benefits of use and enjoyment that would accrue to him if he were the owner of the right. He may, therefore, use the right according to its nature for the duration of his usufruct.

Acts 1974, No. 50, §193, eff. Jan. 1, 1975. Amended by Acts 1975, No. 589, §2, eff. July 17, 1975.

Comment

This article solves a problem not yet treated by the courts. That a usufruct may exist on mineral rights is unquestioned. La. Civil Code art. 541 (1870) [see, now, C.C. art. 544]. The very nature of usufruct is that it is the "use and enjoyment of a thing." If the thing is an incorporeal which must be exercised to be enjoyed, such as a mineral servitude or mineral lease, there can be little question that the usufructuary should be entitled to make use of it according to its nature. Further, the usufructuary is charged to preserve the thing subject to the usufruct. Mineral rights, particularly servitudes and leases, cannot be preserved without being used. La. Civil Code arts. 535, 567 (1870) [see, now, C.C. arts. 539 and 628]. All of these principles are buttressed by common sense in this situation.

The usufruct would be meaningless without the right to exercise the mineral right in question. The right to lease in this situation is granted in Article 118.

Art. 194. Usufructuary not obligated to account to naked owner

A usufructuary of land benefitting under Article 190 or 191 or a usufructuary of a mineral right is not obligated to account to the naked owner of the land or of the mineral right for production or the value thereof or any other income to which he is entitled.

Acts 1974, No. 50, §194, eff. Jan. 1, 1975. Amended by Acts 1975, No. 589, §2, eff. July 17, 1975.

Art. 195. Right of naked owner of land to enjoyment of minerals

If a usufruct of land does not include mineral rights, the naked owner of the land has all of the rights in minerals that he would have if the land were not subject to the usufruct. The rights may not be exercised in coal or lignite which is to be produced through surface mining techniques without first obtaining the consent of the usufructuary. If the usufructuary is entitled to the benefits provided in Article 190 and 191, the rights of the landowner are subject thereto.

Acts 1974, No. 50, §195, eff. Jan. 1, 1975. Amended by Acts 1982, No. 780, §1.

Comment

Article 195 complements Article 188. It makes it clear that the naked owner under the circumstances treated has all of the rights in minerals which he would have if he were the full owner. This includes the right to operate, the right to create mineral rights, including mineral leases, and the right to the economic benefits flowing from the creation of mineral rights, such as bonuses and rentals. Also, it includes the right to such production as does not

0

accrue to a usufructuary entitled to the benefits of Articles 190 or 191.

Comment-1982

Article 195 has been amended because without it the effect of Articles 195 and 196 could be to deprive the usufructuary of the use of the land entirely when lignite or coal would be strip-mined.

Art. 196. Obligations of naked owner arising from enjoyment of rights in minerals

In enjoying the right recognized by Article 195, the naked owner is entitled to use only so much of the surface of the land as is reasonably necessary for his operations, but he is responsible to the usufructuary or those holding rights under him for the value of such use and for all damages caused by the naked owner's mining activities or operations. If the activities or operations are conducted by one to whom the naked owner has granted a mineral right, the naked owner and his grantee are liable in solido for damages suffered by the usufructuary or those holding rights under him.

Acts 1974, No. 50, §196, eff. Jan. 1, 1975.

Comment

Article 196 solves another outstanding problem in this area. The question has never been treated in the jurisprudence. Article 600 of the Civil Code [see, now, C.C. art. 605] provides that the naked owner "must neither interrupt nor in any way impede the usufructuary in the enjoyment of the usufruct, or in any manner impair his rights." Article 196 infringes on that general principle. The infringement is, however, justifiable on the ground that the public interest in securing the extraction of valuable minerals is strong. However, the naked owner cannot engage in mining if by so doing he would effactually deprive the usufructuary of his right to use the surface of the land. If, for example, the usufruct were of a very small tract and drilling would require the entirety of it, the naked owner could not deprive the usufructuary of his right. However, most forms of mining activity in this state can be conducted compatibly with other surface uses. For this reason, it achieves a valuable public goal to make it possible to put land to maximum economic utilization. The naked owner can, therefore, use as much of the surface as he reasonably needs for mineral operations but must repair all damage to the usufructuary. The items of damage are stated in this manner because it is possible that operations by the naked owner might cause damage to the land in which the usufructuary has no interest. Thus damages are limited to property of the usufructuary, or those holding rights under him, and the value of their property rights. The provision making the naked owner liable in solido with his lessee or other mineral right owner is in keeping with delictual principles previously in operation.

CHAPTER 12. SECURED RIGHTS IN MINERAL RIGHTS

PART 1. PLEDGE OF MINERAL RIGHTS

Art. 197. Repealed by Acts 1990, No. 1079, §8, eff. Sept. 1, 1990.

Repealed Article below is listed for historical purposes

Art. 197 A landowner or mineral servitude owner may pledge in the manner hereafter provided, all bonuses or other amounts which he is or may be entitled to receive from the sale, lease or other disposition of mineral rights; the royalties, rentals or other payments or benefits receivable from mineral rights affecting the land; and his share of any minerals reduced to possession from the land or a unit including all or a portion of the land, or the proceeds from the sale or other disposition thereof. A pledge may be made whether or not mineral rights are owned separately from the land or minerals are being produced when the pledge is made.

(Added by Acts 1974, No. 50, §1, eff Jan. 1, 1975.) Repealed by Acts 1990, No. 1079, §8, eff. Sept. 1, 1990.

Comment

Although a landowner cannot mortgage or pledge mineral interests separately from the land, Article 197 permits him to pledge the bonuses, delay rentals, royalties and other payments which he may be entitled to receive from mineral rights affecting the land and which are at the time of the pledge or thereafter owned by others, and to pledge his interest in the minerals thereafter produced and reduced to possession from the land. The landowner's interest in such minerals includes minerals produced from units to the extent they are attributable to the land.

Art. 198. Repealed by Acts 1990, No. 1079, §8, eff. Sept. 1, 1990.

Repealed Article below is listed for historical purposes

Art. 198. The owner of a royalty overriding royalty production payment or other mineral right who does not have the right to explore for or actually reduce minerals to possession, may pledge it in the manner hereafter provided.

(Added by Acts 1974. No. 50, §1, elf Jan. 1, 1975.) Repealed by Acts 1990, No. 1079, §8, eff. Sept. 1, 1990.

Comment

Mineral interests that do not vest in their owner the right to explore for or actually reduce minerals to possession may be pledged under Article 198. The source for Article 198, (La. R.S. 9:4301 (1950) (repealed)) appeared to refer not only to the mineral rights as such, but also to minerals after severance and contracts pertaining to them. The two concepts should be separately dealt with. Article 198 pertains only to the pledge of mineral rights. The hypothecation of the minerals after severance or of contracts pertaining to minerals after they have been severed, Me subject to pledge as provided in Articles 187 and 203, and, of course, may also be hypothecated in the same manner as other movable property.

Art. 198.1. Repealed by Acts 1990, No. 1079, §8, eff. Sept. 1, 1990.

Repealed Article below is listed for historical purposes

Art. 198.1. Rights under contracts for the sale of minerals, by the landowner or owner of a mineral right, after they are severed may be pledged and hypothecated by the seller or purchaser in the manner hereinafter provided.

(Added by Acts 1979, No. 269, §1.) Repealed by Acts 1990, No. 1079, §8, eff. Sept. 1, 1990.

Comment

A chattel mortgage under R.S. 9:5351 et seq., is not an adequate security device because it does not apply to intangibles.

Art. 199. Repealed by Acts 1990, No. 1079, §8, eff. Sept. 1, 1990.

Repealed Article below is listed for historical purposes

Art. 199. A pledge shall be in writing and shall identify the right or benefit pledged, the land or lands affected thereby and the debt secured by the pledge including, if it secures future obligations, a general description of their nature and the minimum amount secured by the pledge.

(Added by Acts 1974, No. 50, §1, eff. Jan. 1, 1975.) Repealed by Acts 1990, No. 1079, §8, eff. Sept. 1, 1990.

Art. 200. Repealed by Acts 1990, No. 1079, §8, eff. Sept. 1, 1990.

Repealed Article below is listed for historical purposes

Art. 200. Delivery of the right pledged is unnecessary and, upon execution of the act of pledge, the pledgee is possessed of the right pledged and entitled to receive all benefits accruing to it. A pledge is effective as to third persons when it is filed for registry in the mortgage records of the parish where the land affected thereby is located.

(Added by Acts 1974, NQ. 50, §1, eff. Jan. 1, 1975.) Repealed by Acts 1990, No. 1079, §8, eff. Sept. 1, 1990.

Comment

A pledgee is entitled to possession of the thing pledged (La. Civil Code Art. 3133 (1870)) to receive the fruits or revenues of the thing pledged (La. Civil Code Art. 3168, 3169 (1870)) or other payments made with respect thereto (La. Civil Code Art. 3170 (1870)), and to retain the thing pledged until discharge of the obligation it secures. Furthermore an obligation does not prescribe as long as the pledge continues. These principles are equally applicable to a pledge of rights under Article 197 or 198. Accordingly, the pledgee is deemed to be in possession of the mineral right or benefit pledged and is entitled to receive the minerals severed or sums accruing to the interest pledged. Until the debt is di8chargecl, he continues to hold the pledged right or benefit and is entitled to receive such amounts. No foreclosure or other execution is required to permit him to enjoy these benefits. When the proceeds received are sufficient to discharge the debt, the pledge will be extinguished and the pledgor will be restored to possession. A pledgee is not prohibited from executing upon and selling the pledged property in accordance with applicable law.

Art. 201. Repealed by Acts 1990, No. 1079, §8, eff. Sept. 1, 1990.

Repealed Article below is listed for historical purposes

Art. 201. A person who pays, delivers, or accounts to a pledgor, under a contract or agreement or a valid regulatory order of a state or federal agency effective at the time the act of pledge is filed for registry, for minerals produced, or proceeds from the sale thereof, or royalties, rentals, or other sums that the pledgee is entitled to receive under the pledge, may make the payments or deliver or account for the minerals to the pledgor without liability to the pledgee until the person has been delivered a certified copy of the act of pledge or until he has acknowledged in writing to the, pledgee notice of the pledge. The privilege enjoyed by the pledgee attaches to all amounts received by the pledgor that accrue to the rights pledged as long as they remain in the hands of the pledgor and can be identified, and the pledgor shall promptly account to the pledgee for them unless excused from doing so by the act of pledge.

(Added by Acts 1974, No. 50, §1, eff. Jan. 1, 1975.) Repealed by Acts 1990, No. 1079, §8, eff. Sept. 1, 1990.

Comment

Article 201 covers the situation of a person who may be required to make payments prior to the time the pledge is recorded. Such a person is not required to take notice of the pledge and may continue to deal with the pledgor until notice of the pledge has been received as set forth in Article 201. Any amounts received by the pledgor under such circumstances are subject to the pledge and must be surrendered by him to the pledgee unless the act of pledge excuses him from doing so. The pledgee may pursue the proceeds of the pledged rights in the hands of the pledgor as long as they can be identified.

Art. 202. Repealed by Acts 1990, No. 1079, §8, eff. Sept. 1, 1990.

Repealed Article below is listed for historical purposes

Art. 202. The effect of registry of a pledge ceases ten years from the date of its filing unless prior thereto it is duly reinscribed, and such effect shall thereafter cease at the end of any ten year period during which the pledge has not been reinscribed.

(Added by Acts 1974, No. 50, §1,eff. Jan. 1, 1975.) Repealed by Acts 1990, No. 1079, §8, eff. Sept. 1, 1990.

PART 2. MORTGAGE OF MINERAL RIGHTS

Art. 203.   Mineral rights susceptible of mortgage; effect of mortgage

A mineral right is susceptible of mortgage to the same extent and with the same effect, and subject to the same provisions of rank, inscription, reinscription, extinguishment, transfer, and enforcement as is prescribed by law for mortgages of immovables under Article 3286 of the Civil Code. Unless expressly excluded by the terms of the act creating it, a mortgage entered into prior to the time Chapter 9 of the Louisiana Commercial Laws becomes effective attaches to the interest of the mortgagor in all corporeal movables placed on the land, or on a unit including all or part of the land, and dedicated to the use and exploitation of the mineral right. The interest of the mortgagor in movables placed on a unit including all or part of the land affected by the mineral right is subject to such a mortgage only to the extent of the interest in the unit attributable to the mineral right mortgaged. Movables only temporarily or transiently on the premises for purposes such as drilling, reworking, servicing, or testing a well or mine located thereon shall not be deemed dedicated to the use or exploitation of the mineral right. The movables shall remain movable and be subject to separate mortgage or encumbrance under Chapter 9 of the Louisiana Commercial Laws as permitted by law with the rank and priority so provided.

Acts 1974, No. 50, §203, eff. Jan. 1, 1975; Acts 1989, No. 137, §10, eff. Sept. 1, 1989; Acts 1991, No. 652, §3, eff. Jan. 1, 1992.

Comment

Mineral rights of all kinds remain subject to mortgage. The source of Article 203 (La.R.S. 9:5101 (1950) (repealed)) has been modified in several respects. R.S. 9:5101 is not clear as to whether judicial and legal mortgages affect mineral interest. Article 203 makes all mineral rights subject to legal and judicial mortgages, as well as conventional mortgages. The presumption as to whether a mortgage covers equipment and accessories on the property affected by the mineral right has been changed, and unless expressly excluded the mortgage will cover all movables on the property which are placed there by the mortgagor for the operation of the mineral right as well as the mortgagor's interest in such equipment on a unit even if it is not actually on the premises covered by the mortgage. Equipment only temporarily or transiently on the premises will not be covered, nor will equipment be covered once it is removed from the mortgaged premises or a unit including all or part thereof.

{{NOTE: SEE ACTS 1989, NO. 137, §§20 AND 21.}}

Section 20 of Act 137 Provides

"It is the intent of the Legislature in enacting this Act to amend the preexisting Louisiana security device laws to accompany and accommodate implementation of Chapter 9 of the Louisiana Commercial Laws (R.S. 10:9.101, et seq.) as previously enacted under Act 528 of 1988. It is further the intent of the legislature that these preexisting Louisiana laws, including without limitation the various statutes and code articles amended and reenacted under this Act, not be expressly or impliedly repealed by Chapter 9 of the Louisiana commercial Laws, but that such laws remain in effect and be applied to preexisting secured transactions and, at times when so provided, be applied to secured transactions subject to Chapter 9 of the Louisiana Commerical Laws."

Art. 204. Security interest in minerals and proceeds thereof

The Uniform Commercial Code - Secured Transactions governs the manner of creation of security interests in minerals produced and the proceeds from their sale or other disposition, as well as the rights of the holders of these security interests against obligors and third persons.

Acts 1974, No. 50, §204, eff. Jan. 1, 1975; Acts 1989, No. 137, §10, eff. Sept. 1, 1989; Acts 2023, No. 88, §1.

{{NOTE: SEE ACTS 1989, NO. 137, §§20 AND 21.}}

Comment

A mortgagor of mineral interests is permitted by Article 204 to pledge the minerals or proceeds thereof severed from the mortgaged premises. Article 204 contains provisions similar to those in Article 201 in that persons who commence dealing with the mortgagor prior to the filing of the mortgage are not bound to take notice of the provisions of the pledge and may continue to deal with the mortgagor with respect to such minerals as they are severed until such notice of the pledge is given in the manner prescribed by the Article. The pledge contained in the act of mortgage deals only with the minerals as they are severed and the Article provides that the extinction of the mortgage carries with it the extinction of the pledge.

{{NOTE: SEE ACTS 1989, NO. 137, §§20 AND 21.}}

Section 20 of Act 137 Provides

"It is the intent of the Legislature in enacting this Act to amend the preexisting Louisiana security device laws to accompany and accommodate implementation of Chapter 9 of the Louisiana Commercial Laws (R.S. 10:9.101, et seq.) as previously enacted under Act 528 of 1988. It is further the intent of the legislature that these preexisting Louisiana laws, including without limitation the various statutes and code articles amended and reenacted under this Act, not be expressly or impliedly repealed by Chapter 9 of the Louisiana commercial Laws, but that such laws remain in effect and be applied to preexisting secured transactions and, at times when so provided, be applied to secured transactions subject to Chapter 9 of the Louisiana Commerical Laws."

PART 3. GENERAL PROVISIONS

Art. 205. When transfer, assignment, or termination of mortgage or pledge effective against parties dealing with mortgagee or pledgee

Notwithstanding any other knowledge or notice, no transfer, assignment, or termination of the right of a mortgagee or pledgee under a mortgage or pledge permitted by these articles shall be binding upon any person dealing with the mortgagee or pledgee until thirty days after there has actually been delivered to him a certified or duplicate original copy of the act evidencing the transfer or assignment or proper evidence of the cancellation of the mortgage or pledge from the mortgage records. Any payments made to the mortgagee or pledgee whose rights have been transferred or terminated shall discharge the person paying them in the amount thereof. The mortgagee or pledgee shall hold any amounts so paid for the account of the person properly entitled to receive them.

Acts 1974, No. 50, §205, eff. Jan. 1, 1975.

CHAPTER 13. MISCELLANEOUS PROVISIONS

PART I. DEMAND FOR AUTHORIZATION TO CANCEL EXTINGUISHED MINERAL RIGHT FROM PUBLIC RECORDS

Art. 206. Obligation of owner of expired mineral right to furnish recordable act evidencing extinction or expiration of right; mineral lease

A. Except as provided in Paragraph B of this Article, when a mineral right is extinguished by the accrual of prescription of nonuse, expiration of its term, or otherwise, the former owner shall, within thirty days after written demand by the person in whose favor the right has been extinguished or terminated, furnish the person with a recordable act evidencing the extinction or expiration of the right.

B. When a mineral lease is extinguished prior to the expiration of its primary term, the former lessee shall, within ninety days after the extinguishment, record an act evidencing the extinction or expiration of the lease in the official records of all parishes wherein the lease is recorded.

Acts 1974, No. 50, §1, eff. Jan. 1, 1975. Amended by Acts 1981, No. 612, §1; Acts 1982, No. 358, §1, eff. July 18, 1982; Acts 2023, No. 88, §1.

Comment

Articles 206 through 209 are a redraft of former La.R.S. 30:101-102 (1950). No change in substance is intended. The term "mineral rights" used is inclusive of all forms of mineral rights, including mineral leases, under Article 16. There is, therefore, no need for two separate statutory sections as found in the present legislation.

Articles 206 through 209 give any person whose title is freed of any form of mineral right the right to demand an instrument sufficient to authorize cancellation of the previously outstanding right from the public records. If the authorization is not furnished by the owner of the expired right, the person demanding the cancellation is entitled to damages and attorney's fees. In the case of interests other than mineral leases, the party demanding the cancellation is not entitled to damages or attorney's fees if there is a good faith dispute concerning whether the interest in question has expired. Perkins v. Long-Bell Petroleum Co., 227 La. 1044, 81 So.2d 389 (1955). The provision concerning the effect of a good faith dispute is not applicable to cancellations of mineral leases under Article 208.

Art. 207. Effect of failure to furnish act evidencing extinction or expiration of right; mineral lease

If the former owner of the extinguished or expired mineral right fails to furnish the required act within thirty days of receipt of the demand or if the former lessee of a mineral lease fails to record the required act within ninety days of its extinguishment prior to the expiration of its primary term, he is liable to the person in whose favor the right or the lease has been extinguished or expired for all damages resulting therefrom and for a reasonable attorney's fee incurred in bringing suit.

Amended by Acts 1981, No. 612, §1; Acts 1982, No. 358, §1, eff. July 18, 1982.

Comment

This Article is discussed in the comment following Article 206.

Art. 208. Effect of good faith dispute as to extinction or expiration of right

The former owner of a mineral right other than a mineral lease is not liable for damages or attorney's fees under Article 207 if there is a good faith dispute as to whether prescription has accrued, the term of the right has expired, or it has been otherwise extinguished.

Acts 1974, No. 50, §208, eff. Jan. 1, 1975.

Comment

This Article is discussed in the comment following Article 206.

Art. 209. Applicability to demand for dissolution of mineral lease

The right to secure damages and attorney's fees under Article 207 is applicable also to a demand for dissolution of a mineral lease for failure to comply with its obligations.

Acts 1974, No. 50, §209, eff. Jan. 1, 1975.

Comment

Article 209 is a statement of prior law arising perhaps more by judicial interpretation than by the express terms of La. R.S. 30:102 (1950) (repealed). Nevertheless, it preserves an idea well embedded in the jurisprudence and the right to damages and attorney's fees recoverable under Article 207 exists in cases demanding dissolution for failure to comply with the obligations of a mineral lease as well as suits seeking to have a court declare that a lease has expired because of the running of its term or the occurrence of some other express resolutory condition. See Sohio Petroleum Co. v. Miller, 237 La. 1013, 112 So.2d 695 (1959).

PART 2. PROTECTION OF PURCHASERS OF PRODUCTION; COMPELLING PAYMENT FOR PRODUCTION

Art. 210. When purchaser protected in paying party in interest under lease for minerals produced

A purchaser of minerals produced from a recorded lease granted by the last record owner holding under an instrument translative of title to the land or mineral rights leased is fully protected in making payment to any party in interest under the lease unless and until a suit is filed testing title to the land or mineral rights embraced in the lease and the purchaser receives notification of it by registered mail. The purchaser is not entitled to this protection unless he has filed for registry in the conveyance records of the parish in which the land subject to the lease is located notice that the minerals produced have been and will be purchased by him.

Acts 1974, No. 50, §1, eff. Jan. 1, 1975.

Comment

Articles 210 through 212 are a redrafted version of former La.R.S. 30:105-107 (1950). These articles differ, however, from the prior legislation in some respects. La.R.S. 30: 105 formerly provided that no person "acquiring mineral rights from, or mineral rights under a lease by, the last record owner holding under an instrument translative of title" could withhold payment of "any rentals, royalties, or other sums due to a party holding an interest in the minerals or under the lease." Similarly, purchasers of production could not withhold payment for it. It is provided in Article 123 that production royalties, rentals, and other sums paid to maintain a lease are rent and must be paid timely according to the terms of the lease or industrial custom. Articles 137 through 141 provide procedures and special remedies for lessors complaining of nonpayment of royalties. These are thought to be fully adequate. The thrust of the prior legislation was to provide protection to third party purchasers of production and at the same time to make them diligent in paying for production purchased. In light of the provisions of the Mineral Code providing specifically for the lessee's obligation to pay royalties, Articles 206 through 209 have been redrafted to deal strictly with the third party purchaser of production. Article 210 provides protection to the third party purchaser under a recorded lease granted by the last record owner holding under an instrument translative of title "unless and until a suit is filed testing title to the land or mineral rights embraced in the lease and the purchaser receives notification of it by registered mail." To be entitled to this protection a third party purchaser must file notice of his purchase agreement in the conveyance records of the parish in which the land subject to the lease is located. There has always been some lack of preciseness to the term "last record owner," but there seemed to be no ready drafting solution to this problem of definition.

Art. 210.1. Interest on purchase payment of production

A.   When mineral production has been delivered under a purchase contract but the purchaser is delaying payment for the production, pending receipt of proof of clear title or a valid division order or both, interest at the legal rate over the time period of the delay shall be paid by the purchaser on all money held for more than thirty days after payment would be due after delivery under the purchase contract. The interest earning period shall be from the date payment is due under the contract to the day disbursement is made.

B.   The provisions of this section shall not apply to payments due to any person who is afforded a remedy under R.S. 31:137 through 31:142 or under R.S. 31:212.21 through 212.23 for nonpayment or delayed payment of sums due.

Added by Acts 1982, No. 534, §1.

Art. 210.2. Declaration of interest; when third party purchasers of oil may withhold payment

A. For purposes of this Article, "declaration of interest" means a signed statement by a party claiming an interest in mineral production, including the authority to sell production belonging to others, and containing the name, address, and taxpayer identification number, a description of the property from which the oil and condensate are produced, and a certification and representation of the claimant's fractional or decimal interest in the production.

B. Until receipt of a declaration of interest, a third party purchaser of oil and condensate is fully protected and may withhold payment for the production.

C.(1) Any party claiming an interest in oil and condensate production must notify a third party purchaser by registered mail.

(2) If the third party purchaser has received a declaration of interest from the claimant, the third party purchaser shall pay the claimant any amounts due for the production within sixty days.

(3) If the third party purchaser fails to pay a claimant who has provided a declaration of interest or fails to inform the claimant of reasonable cause for nonpayment within sixty days of receipt of the notice of interest, the court may impose damages in an amount not to exceed fifty percent of the amount due, plus legal interest on the amount due on the date the required notice was received and reasonable attorney's fees and court costs.

(4) If reasonable cause for nonpayment exists or the third party purchaser has not received a declaration of interest from the claimant, the third party purchaser shall deposit any payments due into an interest-bearing account.

(5) The provisions of this Article shall not apply to payments due to a mineral lessor or any person who is afforded a remedy under Articles 137 through 142 for nonpayment or delayed payment of sums due, except where such persons elect to contract directly with the third party purchaser for the sale of his share of production.

(6) The withholding of payments by a third party purchaser pursuant to this Article shall not constitute reasonable cause for nonpayment of royalty pursuant to Article 138.

D. A third party purchaser of oil and condensate may suspend payment without incurring any interest or penalties to any payee if the aggregate twelve-month accumulation of proceeds totals twenty-five dollars or less.

E. Notwithstanding any other provision of this Code, this Article affords protection to a third party purchaser.

Acts 1992, No. 155, §1, eff. June 5, 1992.

Art. 211. Availability of mandamus for nonpayment of sums due for production

A purchaser of production under Article 210, a purchaser of production under any division order, or a purchaser of production from a lease under which the lessee's royalty obligation to the lessor has been satisfied by the delivery of production to the purchaser may be compelled by writ of mandamus issued by a court of competent jurisdiction to pay sums due for production purchased by him.

Acts 1974, No. 50, §211, eff. Jan. 1, 1975.

Comment

As a corollary to Article 210 protecting third party purchasers from operators holding leases from "the last record owner," Article 211 provides a spur to diligent payment for production. Article 211, however, goes beyond the ambit of Article 210 somewhat and extends the remedy of mandamus for nonpayment not only to third party purchasers protected by Article 210 but also to purchasers under any division order or under any lease under which the lessee's royalty obligation is satisfied by the mere act of delivery into the hands of the third party purchaser.

Several aspects of this provision are noteworthy. First, it was established jurisprudence that the writ of mandamus under La.R.S. 30: 105-107 (1950) (repealed) could not be issued unless the sums claimed were "certain, definite and fixed amounts." *E.g.*, State ex rel. Superior Oil Co. v. Texas Gas Transmission Corp., 242 La. 315, 136 So.2d 55 (1962). This limitation on the availability of the remedy will continue. Second, careful note should be taken of the extension of the remedy of mandamus to the two new classes of persons: (1) purchasers under division orders, and (2) purchasers under leases providing for satisfaction of the royalty obligation by delivery of royalty oil or gas into the hands of a third party purchaser. Many commonly used lease forms provide that as one alternative mode for the payment of royalties, the lessee may deliver royalty oil free of cost into a pipeline connected to the well. Under these circumstances, it has been held that the royalty obligation is satisfied by the act of delivery. Sohio Petroleum Co. v. V.S. & P.R.R., 222 La. 383, 62 So.2d 615 (1952). In circumstances of this kind, it was felt that extension of the remedy of mandamus as a spur to diligence in paying the lessor for production was justified. The same is true of division order arrangements. If a lessor executes a division order providing for a third party purchase arrangement, the availability of the remedy of mandamus is intended to assure prompt payment for production. These provisions are in harmony with the policy of Articles 137-141 providing special procedures and remedies for a lessee's failure to pay royalties.

Art. 212. Right to attorney's fee incurred in securing writ

A party obtaining a properly issued writ of mandamus under Article 211 shall be entitled to reasonable attorney's fees incurred in securing the writ.

Acts 1974, No. 50, §212, eff. Jan. 1, 1975.

Comment

Article 212 makes the remedy of mandamus provided in Article 211 meaningful to persons of limited means who have not been paid for their share of production by a third party purchaser by granting the right to recover reasonable attorney's fees incurred in securing a writ of mandamus. The provision for attorney's fees is an addition to the legislation.

Art. 212.1. Sales relative to minerals after they are severed are subject to the laws of registry

Contracts by a landowner or owner of a mineral right disposing of minerals after they are severed, if filed for registry in the conveyance records at the situs of the land or mineral right from which produced, are subject to the laws of registry.

Added by Acts 1979, No. 269, §2. Acts 1993, No. 948, §5, eff. Jan. 1, 1994.

Comment

Articles 6, 8, and 16 provide for the landowner's right to produce minerals. Article 16 provides for the basic mineral rights which the landowner may create. Article 18 makes mineral rights immovables and fixes their situs. Proposed Article 212.1 is compatible with those articles, but preserves the distinction between a mineral right and contracts disposing of or hypothecating the minerals themselves after severance.

PART 2-A. PRODUCTION PAYMENTS AND ROYALTY PAYMENTS TO OTHER THAN MINERAL LESSOR; REMEDIES OF OBLIGEE

Art. 212.21. Nonpayment of production payment or royalties; notice prerequisite to judicial demand

If the owner of a production payment created out of a mineral lessee's interest or a royalty owner other than a mineral lessor seeks relief for the failure of a mineral lessee to make timely or proper payment of royalties or the production payment, he must give his obligor written notice of such failure as a prerequisite to a judicial demand for damages.

Added by Acts 1982, No. 249, §1; Acts 2020, No. 76, §1.

Art. 212.22. Required response of obligor to notice

The obligor shall have thirty days after receipt of the required notice within which to pay the royalties or production payments due or to respond by stating in writing a reasonable cause for nonpayment. The payment or nonpayment of the sums due or stating or failing to state a reasonable cause for nonpayment within this period has the following effect.

Added by Acts 1982, No. 249, §1.

Art. 212.23. Effects of payment or nonpayment with or without stating reasonable cause therefor; division order

A. If the obligor pays the royalties or production payments due plus the legal interest applicable from the date payment was due, the owner shall have no further claim with respect to those payments.

B. If the obligor fails to pay within the thirty days from notice but states a reasonable cause for nonpayment, then damages shall be limited to legal interest on the amounts due from the date due.

C. If the obligor fails to pay and fails to state a reasonable cause for failure to pay in response to the notice, the court may award as damages double the amount due, legal interest on that sum from the date due, and a reasonable attorney's fee regardless of the cause for the original failure to pay.

D. Repealed by Acts 1992, No. 1110, §2.

Acts 1982, No. 249, §1; Acts 1990, No. 986, §1; Acts 1992, No. 1110, §2.

PART 2-B. GENERAL PROVISIONS RELATING TO PAYMENT

Art. 212.31. Payment information to interest owners

A. As used in this Article:

(1) "Check stub" means the financial record attached to a check.

(2) "Division order" means a contract of sale to the purchaser of oil or gas directing the purchaser to make payment for the value of the products taken in the proportions set out in the division order, which division order is prepared by the purchaser on the basis of the ownership shown in the title opinion prepared after examination of the abstracts and which is executed by the operator, the royalty owners, and the other persons having an interest in the production.

(3) "Interest owner" means a person owning a royalty interest or a working interest in an oil or gas well or unit.

B. Whenever payment is made for oil or gas production to an interest owner, whether pursuant to a division order, lease, servitude, or other agreement, all of the following information shall be included on the check stub or on an attachment to the form of payment, unless the information is otherwise provided on a regular basis:

(1) Lease identification number, if any, or reference to appropriate agreement with identification of the well or unit from which production is attributed.

(2) Month and year of sales or purchases included in the payment.

(3) Total barrels of crude oil or MCF of gas purchased.

(4) Owner's final realizable price per barrel or MCF.

(5) Total amount of severance and other production taxes, with the exception of windfall profit tax.

(6) Net value of total sales from the property after taxes are deducted.

(7) Interest owner's interest, expressed as a decimal fraction, in production from (1) above.

(8) Interest owner's share of the total value of sales prior to any tax deductions.

(9) Interest owner's share of the sales value less his share of the production and severance taxes, as applicable.

Added by Acts 1983, No. 660, §1, eff. Jan. 1, 1984.

Art. 212.32. Accumulation of proceeds from production

A. Unless otherwise requested, proceeds from production of oil and gas may be accumulated and remitted to the persons entitled thereto annually for the twelve months accumulation of proceeds totaling less than one hundred dollars.

B. Proceeds totaling less than one hundred dollars but more than twenty-five dollars shall be remitted monthly if requested in writing by the person entitled to the proceeds. Amounts less than ten dollars shall be remitted annually if requested in writing by the person entitled to the proceeds.

C. Before proceeds may be accumulated, the payor shall provide notice to the person entitled to such proceeds that there is an option to be paid monthly when the accumulated proceeds exceed ten dollars. Such notice to the person shall also provide directions for requesting monthly payment, and constitutes notice to all heirs, successors, representatives, and assigns of the person.

D. Notwithstanding any other provision of this Section to the contrary, all accumulated proceeds shall be paid to the owner thereof when production ceases or upon relinquishment or transfer of the payment responsibility.

Acts 1995, No. 1116, §2.

PART 3. DEFINITIONS

Art. 213. Definitions

Unless otherwise defined by express agreement, the following terms used in this Code shall have the following meanings:

(1) "Bonus" means money or other property given for the execution of a mineral lease, except interests in production from or attributable to property on which the lease is given.

(2) "Mining Plan" means that plan for development of lignite or other form of coal filed with the appropriate government official in connection with an application for a surface mining permit to conduct operations within some portion of the mining plan. The mining plan indicates the area ultimately to be mined or used for mining operations, and an area of land may be included in a mining plan even though a surface mining permit for operations is limited to a portion of the land in the mining plan or to a specified period of time shorter than the time necessary for full implementation of the mining plan. For purposes of filings under Articles 61, 115, and 191, a mining plan shall consist of a description of the land covered by the filing with the appropriate government official or a plat showing the same. If that official shall disapprove of inclusion of land in the mining plan under his authority under the Surface Mining and Reclamation Act or successor legislation, then the filing of the mining plan will have no effect under Articles 61, 115, and 191 with respect to the land disapproved. If he shall require under his authority under the Surface Mining and Reclamation Act or successor legislation the amendment of a mining plan to include land not included in a previous filing, then the amendment of the mining plan shall have the same effect from the date of the amendment under Articles 61, 115, and 191 as though such additional land had been included in the mining plan. When used in this definition, "appropriate government official" means the commissioner of conservation or other state or federal official who issues permits to conduct surface mining of lignite or other forms of coal within the state of Louisiana.

(3) "Pool" means an underground reservoir containing a common accumulation of crude petroleum or gas or both. Each

zone of a general structure that is completely separated from any other zone in the structure is covered by the term "pool."

(4) "Rental" means money or other property given to maintain a mineral lease in the absence of drilling or mining operations or production of minerals. "Rental" does not include payments classified by a lease as constructive production.

(5) "Royalty," as used in connection with mineral leases, means any interest in production, or its value, from or attributable to land subject to a mineral lease, that is deliverable or payable to the lessor or others entitled to share therein. Such interests in production or its value are "royalty," whether created by the lease or by separate instrument, if they comprise a part of the negotiated agreement resulting in execution of the lease. "Royalty" also includes sums payable to the lessor that are classified by the lease as constructive production.

(6) "Unit" means an area of land, deposit, or deposits of minerals, stratum or strata, or pool or pools, or a part or parts thereof, as to which parties with interests therein are bound to share minerals produced on a specified basis and as to which those having the right to conduct drilling or mining operations therein are bound to share investment and operating costs on a specified basis. A unit may be formed by convention or by order of an agency of the state or federal government empowered to do so. A unit formed by order of a governmental agency is termed a "compulsory unit."

(7)(a) "Actual mining operations", as used in connection with the mining of lignite or other forms of coal, means good faith operations to obtain or establish the production of lignite or other forms of coal.

(b) Such operations shall be deemed to have commenced with the good faith initiation of any of the following or other similar types of activity: the removal of existing improvements, construction of railroad spurs, conveyor or transportation facilities for lignite and other forms of coal, and haul roads, construction of electric power lines, relocation of existing pipelines, construction of sedimentation ponds, on-site erection of major equipment for removal or transportation of lignite and other forms of coal and overburden, construction and installation of de-watering facilities, construction of office, shop, or other facilities, the removal of overburden, and other such necessary operations conducted to obtain or utilize lignite or other forms of coal.

(c) The initiation of any of the above or similar activities shall constitute a commencement of actual mining operations when conducted by or under the authority of:

(i) The party mining or commencing the mining of lignite or other forms of coal;

(ii) An affiliated synthetic fuel facility; or

(iii) An affiliated specific major electric generating facility.

Acts 1974, No. 50, §213, eff. Jan. 1, 1975. Amended by Acts 1982, No. 780, §1; Acts 1983, No. 203, §1.

Comment

Precise definitions of the terms "bonus," "rental," and "royalty" provide standards for interpretation of all instruments using them, but they are of particular importance in connection with Articles 105 through 113 dealing with executive rights. Considerable difficulty has been encountered in other jurisdictions in defining exactly what constitutes a bonus and what constitutes a royalty. Thus, if a production payment is created at the time a lease is executed, does the holder of a nonexecutive mineral servitude or a mineral royalty have a right to share in production attributable to it or is it to be considered as "bonus"? The definition of "bonus" in Article 213(1), complemented by the definition of "royalty," in Article 213(2) results in characterization of a production payment from the property being leased as royalty rather than bonus. If, however, the production payment were granted by the lessee out of another producing lease, the definitions would require treatment of the interest as bonus. Generally, then, under subparagraphs (1) and (2) of Article 213, any interest in production or its value from or attributable to a lease granted by the holder of an executive right would be royalty and not bonus, even though it might be termed in the documentation as an overriding royalty or a production payment taken out of the working interest. Coupled with the provisions concerning executive rights, this means that one holding an executive interest cannot, by the device of calling an interest in production an overriding royalty rather than a lessor's royalty, deprive the holder of a mineral royalty or other nonexecutive interest of the right to share in production.

The definition of "royalty" in Article 213(2) is important as a complement to the definition of "bonus." For example, if landowner A grants a mineral royalty to B, A retains the executive rights. He retains, also, all other elements of ownership that he has not specifically granted. It is conceivable that without this definition, the landowner might make an argument such as the following: admitting that a particular interest in production, such as a production payment, is not "bonus" as defined in subparagraph (1), it is not royalty to which the owner of a mineral royalty would be entitled. Thus, if B in the example given were entitled by his deed to 1/4 of all royalties to be stipulated for under any mineral lease, he might not be entitled to participate in the production payment or in an overriding royalty or other interest in production or its value. In this regard, see Uzee v. Bollinger, 178 So.2d 508 (La. App. lst Cir. 1965). The definition would also foreclose the executive from dealing unfairly by using a side agreement to obtain an additional share of production to the detriment of the mineral royalty owner. The term "royalty" also is defined to include payments classified as constructive production. This characterization would commonly include shut-in royalty payments and compensatory royalty payments that, when paid under the terms of some leases, are regarded as production under the habendum clause of the lease or otherwise as the equivalent of production. This type of payment is more fully discussed in connection with the definition of "rental," which is expressly defined to exclude payments designated as constructive production.

The definition of the term "rental" in Article 213(3) is also necessary, particularly in connection with Articles 105-113 dealing with executive rights. The definition here given would include not only sums designated as delay rentals payable prior to drilling or mining operations or after unsuccessful operations but would also include so-called "shut-in rentals" commonly found in many oil and gas lease forms as a means of maintaining leases when a well producing gas or gaseous substances in paying quantities is shut in. Payments of this type are to be distinguished from other payments deemed to be constructive production under certain lease forms. For example another common type of lease form provides for the making of shut-in payments in the royalty clause of the lease and states that when such payments are made, it shall be considered that there is production under the habendum clause of the lease. Compensatory royalty payments may also be classified as constructive production for purposes of maintaining a lease.

The definition of "pool" in Article 213(4) is the same as that found in the conservation act. La. R.S. 30:3(6) (1950). For purposes of the Mineral Code, the term is of particular importance in connection with the rights of usufructuaries of land under the open mines doctrine as specified in Articles 188-196.

The term "unit" requires definition as it is used in several places throughout the code. Of particular importance are those articles dealing with the effect of unit operations or production on mineral servitudes, mineral royalties, and mineral leases. See Articles 33, 34, 35, 38, 89, 90, and 91. The definition used is a functional one that comports with standard industrial practices. This definition includes conventional units of all kinds, whether established by declaration under a pooling power, by a contract executed by all parties affected, or otherwise. The reference to compulsory units includes all types of units which may presently be established by the Commissioner of Conservation as well as any others that might be authorized in the future. See La. R.S. 30:5, 9, and 10 (1950).

Comment-1982

A definition of mining plan has been added since the term has been used in several articles of the Mineral Code. It does not change the meaning the term has had in Article 115 but merely reflects the usage of the term there for integration of that concept with other articles of the Mineral Code which have been amended subsequent to amendments of Article 115. The Commissioner of Conservation has authority under the Surface Mining and Reclamation Act, La. R.S. 30:905 B(2), (5), and (11) to adopt rules and regulations pertaining to surface coal mining and reclamation, to issue orders reasonably necessary or take actions necessary to carry out the provisions of the Surface Mining and Reclamation Act and regulations, and to exercise discretionary review over all aspects of surface coal mining and reclamation operations performed within the state. The definition of mining plan in Article 213 does not expand or restrict the authority of the Commissioner but merely specifies the effect under Articles 61, 115, and 191 of the lessee or servitude owner's filing where the Commissioner has concluded that an area of land is or is not reasonably subject to being mined under a plan of development. The term "appropriate government official" has been used in the event that another State or Federal official becomes charged with the responsibility for issuing permits to conduct surface mining operations.

PART 4. APPLICATION OF CODE

Art. 214. Applicability of Code to existing rights

The provisions of this Code shall apply to all mineral rights, including those existing on the effective date hereof; but no provision may be applied to divest already vested rights or to impair the obligation of contracts.

Acts 1974, No. 50, §214, eff. Jan. 1, 1975.

Comment

There are three constitutional provisions of relevance to this Article. Article I, § 10 of the United States Constitution provides that "no State shall ... pass any ... ex post facto law, or law impairing the obligation of contracts." Article 4, § 15 of the Louisiana Constitution of 1921 provides that "no ex post facto law, nor any law impairing the obligation of contracts, shall be passed; nor shall vested rights be divested, unless for purposes of public utility and for just and adequate compensation previously paid." Article 1, § 23 of the Louisiana Constitution of 1974 provides that "No bill of attainder, ex post facto law, or law impairing the obligation of contracts shall be enacted." The due process clause of the Fourteenth Amendment to the federal constitution would also prohibit divestiture of vested rights.

These provisions do not prohibit the retrospective application of all laws but only retrospective application that would violate their specific terms. That is, invalid laws under the combined prohibitions of these provisions are: (1) ex post facto laws; (2) laws that impair the obligations of contracts; and (3) laws divesting vested rights unless for purposes of public utility and for just and adequate compensation.

Article 8 of the Louisiana Civil Code [see, now, C.C. art. 6], however, provides: "A law can prescribe only for the future; it can have no retrospective operation, nor can it impair the obligation of contracts." Because this blanket prohibition of retroactivity is legislative, the legislature may make specific legislation retroactive provided there is no violation of the constitutional prohibitions. Under the terms of Article 2 of the Mineral Code, the provisions of the code are supplemental to those of the Louisiana Civil Code. Thus, in the absence of specific provisions in the Mineral Code, Article 8 of the Civil Code might have governed. This prohibition in Article 8 has been interpreted as applying only to substantive laws and not to procedural or remedial statutes. *E.g.*, Oil Well Supply Co. v. Red Iron Drilling Co., 210 La. 222, 26 So.2d 726 (1946). Changes in prescriptive limitations have been considered as remedial in nature. *E.g.*, Shreveport Long Leaf Lumber Co. v. Wilson, 195 La. 814, 197 So. 566 (1940).

The situation was also clouded by La.R.S. 1:2 (1950), which provides that "no section of the Revised Statutes is retroactive unless it is expressly so stated." No cases were found interpreting this section to determine whether it would be given the same construction as Article 8 of the Civil Code. It is at least arguable, however, that as the Revised Statutes contain so many purely procedural and remedial provisions, the redactors must have meant that intent to have retrospective application must be express regardless of the nature of the legislation. Additionally R.S. 1:2 states that "no section" shall be retroactive whereas Article 8 of the Civil Code speaks generally in terms of "laws." This might furnish the basis for a distinction between the two. Support for the contrary argument is found in the fact that the Civil Code also contains provisions considered to be procedural or remedial as well as those that are substantive. Yet Article 8 is not applied to procedural or remedial laws. The plain fact is, however, that the confusion presented by these two provisions of the Civil Code and the Revised Statutes made some treatment of the matter of retrospective application of the Mineral Code a necessity.

There are strong reasons why the Mineral Code should be retrospective, at least in the sense that to the extent possible it should apply to existing rights. There are many mineral servitudes, mineral royalties, and mineral leases outstanding at any given point in time. If comprehensive mineral legislation were made applicable only to rights created after its effective date, the number of outstanding rights at that time would assure that there would be two clear and distinct bodies of mineral law in the state for many years to come. One would be the "old law" as developed by analogy to provisions of the Civil Code which would apply to rights already existing on the effective date of the legislation. The other would consist of the Mineral Code and the interpretive jurisprudence applicable to rights created after enactment of the Mineral Code. The resultant difficulties in judicial administration are readily discernible. Additionally, the purpose of codification would be substantially frustrated.

The chosen approach to this problem is to adopt a general principle making the provisions of the code retrospective in operation to the extent not violative of the state and federal constitutions. Thus, unless an individual can satisfy a court that he is deprived of a vested right without just compensation or that the obligations of a contract are impaired, the rules specified in the Mineral Code apply to both existing and future rights. This approach was regarded as the only practical one. A second possible approach would have been to specify those provisions deemed not violative of the constitutional prohibitions. This would have been a cumbersome undertaking. In addition to being cumbersome, there was a high level of risk that judgments by the draftsmen as to which provisions should be placed in which categories would prove erroneous, lending complication rather than simplicity to the situation.

PART 5. OPERATING AGREEMENTS

Art. 215. Contracts; partnership status

A written contract for the joint exploration, development, or operation of mineral rights does not create a partnership unless the contract expressly so provides.

Added by Acts 1980, No. 150, §2, eff. Jan. 1, 1981.

Art. 216. Filing

An agreement entered into by or among the owners of mineral rights for the joint exploration, development, operation or production of minerals thereunder shall be binding upon third persons when the agreement is filed for registry in the conveyance records of the parish or parishes where the lands affected by the mineral rights are located.

Added by Acts 1974, No. 545, §1, eff. Jan. 1, 1975; Acts 2005, No. 169, §7, eff. July 1, 2006; Acts 2005, 1st Ex. Sess., No. 13, §1, eff. Nov. 29, 2005. Redesignation of R.S. 9:2731 by Acts 2005, No. 169

Art. 217. Declaration in lieu of agreement

In lieu of filing an agreement as provided in R.S. 31:216, the parties thereto may file a declaration signed by them, or signed by any person designated in the agreement as the general operator or agent of the parties, describing the lands affected by the mineral rights that are the subject of the agreement, stating in general terms the nature or import of the agreement, and stating where the agreement may be found. The recording officer of the parish in which the declaration is filed may copy into his records only the declaration, without the exhibit attached thereto. The declaration when so filed shall serve as full and complete notice of the agreement to the same extent as if the original agreement had been filed and recorded. The recording officer shall charge only the fees for filing and recording the declaration.

Added by Acts 1974, No. 545, §1, eff. Jan. 1, 1975; Acts 1985, No. 325, §1; Acts 2005, No. 169, §7, eff. July 1, 2006 ; Acts 2005, 1st Ex. Sess., No. 13, §1, eff. Nov. 29, 2005. Redesignation of R.S. 9:2731 by Acts 2005, No. 169

www.ingramcontent.com/pod-product-compliance
Lightning Source LLC
Chambersburg PA
CBHW060340220326
41598CB00023B/2761